Muriel Spark's Early Fiction

Muriel Spark's Early Fiction

Literary Subversion and Experiments with Form

James Bailey

EDINBURGH
University Press

Edinburgh University Press is one of the leading university presses in the UK. We publish academic books and journals in our selected subject areas across the humanities and social sciences, combining cutting-edge scholarship with high editorial and production values to produce academic works of lasting importance. For more information visit our website: edinburghuniversitypress.com

© James Bailey, 2021, 2022

Edinburgh University Press Ltd
The Tun – Holyrood Road
12(2f) Jackson's Entry
Edinburgh EH8 8PJ

First published in hardback by Edinburgh University Press 2021

Typeset in 10.5/13 Adobe Sabon by
Servis Filmsetting Ltd, Stockport, Cheshire

A CIP record for this book is available from the British Library

ISBN 978 1 4744 7596 9 (hardback)
ISBN 978 1 4744 7597 6 (paperback)
ISBN 978 1 4744 7598 3 (webready PDF)
ISBN 978 1 4744 7599 0 (epub)

The right of James Bailey to be identified as the author of this work has been asserted in accordance with the Copyright, Designs and Patents Act 1988, and the Copyright and Related Rights Regulations 2003 (SI No. 2498).

Contents

Acknowledgements   vi

    Introduction: The Desegregation of Spark   1
1. 'Author's Ghosts': Manifestations of the Supernatural in
    Spark's Early Fiction   34
2. 'The role in which you've cast me': Reassessing the Myth of
    Spark   63
3. 'Drama[s] of exact observation': Spark and the *Nouveau*
    Roman   103
4. 'A study, in a way, of self-destruction': *The Driver's Seat* and
    the Impotent Gaze   142
    Conclusion: Leaving the Hothouse   171

Notes   184
Bibliography   190
Index   207

Acknowledgements

A number of people have played a crucial role in the completion of this book. My PhD supervisors, Professors Adam Piette and Sue Vice, have been invaluable sources of insight and guidance throughout my years as a frazzled doctoral candidate.

Thanks are due to the remarkably patient staff at the National Library of Scotland and the McFarlin Library at the University of Tulsa, who helped me locate all manner of letters, notebooks and draft fragments from each of Spark's vast public archives. Thanks, too, to Spark's estate, for granting me permission to quote from various unpublished materials in this book.

I am extremely grateful to Dr Jackie Jones at Edinburgh University Press for her support and guidance, along with her longstanding enthusiasm for all things Sparkian. Sincere thanks, too, to Dr Ersev Ersoy, for answering innumerable questions as I prepared the manuscript for submission. I am also indebted to the readers, whose recommendations have shaped the book and encouraged me to look for what Spark herself would call 'hidden possibilities'.

I have my friends and family to thank for encouragement and understanding when I needed them most. My colleagues at Arts Council England offered motivation and humour in equal measure, as I balanced full-time work with late-night writing. Finally, none of this would have been possible without the love and support of my partner, Richard, whose kindness and patience seemingly know no bounds (although both were surely tested as the book neared its completion . . .). This book is dedicated to you.

* * *

Some sections of this book have been published, in earlier forms, in journal articles and book chapters. The final section of Chapter One is adapted from my chapter 'The Ghost Stories of Muriel Spark', in *British*

Women Short Story Writers: The New Woman to Now (2015); thank you to Edinburgh University Press and my co-editor, Dr Emma Young, for allowing me to reproduce elements of this work in my book. Thanks are also due to Dr Kaye Mitchell, for permission to expand on aspects of my 2015 article 'Salutary Scars: The "Disorienting" Fictions of Muriel Spark' when discussing *Not to Disturb* and *Doctors of Philosophy* in Chapter Two. The analysis of *The Mandelbaum Gate* in Chapter Three is expanded from my chapter '"Repetition, boredom, despair": Muriel Spark and the Eichmann Trial', published in the *Holocaust Studies* journal; I am grateful to Professor Sue Vice and Dr Jenni Adams for allowing me to expand on ideas first explored in this chapter.

Introduction:
The Desegregation of Spark

Readers of novels were not yet used to the likes of me, and some will never be.
Muriel Spark, *Curriculum Vitae* (208)

In a short essay entitled 'The Sitter's Tale' (1999), Muriel Spark recalls accepting an invitation from the Scottish National Portrait Gallery to have her portrait painted by the artist Sandy Moffat, and her later disappointment at seeing a finished work to which she bore little resemblance. On the painter's canvas, the author noticed that her 'light reddish hair' had become 'yellow hair with a navy blue parting', while the thin lines that patterned her sweater had been 'made into broad footballer's stripes'. The artist, Spark surmised, had been less interested in capturing *her* in his painting than the brightly coloured scarf that she happened to be wearing:

> He said to me, the picture is called *The Red Scarf*, and that, in fact, is what it is. I was just a model for *The Red Scarf* by Sandy Moffat. It isn't me at all; the author of my books is just not there. (2014b: 99)

For a contemporary Spark scholar – one who has examined the wealth of critical commentary written on the author over the past six decades – Spark's self-professed struggle to recognise herself in Moffat's portrait may acquire a certain resonance. Critical responses to Spark, as Patricia Waugh notes, have largely 'focused on theorising, historicising, or claiming' the author 'for various identity politics or ethnic, national, religious, and cultural groupings' (2010: 64), while also striving to position her fiction, as Matthew Wickman observes, under 'classifications like "tradition", "modernism" or "postmodernism"', often to the exclusion of all others (2010: 73). This is due in no small part to what Bryan Cheyette terms the 'abiding doubleness' that distinguishes both Spark's life and work. Spark's fiction, Cheyette explains, bears the influence of 'the long tradition of English social realism and literary satire', yet is also informed by 'avant-garde movements such as the French *nouveau roman* of Alain Robbe-Grillet and the British "experimentalism" of B. S. Johnson'. Similarly, the author's 'hybrid background', which is 'part English, part Scottish, part Protestant, part Jewish', as well as her later conversion to Catholicism and expatriate status in Africa, America and Italy at various stages of her life, leave her open to competing, and often essentialising, identity claims (2000: 9–10). Any such attempt to stamp Spark or her fiction with a definitive label, Waugh warns, will thus inevitably risk 'displacing and marginalising what fails to fit the confirmatory bias of the perspective adopted' (2010: 64). At worst, then, a study can become its own version of *The Red Scarf*, its focus tethered so tightly to a singular focal point that whatever falls outside of the narrow, prescriptive line of enquiry applied is distorted, relegated to the background, or expelled entirely from the frame.

As an alternative to this critical tendency (one which is particularly ironic, given the concern, raised recurrently throughout Spark's œuvre, with that which eludes and consequently undermines the rigid modes of categorisation which certain characters or institutions either myopically subscribe to or tyrannically enforce), we might follow Marina MacKay in conceptualising Spark as a curiously 'amphibious figure', whose fiction finds itself situated indeterminately between postwar British literature's 'starkly divided possibilities' (2010: 506). Spark's novels and short stories, MacKay observes, exhibit qualities drawn from both of these apparently polarised 'possibilities' – represented on one side by 'the so-called Angry Young Men, all intent on restoring fiction to a condition of panoramic social documentary', and on the other by 'the domestic *nouveaux romanciers*' identified by Cheyette above (Ibid.). Echoing the views of Cheyette and MacKay in his introduction to the *Modern Fiction Studies* special issue on Spark, David Herman claims that the author 'in effect opted out of the two responses to modernism' by taking a productive 'third path' that was all her own:

> [Spark's] fiction embraces (or rather extends and radicalises) the modernist emphasis on technique while *also* projecting complex social worlds – worlds in which [. . .] characters are impinged on by powerful historical and political forces, their psychologies and interactions shaped by entrenched educational and religious institutions, ideologies of gender, and more or less dominant assumptions about the possibilities and limitations of human agency. [. . .] [I]n other words, her novels encompass tendencies displayed by both antimodernists advocating a midcentury return to realism and by postmodernist practitioners. (2008: 473–4)

By combining a 'reflexive focus on narrative form' with a sustained 'engagement with the historical contingencies of lived experience',

Herman observes, Spark's 'third path' involves engaging in a dynamic interplay between various modes of 'mind-bending formal innovation' and a 'nuanced representation of sociohistorical circumstances'. Her writing practices, he concludes, are thus 'dependent on the *nonresolution* of this dialectical tension', with each text setting 'a different balancing point for these two sets of concerns' (Ibid.). Whether intentionally or otherwise, Herman's argument evokes the sentiment (as well as the central metaphor) of David Lodge's well-known meditation on the state of mid-century fiction, 'The Novelist at the Crossroads' (1969). 'The novelist who has any kind of self-awareness', Lodge famously contends, 'must at least hesitate at the crossroads [between the 'starkly divided possibilities' outlined above]; and the solution many novelists have chosen [. . .] is *to build their hesitation into the novel itself*' (1977: 104, emphasis mine). This 'hesitation' led to the emergence of what Lodge terms 'the problematic novel':

> This kind of novel [. . .] clearly has affinities with both the non-fiction [realist] novel and fabulation [Lodge is here referencing Robert Scholes's 1967 study of self-reflexive, non-realistic and supernatural fiction, *The Fabulators*], but it remains distinct precisely because it brings both into play. [. . .] In the kind of novel I am thinking of [. . .] the reality principle is never allowed to lapse entirely – indeed, it is often invoked [. . .] to expose the artificiality of conventional realistic illusion. (105)

Perceiving Spark as an author who 'hesitate[s] at the crossroads', before embarking on a 'third path' of her own devising, offers a valuable means of comprehending a body of fiction which occupies an ambiguous (or indeed 'amphibious') position between realism and experimentation, sincerity and self-consciousness, and the quotidian and the otherworldly. As Spark herself would assert, however, these possibilities need not be considered as diametrically opposed or irreconcilable; her practice of fiction, she insisted, was geared towards *redefining* traditional realism through varied modes of literary innovation rather than abandoning it entirely. 'I might claim to be the opposite of C. P. Snow in every possible way,' she remarked in 1971, referencing the attacks made upon the experimental novel by self-proclaimed realists such as Snow, William Cooper and Kingsley Amis during the previous two decades: 'he thinks he's a realist: I think *I'm* a realist and he's a complete fantasist' (Toynbee 1971: 74).[1] So-called 'realistic novels', she maintained in one of her final interviews, 'are more committed to dogmatic and absolute truth than most other varieties of fiction. I would say that the novels of George Eliot are extremely realistic and rather dogmatic, and more absolute in their tone' (Hosmer 2005: 147). Spark's reconceptualised model of realism thus functions, as Lodge writes of 'the problematic novel' more generally, 'to expose the artificiality of conventional realistic illusion' (1977: 105), by defamiliarising and dismantling the 'dogmatic and absolute truth' propagated therein.

An effective reading of Spark's fiction must therefore attend to the nature and purpose of its disorienting indeterminacy. I borrow 'disorienting' from its use in a letter written to Spark in 1986 by her friend and sometime mentor, Christine Brooke-Rose, which bemoaned the typically bemused critical responses to which both authors had grown accustomed.[2] Because she and Spark 'keep doing something quite different' from one text to the next, Brooke-Rose reasoned, their work had proved 'disorienting for critics who like labels', so that 'the only one they can think of is "experimental" (which annoys them), or "French", "*nouveau roman*" (completely untrue, but that label annoys them too) – I now occasionally get "postmodern" – all nonsense' (NLS 1986). Brooke-Rose was not, I would argue, denying the suitability of these terms to her and Spark's respective fictions (indeed, she has written in detail of their relevance to both authors),[3] but taking issue instead with their clumsy, catch-all application at the hands of critics who begrudged their use to begin with. A more considered critical approach to both authors, her letter suggests, is long overdue.

Although Brooke-Rose adopts 'disorienting' to refer to the critical bafflement induced by texts that defy easy categorisation, her choice of word bears additional relevance to Spark's own authorial intent. 'Disorient', derived from the French *désorienter* and defined in the *Oxford English Dictionary* as 'to turn from the east; to cause to "lose one's bearings"; *to put out, disconcert, embarrass*', neatly encapsulates the derisive and unnerving effects that Spark, in her artistic manifesto 'The Desegregation of Art' (1970), recommended that 'effective' writing such as her own ought to possess. In place of the 'literature of sentiment and emotion' which she found to be characteristic of an outdated mode of 'socially conscious art' that 'isn't achieving its ends or illuminating our lives anymore', Spark advocated for 'a less impulsive generosity, a less indignant representation of social injustice, and a more deliberate cunning, a more derisive undermining of what is wrong' (1992c: 35). It is 'the *art of ridicule*', she proposed, that could 'penetrate to the marrow' and 'paralyse its object', leaving 'a salutary scar' in its wake:

> Our noble aspirations, our sympathies, our elevated feelings should not be inspired merely by visits to an art gallery, a theatre, or by reading a book, but rather the rhetoric of our times should *persuade us to contemplate the ridiculous nature of the reality before us*, and teach us to mock it. We should know ourselves better by now than to be under the illusion that we are all essentially aspiring, affectionate, and loving creatures. We do have these

qualities, but we are aggressive, too. And so when I speak of the desegregation of art I mean by this the liberation of our minds from the comfortable
cells of lofty sentiment in which they are confined and never really satisfied.
(35–6, emphasis mine)

In choosing 'A Salutary Scar' as the title of his introductory essay on
the author, David Herman attests to the pertinence of 'The Desegregation
of Art' to future Spark studies. In his brief but insightful discussion of
the manifesto, Herman proposes that the 'deliberate cunning' advocated by Spark is 'exemplifie[d] in her own fictional methods', which
'call attention to the constructedness of the fictional scenarios being
portrayed in order to inhibit readerly immersion and promote instead
a critical engagement with those situations and events' (2008: 477–8).
A link is thus forged between the subversive, derisory and 'aggressive'
intent held by Spark and the experimental and often self-reflexive narrative techniques encountered throughout her fiction; the 'salutary scar'
announces itself as a mark of *severance*, brought about by strategies
which encourage detached scrutiny rather than passive absorption.

Muriel Spark's Early Fiction has been written in the conviction that
the form and function of Spark's 'abiding doubleness' remain inad-
equately explored. It contends that there is a great deal more to be said
of the author's development of a mode of fiction that unites a degree
of postmodern narrative 'play' with a realist approach to character
construction and a serious moral–political vision. Indeed, this is a book
about Spark at her most strange and subversive, and one which claims –
by focusing on instances of narrative daring during the first two decades
of her literary career – that her various narrative experiments combine
formal innovation with an ethically driven and often feminist method
of storytelling; in particular, I argue that Spark's fiction demonstrates
relentlessly and in different ways how modern life constricts and shapes
human performativity and language. Spark emerges from this book as a
writer whose developments in style are neither introspective nor overtly
preoccupied with Catholicism, but are restlessly concerned instead with
exploring the possibilities of literary form to produce an agile kind of
social critique.

In the sections that follow, I examine how Spark has been (and indeed
continues to be) discussed in limited terms as a rather cruel Catholic
comic novelist, whose literary experiments – however complex, outlandish or confrontational – are nevertheless reducible to a narrowly didactic
God-game played out between an all-powerful author, 'indifferent to
creation' (Bradbury 1992: 187), and an ensemble of thinly drawn caricatures. This book attempts to remedy such shortcomings by reconsidering
Spark's self-reflexive approach to matters of narration, characterisation,

genre and plot, while attending to the largely unexamined influence of the *nouveau roman* on texts which aspire to the same 'disorienting' *detachment* advocated by the author in 'The Desegregation of Art'. Before doing so, it is necessary to trace the refinement of Spark's authorial intent, by examining unpublished notes and correspondence (as well as the author's debut short story) through which her desire for a derisory 'doubleness' can be seen to originate and evolve.

'An honest creative process': Spark's Pack of Lies

I was brought up in Edinburgh during the period described in this novel. But it would be personally embarrassing if anyone should quite wrongfully imagine it to be a literal record of my own happy schooldays.

I think it is well enough known that when I say I write fiction I mean it with all the intensity that I am capable of concentrating on the idea of fiction.

It has always been my intention to practise the arts of pretence and counterfeit on the reader. My fiction does not pretend that it is doing otherwise [. . .]. And so I should be embarrassed as a writer, also, if anyone should think this novel to be a literal history.

And I hope it bears whatever truth is proper to it, or emerges by chance from an honest creative process.

(MFL 1961)

The 'Author's Note' quoted above was drafted by Spark as the intended Preface to her 1961 novel, *The Prime of Miss Jean Brodie*, yet never included in the published text. Spark's words, while ostensibly concerned with denying any meaningful similarities between her novel's lively and often sinister plot and her own 'happy schooldays' in 1930s Edinburgh, double as a broader statement of authorial intent that can be applied across her œuvre. As Spark asserts, 'practis[ing] the arts of pretence and counterfeit' in a mode of fiction that 'does not pretend that it is doing otherwise' constitutes 'an honest creative process' from which emerges a 'truth [. . .] proper to it'. Spark, who shortly thereafter described her body of work as 'a pack of lies' that contained within it 'a kind of truth' (Kermode 1963: 78), was firming up a stance on her own practice of fiction that would be conceptualised more thoroughly in 'The Desegregation of Art'.

Spark knew 'an honest creative process' from a dishonest one. Her wartime work in black propaganda, conducted at Sefton Delmer's Political Intelligence Compound at Milton Bryan in Bedfordshire, saw her combine 'detailed truth with believable lies' in radio broadcasts, seemingly transmitting from within Germany, that were designed to weaken enemy morale by undermining the leadership and authority of the Nazi Party (1992a: 148). Destabilising fabrications, in other words, were presented in the form of compelling facts, written to be read on air by 'truly patriotic Germans' (151) who were intent on contributing toward the Nazis' downfall. In her novels, short stories and dramatic works, Spark sought to do the exact opposite; such works are often *overtly* fictional rather than convincingly realistic, yet each is concerned with communicating a certain 'truth [...] proper to it'. In many of these works, the quotidian surface of everyday life finds itself disrupted by extraordinary intrusions in the form of unquiet spirits, heavenly bodies, disembodied voices, maniacal authors, flying saucers, ghostly shadows, vanishing and reappearing characters, oracles and occultists, unfathomable coincidences, wild chronological leaps, and the disorienting metaleptic (or metatheatrical) implication that even the most banal occurrences and conversations might in fact be meticulously stage-managed and elaborately scripted. While such intrusions can hardly be said to exist in the service of verisimilitude, they often function rhetorically to enhance rather than diminish the particular *quality* of realism that Spark desired her work to attain, while supplementing her fiction with an emphasis on multiplicity and play. As Spark would reflect in one of her final interviews, her principle 'achievement' as a novelist had been to 'liberat[e] the novel in many ways', by 'opening doors and windows in the mind, and challeng[ing] fears – especially the most inhibiting fears about what a novel should be' (Taylor 2004: 27).

Spark's restless experimentation with narrative form, meanwhile, expresses her need for a sense of correlation between *what* and *how* she writes. This is perhaps unsurprising, given her origins in poetry and continued self-identification as a poet as opposed to a novelist: 'I think of myself as a narrative poet – I think of my novels as poems,' reads a brief handwritten note entitled 'My Contribution to Literary History', compiled among the notes and drafts relating to the author's 1992 autobiography, *Curriculum Vitae*, that are held in her Edinburgh archive (NLS c.1991). As Spark recalls in that book, her correspondence with the then Poet Laureate, John Masefield, during the early 1950s coincided with her own writing 'moving [...] from lyric poetry to narrative verse', a transition which marked 'the start of [her] move in literature towards the short story and then the novel' (197). Indeed, to consult the unpublished letters sent between the pair is to catch a glimpse into Spark's careful reconsideration of the narrative form best suited to her intentions. 'We have to address a disintegrated world', she wrote to Masefield in 1951:

The world we draw our inspiration from is disintegrated. When we write poems we are trying, in a manner, to write several poems at once and to speak on different levels. Our next job should be to do this and at the same time to make our meanings accessible, and I think this will come about through a rediscovery of form and the dramatic uses of rhetoric. (NLS 1951)

There is much that is insightful in Spark's letter, which expresses ideas concerning 'the dramatic uses of rhetoric', and writing for 'living audiences', that the author would theorise in far greater detail in 'The Desegregation of Art' two decades later. Spark's assertion of her need to 'address a disintegrated world' is especially intriguing, if ambiguous. Her comment could apply just as readily to the fractured conditions of postmodernity (famously described by Jean-François Lyotard as being defined by an 'incredulity toward metanarratives', and particularly an incredulity toward the 'grand narrative' of the Enlightenment and the advancement of knowledge [1984: xxiv]) as to what Adam Piette has discussed at length as the disquieting 'amnesias, lies and repressions of the postwar [and Cold War] world' (2009: 20). There may well be a more personal significance to such a remark, however. The Edinburgh-born daughter of a Jewish father and English mother, who attended a Presbyterian school and who, at the time of writing to Masefield, had escaped an abusive marriage in South Africa, before moving to England, devising convincing untruths in Political Intelligence, and then immersing herself among the London literati (as a critic and poet, and as editor of the *Poetry Review*), Spark certainly understood what it was to inhabit a 'disintegrated world' of unfixed identity, fabricated reality, and drastically changing personal circumstances and world events. Just as her varied and mobile life could hardly be contained within any singular, unifying narrative, so her artistic practice – her intention, that is, to 'write several poems at once and to speak on different levels' – would also come to undermine (or indeed *disintegrate*) any stable conception of selfhood and story.

In seeking in her work to 'speak on different levels' in an attempt to 'address a disintegrated world', it is understandable that Spark should also wish to pursue what she describes as 'a rediscovery of form' – arriving, as would come to be the case, at a mode of narrative prose which draws upon the ludic, intertextual and metafictional techniques and strategies associated with literary postmodernism. As numerous critics have noted, postmodernist fiction's characteristic ontological disruptions have the effect of foregrounding the mediated, relative and pluralistic nature of 'reality' itself. In her seminal critical study, *Metafiction: The Theory and Practice of Self-Conscious Fiction* (1984), Patricia Waugh argues that metafictional texts must demonstrate a self-reflexive awareness of their own inability to 'imitate or "represent" the world'; instead, such texts recognise that they can only represent those 'discourses which in turn *construct* that world'. It is because of this, Waugh affirms, that even the most outlandish work of metafiction 'always implicitly evokes the contexts of everyday life' (1988: 100):

> Contemporary metafictional writing is both a response and a contribution to an even more thoroughgoing sense that reality or history are [*sic*] provisional: no longer a world of eternal verities but a series of constructions, artifices, impermanent structures. The materialist, positivist, and empiricist world-view on which realistic fiction is premised no longer exists. It is hardly surprising, therefore, that more and more novelists have come to question and reject the forms that correspond to this ordered reality (the well-made plot, chronological sequence, the authoritative omniscient author). (7)

'Metafiction', Waugh asserts elsewhere in her study, 'does not abandon "the real world" for the narcissistic pleasures of the imagination', but rather 're-examine[s] the conventions of realism in order to discover – through its own self-reflection – a fictional form that is culturally relevant and comprehensible to contemporary readers' (18). In the absence of faith in any totalising 'grand narrative', such strategies disrupt the 'ordered reality' of conventional realism by placing a marked emphasis on, among other aspects, epistemological impotence over narrative authority, contradiction over consistency, and lasting irresolution over anything approaching a conclusive ending.

A few months after writing to Masefield, Spark embarked on the composition of her first short story, the vibrantly metafictional 'The Seraph and the Zambesi', which went on to win *The Observer*'s 1951 Christmas short story competition ('a glass of postmodern champagne among the musty realism of the other entries', in the words of her biographer, Martin Stannard [2009: 124]) and which became, as Spark remarked in *Curriculum Vitae*, 'the first real turning point of [her] career' as an author (198). The story, in which a luminous, six-winged seraph intrudes upon the unremarkable life of Samuel Cramer (the very same poet–protagonist from Charles Baudelaire's *Fanfarlo* [1847], now the incongruous proprietor of a petrol pump close to the Zambezi River in 1946), juxtaposes elements of the fantastical and the commonplace in a manner which would become a characteristic trait of Spark's subsequent works. Having long since abandoned his literary career, Cramer's artistic ambitions now extend only as far as writing and directing a local Nativity play, in which he has claimed for himself the leading role of First Seraph. When the celestial seraph interrupts the performance, Cramer's artistic failings are thrown into sharp relief. Next to the 'completed look' of the heavenly being, whose 'outline lacked the signs of confusion and ferment which are commonly the signs of living things', Cramer is defined witheringly as a spent creative force, and thus a shadow of his former self; his unimaginative and poorly designed costume, assembled from 'several thicknesses of mosquito-net', is 'not thick enough to hide his white shorts underneath' (122). The story ends with the destruction of Cramer's shoddily built stage set in a violent inferno whipped up by the seraph's enormous wings, before the creature glides gracefully along the river and out of sight.

Perhaps unsurprisingly (for reasons I shall detail shortly), 'The Seraph and the Zambesi' has been viewed predominantly as an eccentric yet didactic meditation on the disastrous consequences of neglecting one's religious beliefs, as well as a commentary on the 'degraded status' of human life and art when witnessed from the elevated 'spiritual perspective' of celestial beings (Gregson 2006: 6–7). I would argue that the focus of such criticism is misdirected, however. Cramer, after all, is not a mortal being but an exhausted literary relic, whose powers of imagination are shown to have diminished severely since he appeared in the pages of Baudelaire's novella a century earlier. The seraph's extraordinary arrival only emphasises this, by establishing a powerful rhetorical counterpoint to the otherwise unremarkable 'reality' of Cramer's lethargic and creatively stagnant existence in South Africa. The story thus stages the metafictional destruction (and possible revivification) of what John Barth, writing in 1967, describes as 'the literature of exhausted possibility' (64), by having the products of Cramer's insipid imagination be incinerated, before shifting focus – thrillingly – to the seraph's fiery flight to a new land. By way of its combination of irony, fantasy, realism and intertextuality, Spark's defamiliarising wit paves (or indeed *blazes*) fresh avenues of thought, while fulfilling her later-stated aim of 'writ[ing] fiction [. . .] with all the intensity that I am capable of concentrating on the idea of fiction'.

As Spark's first foray into narrative fiction, 'The Seraph and the Zambesi' constitutes an act of narrative daring, experimenting as it does with a mode of playful, self-reflexive fictionality in order to articulate a serious statement of artistic intent. In the novels, short stories and dramatic works that followed, Spark continued to pursue what she described to Masefield as a 'rediscovery of form' by developing a diverse range of innovative narrative strategies derived from modes of metafiction and metatheatre, the *nouveau roman*, and her own subversive spins on the familiar formal and thematic conventions of genres including the ghost story, crime caper, Wildean social comedy, Gothic melodrama, detective mystery and ancient tragedy. In these subsequent works, Spark gears her self-described practice of overt 'pretence and counterfeit' toward more nuanced instances of satire and social critique, placing particular emphasis on the plight of individuals (women, especially) who find themselves ensnared in self-alienating structures of conformity and control, within which they are forced to occupy roles intended to silence and tame them. Self-reflexive, illusion-breaking narrative techniques are remarkably well suited to conveying – and undermining – such structures; if, as Patricia Waugh asserts, metafiction can present reality as 'a series of constructions, artifices [and] impermanent structures' (1988: 7), then subversive potential exists in texts that stage the construction and dismantling of oppressive realities. Such is the nature of Spark's 'pack of lies', from which emerge fanciful fictions that carry urgent truths.

With all of this in mind, it must be noted that Spark's particular ingenuity has not always received the same degree of critical recognition afforded to her contemporaries. In her incisive comparative analysis of the experimental narrative strategies encountered in Spark's *The Driver's Seat* and Marguerite Duras's *The Ravishing of Lol Stein* (1964), for example, Judith Roof concludes by noting that, while Duras 'wrote works of serious mien within a tradition that venerates authors [including the likes of Alain Robbe-Grillet, Nathalie Sarraute and Michel Butor]', Spark's 'superficially more whimsical offerings landed in English-speaking populations less interested in the idiosyncratic experiments of an expatriate Scot', thus denying her a critical reception that '*takes her textuality seriously*' (2001: 64, emphasis mine). Roof is correct to identify significant contextual differences in terms of the critical standing of both authors, but her comment overlooks a central component of Spark's public image and critical reception. The author's well-documented conversion to Catholicism in 1954 came to dictate the tone of the reviews and readings of her subsequent fictions, including each of her twenty-two novels. The same perceived 'whimsical[ity]' identified by Roof can be seen to derive, in fact, from the longstanding critical conception of Spark as an author merrily playing God, whose narratives are seen to revel in a capricious cruelty derived from the relative inconsequentiality of human life. It is to Spark's disappointingly one-dimensional critical reception that I now turn.

'A light and heartless hand': Catholicism, Control and the Aesthetics of Cruelty

'Here is the recipe for a typical Muriel Spark novel', writes Michiko Kakutani at the beginning of her review of the author's 1996 novel, *Reality and Dreams*:

[T]ake a self-enclosed community (of writers, schoolgirls, nuns, rich people, etc.) that is full of incestuous liaisons and fraternal intrigue; toss in a bomb-shell (like murder, suicide or betrayal) that will ricochet dangerously around this little world, and add some allusions to the supernatural to ground these melodramatics in an old-fashioned context of good and evil. Serve up with crisp, authoritative prose and present with 'a light and heartless hand'. (1997: 29)

Kakutani's 'recipe', which concludes by quoting from the description offered by Fleur Talbot, the narrator–protagonist of *Loitering with Intent* (1981), of her own airily merciless writing style, serves as an accurate indicator of the lens through which critics have tended to view Spark's approach to writing fiction. Given their typical brevity, cloistered and claustrophobic settings, common themes of manipulation, deceit and betrayal, and characteristically 'crisp, authoritative' narrative delivery, Spark's novels – described memorably by John Updike as being 'short, brusque, bleak, harsh and queer' (1975: 76) – have unsurprisingly come to be renowned for 'the cruelty mixed with camp, the lightness of touch, the flick of the wrist that lands the lash' that is apparently discernible throughout (Sehgal 2014: n.p.). The flippancy, or 'lightness', with which Spark has been said to approach much of her 'bleak, harsh' subject matter has led to accusations of what Merritt Moseley, writing about the author in *The Cambridge Guide to Women's Writing in English* (1999), calls an 'Olympian attitude [shown] toward her own characters [which] has not been without its detractors' (592).

Indeed, even admirers of Spark have tended to temper their praise with similar reservations. 'You start deploring Spark's work, love it as you do', remarks Jenny Turner in an otherwise affectionate profile of the author in the *London Review of Books*, 'for its unsisterly cruelty [shown toward female characters] and lack of empathy with human motivation' (1992: 59). Writing about Spark in her critical survey of twentieth-century women writers, *Beyond the Lighthouse* (1981), Margaret Crosland concludes that she had mistakenly 'been looking for depth of character and thought, and had been disappointed at finding none', only to realise that the author's novels ought to be read purely as 'intellec-tualised square dances in which there is a semblance of progression but no real development, presumably because none was intended: it would have spoilt the dance' (55). In a separate study, Richard Todd adopts the adjective 'crystalline' from Iris Murdoch's 1961 essay, 'Against Dryness', but amends its meaning so that it 'suggests [. . .] not just the small-scale, *but also the hard, the impenetrable*' qualities of Spark's typically concise and oblique novels (1986: 177, emphasis mine). To appreciate the meticulously choreographed 'dance' staged in each of Spark's 'crystalline' novels and short stories, such responses suggest, necessitates navigating one's attention away from matters of character psychology, or the moral implications of the author's narrative techniques and treatment of characters (her women, in particular), and learning instead to admire her deft handling of plot, suspense and narrative temporality.

Of each of these elegantly managed components, Spark's inventive play with time is arguably the most distinctive feature of her writing. Her narratives famously flit both analeptically and proleptically from the narrative present to past and future events, with revelations concerning characters' imminent or far-off deaths, illnesses, infamies, betrayals and love affairs strewn throughout the narration of the ongoing plot; readers learn, for instance, that Nicholas Farringdon will be martyred by the end of *The Girls of Slender Means* (1963), and that *The Prime of Miss Jean Brodie*'s Mary Macgregor, though still a schoolgirl during the time at which the novel is set, will burn to death in a hotel fire in her twenties. 'It is like a bizarre textual supermarket', writes Nicholas Royle of the deaths foretold in the morbidly comic and aptly titled *Memento Mori* (1959), 'in which all characters are required to have an age-tag like a price and sell-by date' (2001: 199). When John Crace composed a pastiche of *The Prime of Miss Jean Brodie* for his 'Digested Classics' series in *The Guardian*, it was the novel's proleptic disclosures of the respective fates of its cast of classmates that he took particular pleasure in lampooning:

> 'Miss Brodie seems to have been in her prime for a long time,' replied Sandy, who was famous even then for her piggy eyes. 'That is one of the book's comic conceits,' said Monica, who was famous for maths, 'so we should all say the word prime as often as possible.'
>
> 'There are so many comic conceits going on here,' said Eunice, who was famous for gymnastics and hadn't even noticed all the arch time-shifts, 'that it's becoming a bit laboured. I'd better do a somersault before I get married to a doctor in ten years' time.'
>
> 'I'd better say prime too, I suppose,' said Mary, who was famous for being a silent lump, 'as I'm about to get burned to death in a hotel hell-fire of Calvinist indecision in fourteen years' time.' (2008: n.p.)

What distinguishes Crace's pastiche from Spark's novel, of course, is the schoolgirls' evident awareness of what their futures hold, as well as the attributes for which they will become best known. Spark seldom affords her own characters such a privilege, and it is because of this aspect of her fiction that she has found herself likened by her critics to a malevolent master puppeteer, flaunting her powers of omniscience before the reader. For Patricia Waugh, Spark 'uses the omniscient-author convention not benevolently, to signpost the reader's way through the text, but to express a disturbing authority whose patterns are not quite so easy to understand' (1988: 74).

While Spark's peculiar 'patterns' may remain unnervingly opaque, the power that she appears to exercise over her characters, displayed most overtly through proleptic asides, has proved all too easy for her critics to conceptualise and comprehend. For a vast number of these critics, the overt authority of the Sparkian narrator can be interpreted as a relatively uncomplicated analogy for that possessed by an omnipotent and often callous God, which far exceeds the limited powers and perspectives of mere mortals. Ruth Whittaker, for example, contends that 'the theme of *all* [Spark's] work' is 'the relationship – shown openly or implied – between the secular and the divine, between man's temporal viewpoint and God's eternal vision' (1982: 1):

> Both God and the novelist create a world which they then people with characters simultaneously free and limited. Sometimes in novels, as in real life, characters resent and fight back at authorial or divine omniscience, and the dynamic relationship between creator and character is integral to Mrs Spark's plots. [. . .] God, like the novelist, knows the beginning and the end, and the struggles of his characters to evade their destinies, that is the process of most people's lives. (1979: 162–3)

Each of Whittaker's remarks, which appear to reveal rather more about her own beliefs concerning God and the nature of 'real life' than those necessarily held by Spark, offers a useful means of understanding the particular theological framework through which Spark's fictions have predominantly been interpreted. With such a framework set rigidly in place in the minds of critics, each new novel or short story – however experimental in form or diverse in subject matter – came to be perceived as a new variation on an increasingly familiar theme. 'Restrain your groans', advises Robert Nye in an exasperated early review of *The Driver's Seat*. Spark's latest work, he claims, is the latest in 'a number of novels and stories where the author's function as God's spy has been too apparent'. For Nye, '[Spark's] elbows have been in our ribs a joke too often', and the reader is yet again 'reminded of her liking for saying that this and that is "comical" (viewed from the presumed standpoint of eternity)' (1970: 14). So persuasive is this mode of reading that in a 2018 *Times Literary Supplement* feature, commissioned to mark the centenary of Spark's birth, Margaret Drabble assessed the author's fiction in near-identical terms to Nye by conceptualising Spark once again as 'God's spy':

> Events play themselves out [in Spark's fiction] as though watched by God from a very great distance and another timescale. *Lord, what fools these*

mortals be. The author spies upon her creations, and lets them hurtle towards disaster. Maybe [Spark] sees herself as God's spy, observing with amusement the scurrying antics of a fallen world. (n.p.)

In referencing the contemptuous words of Puck in *A Midsummer Night's Dream*, who gazes upon human follies with detached, half-mocking disdain, Drabble gestures toward the implied effects of Spark's apparently God's-eye (or rather 'God's spy') view. Spark's mortal readers, Drabble's allusion suggests, are invited to share a quasi-divine perspective, from which they can comprehend the relative insignificance of their own 'scurrying antics'. Lorna Sage, having arrived at a similar conclusion in *Women in the House of Fiction* (1992), asserts that 'Spark's concerns are with literary theology, and the way contemporary life looks from the improbable perspective of Almighty irony' (142). Such readings offer a convenient way of comprehending the most unconventional – if not jarring or outright disturbing – elements of Spark's prose: wild leaps in chronology and perspective; a detached, seemingly disaffected view of death and violence; characters who often appear ontologically diminished, or even puppet-like through the compulsive nature of their actions and their apparent lack of free will. '[Spark's] novels are paradoxically oriented *away* from what is most meaningful and towards a spiritually perverse focus on the ultimately meaningless', argues Ian Gregson of the author's depictions of human life; '[her characters'] resultant transformation into puppets works both self-reflexively and ontologically' (2006: 6–7).

To encounter much of the existing scholarship on Spark is thus to be reminded of the address of *The Abbess of Crewe*'s (1974) megalomaniacal protagonist, Abbess Alexandra, to her enraptured congregation: '"We have entered the sphere, dear Sisters, of mythology"' (102). Central to Spark's own particular 'mythology' is her aforementioned conversion to Catholicism in 1954, which came to colour the critical reception of *The Comforters*, published three years later, and set the tone for readings of the numerous thematically and stylistically diverse works which would follow over the subsequent five decades. '[*The Comforters*] is a book in which you've got your myth', remarked Frank Kermode to Spark in 1963, 'but you've deliberately made it in a sense a game about novels, haven't you?' (79). Kermode had good reason to think so. That novel features a protagonist who is herself a Catholic convert, and who is able to overhear an otherworldly voice which appears to dictate a 'plot' that she and her acquaintances seem predestined to follow. Perhaps even more pertinent to Kermode were the circumstances that surrounded *The Comforters*' composition and early promotion. The novel was written in part at a Carmelite priory, to which Spark had retreated while recovering from a period of nervous exhaustion and mental illness, and had been financed by a 'plight fund' contributed to by a fellow Catholic convert, Graham Greene (Stannard 2009: 161). Another notable convert, Evelyn Waugh, joined Greene in supplying a favourable advance notice for the novel (both authors were sent proofs from Spark's literary agent, Alan Barnsley (Ibid.: 176); at Waugh's own suggestion, his words of praise were positioned prominently on the first edition's dust-jacket, as well as on early advertisements.[4] On its eventual publication, therefore, *The Comforters'* reputation preceded it, and the terms on which it was to be read seemed already to have been established. Spark, as Kermode put it, '[had] her myth'.

Spark replied to Kermode, however, by insisting that *The Comforters* had *not* been written with the intended purpose of expressing a theologically informed 'myth' central to her writing practice or attitude towards fiction, but rather to explore a self-reflexive mode of novel-writing suitable to her: 'I was asked to write a novel, and I didn't think much of novels [. . .]. So I wrote a novel to work out the technique first, to sort of make it all right with myself to write a novel at all' (1963: 79). Despite her unambiguous response, Spark appeared to go unheard; for this 'unremittingly Catholic novelist', Kermode later concluded, the 'myth' communicated by way of *The Comforters'* novelistic 'game' revolves around the idea that 'making fictions is in a way a presumptuous thing to do, because the novelist is, unlike God, free at the expense of his creatures'. The novelist's presumptuous power, Kermode argues, is undermined when, with a metafictive flourish, 'the characters fight back' by refusing to honour the will of a false deity (1968: 203). With Spark's essential 'myth' so firmly established by early critics such as Kermode, it is little surprise that subsequent scholarship has followed suit by seeking out analogies between the author and God, and/or the text's didactic unravelling of representations of presumptuous authorial power (so as to emphasise the singular power of God, above all imitators). Examples are wide-ranging, from Joseph Hynes's conviction that the proleptic leaps peppered throughout *The Driver's Seat* reflect the 'conflict between free will and determinism' (1993: 164), to David Lodge's belief that the ultimately thwarted attempts of Jean Brodie to determine her pupils' fates ought to be read purely in terms of a clash 'between the Catholic God who allows free will and the Calvinistic one who doesn't' (1992: 76). Not unlike one of the troubled women who occupy the absent centres of her most experimental novels (*The Driver's Seat* [1970], *Not to Disturb* [1971], *The Hothouse by the East River* [1973] and the tellingly titled *The Public Image* [1968] – all examined over the course of this book), Spark appears to be confined within the rigid parameters of a narrowly defined public persona.

It is not my intention to deny the significance of the theological contexts in which Spark's fiction has predominantly been read. Such readings bear clear relevance to certain texts; in some, such as *The Prime of Miss Jean Brodie*, they are even incorporated into characters' dialogue, as when Sandy Stranger launches into a memorable tirade against her tyrannical teacher: 'She thinks she is Providence [. . .]. She thinks she is the God of Calvin, she sees the beginning and the end' (129). I disagree with Whittaker, however, that the conflicting relationship between the secular/temporal and the divine/eternal ought to be considered 'the theme of *all* [Spark's] work'. I would argue instead that this rigid, prescriptive way of reading Spark has postponed or even precluded more rigorous analysis of the significance of the social and historical contexts and concerns of her fiction, explorations of the relevance of her writing to diverse strands of literary and psychoanalytical theory, as well as considerations of how her literary innovations have facilitated instances of gendered social critique that are often far from 'unsisterly', to return to the term applied by Jenny Turner. Spark's narrative perspectives – which, I shall argue, are multifarious rather than uniform, altering drastically from one text to the next – are concerned intensely with reflecting and subverting the dynamics of power, knowledge and control operating *within* the worlds in which they are set. To begin to explore this possibility, our enduring faith in the unerring omniscience of the Sparkian narrator must first be challenged.

Flawed Crystals: Alternatives to Omniscience

As much of the preceding section makes clear, a common fixture of Spark criticism is a degree of commentary, be it deferential or disparaging, on her fiction's formal economy, structural precision and narrative flair. 'How do you do it? I am dazzled', Evelyn Waugh enthused to Spark of *The Bachelors* on its publication in 1960, before describing the novel as 'the cleverest and most elegant of all your clever and elegant books' (qtd in Stannard 2009: 233). In a not dissimilar reaction to the author's final novel, 2004's *The Finishing School*, Ali Smith wrote admiringly of 'a work of [. . .] glittering Sparkian ice', and expressed her 'wonder' at the paradoxical 'simplicity and [. . .] intricacy of the plot, blowaway as gossamer' (2004: n.p.). Spark's novels, Bernard Harrison complained elsewhere, 'seem all surface, and a rather dry, sparsely furnished, though elegantly mannered surface at that' (1976: 225), while John Updike lauded such texts as works which 'linger in the mind as brilliant shards, decisive as smashed glass' (1975: 76). As with Richard Todd's aforementioned description of Spark's novels as 'crystalline' in their combination of 'the small-scale' and 'the hard, the impenetrable', these critical responses tend to pair a degree of reverence for the stylistic sharpness and concision of the text ('clever and elegant', 'glittering', 'elegantly mannered', 'brilliant shards'), with a pronouncement of its essential intangibility, as well as the critic's own unbridgeable distance ('ice', 'gossamer', 'all surface', 'smashed glass'). The implication is that these are works to be admired from afar rather than intimately understood, as though each ought to come prefaced with the instruction: *look, but don't touch.*

This oddly reverential critical approach is undoubtedly encouraged by the style and structure of the texts themselves, which often appear to delimit the need for extratextual interpretation by foregrounding their own seamless closure and perfect containment. We might note, for instance, the chiastic structures of the sentences with which many of Spark's novels and short stories appear to conclude decisively. These include the closing words of *The Driver's Seat*, 'fear and pity, pity and fear' (107), which seem to smooth the edges of the novel's disquieting story with an elegant allusion to tragic catharsis, as well as the respective endings of 'The Seraph and the Zambesi' and *Reality and Dreams*, which leave their readers 'among the rocks that look like crocodiles and the crocodiles that look like rocks' (131), and 'in the tract of no-man's land between dreams and reality, reality and dreams' (160), and thus emphatically outside the spaces of the preceding plots. We might think, too, of the fable-like first and last words of *The Girls of Slender Means*, which bookend the text and bracket off its plot as taking place '[l]ong ago in 1945' (7; 142), or of *Not to Disturb*'s closing image of 'sunlight [. . .] laughing on the walls' (94), which appears to dispel the novel's sinister content as if it were no more than a bad dream. As with Spark's famous predilection for foreshadowing, such features may be interpreted as manifestations of an authorial desire to control the texts' meanings and thus keep readers on the other side of the 'glittering Sparkian ice'.

For many critics, the elegantly managed style and structure of Spark's writing only underscores its central 'myth' and theological motivation. The implication for Todd, for example, is that the more 'crystalline' Spark's fictions appear in their archness, brevity and structural elegance, the stronger the implied presence of 'an unscrupulous God [. . .] who can be, and often is, ruthlessly decisive with his characters, and intolerant of hesitancy or lingering emotional involvement' (181–2). This need not be seen to be the case, however, and more recent analyses have subjected the narrative dynamics of her novels (and their rhetorical effects) to more rigorous and illuminating critical scrutiny. In his 2006 essay, '"There's Something about Mary": Narrative and Ethics in *The Prime of*

Miss Jean Brodie', Peter Robert Brown offers a careful reconsideration of that novel's narration as emanating not from an omniscient, omnipotent God's-eye view, but from the consciousness of an epistemologically limited being, rather like a first-person narrator recast in a third-person role. Despite its frequent use of prolepses, Brown observes the manifold ways in which 'the narrative's epistemic authority is qualified' by details which remain pointedly obscure, and which therefore allow the narrator to be 'characterised as fallible, even unreliable' (232). Indeed, far from flaunting any powers of omniscience, these recurrent narrative time-shifts come to foreground 'the selection, arrangement and labelling of events' in a manner which emphasises the narrator's partial and personally invested account of Brodie and her pupils (233). Moreover, the narrator displays a pointed interest in belittling the actions and appearance of one of the characters, Mary Macgregor, over all others, in a manner which mirrors the tyrannical tendencies of the novel's titular pedagogue. For Brown, the rhetorical effects of the structure and content of the narrative possess powerful ethical implications:

> [T]he novel illustrates the ways in which institutional authority and power can produce and legitimate malevolent narratives that place limits on how individuals are interpreted. [. . .] [Spark] involves readers in the victimisation of Mary and, through her irony, enables them to become aware of that involvement. Such awareness can have real moral and political impact, since readers are encouraged to acknowledge their participation in victimisation in the actual world and to reflect on the role that narrative plays in the process and justification of victimisation. (229)

According to Brown's reading, *The Prime of Miss Jean Brodie* is instructive in ways that are unrelated to the didactic displays of divine omniscience with which Spark's fiction is so frequently associated. By 'ironically and satirically depicting the activity of narrating and the often dubious authority on which it rests', his essay concludes, the novel encourages readers to 'resist the pernicious narratives we encounter in real life', and to 'question the power and authority of those who construct them' in much the same way that Sandy Stranger attempts to do when she seeks to bring about the dramatic downfall of her teacher (247). Such an interpretation is consistent with Spark's own emphasis, in an account of the composition of her first few novels, on the importance of 'writ[ing] the narratives from a consistent point of view that's not my own', so that 'the narrator of *Memento Mori* [a novel concerned with the lives and deaths of a group of feuding septuagenarians], for example, would be an old wise person who knew how these other old people in the story really felt'. Whether 'first or third person', Spark maintains, 'the narrative [. . .] belongs to a character [. . .]. I have to decide what the author of the narrative is like. It's not me, *it's a character*' (1961: 62, emphasis mine). In interviews conducted since, Spark would maintain that each novel or short story is narrated consistently from a subjective, localised and often humanly limited perspective; speaking in 1987, for example, she described taking pains to write *The Driver's Seat* purely 'from the point of view of someone who doesn't know what anyone is thinking, but who can see, who can observe' (Frankel 1987: 454).

A more varied account of Spark's deflationary conception of authorial power, and the readerly wariness that it ought to invite, is provided in Bran Nicol's 2010 essay, 'Reading Spark in the Age of Suspicion'. Examining the self-reflexive approaches to narration encountered in *The Comforters*, *The Driver's Seat* and *Loitering with Intent*, Nicol contends that 'the analogy between this aspect of Spark's writing and the idea of the "God-like" writer, raised frequently in relation to Catholic writers, needs to be reassessed':

> Unlike those of her contemporaries, such as Iris Murdoch and Graham Greene, Spark's novels do not offer a sustained meditation on religion or spirituality (even though the topic of Catholicism crops up frequently). *God is not one of her 'themes'*. Considering her approach to authorship in relation to the idea of God rather than other paradigms of power and control makes sense only [. . .] in the unsatisfactory terms of 'biographical criticism'. (112–13)

While 'the implicit analogy between the author–character relationship and that between God and his creations seem[s] especially pertinent in the case of a writer who believed in God', argues Nicol, Spark's purportedly 'omniscient' narrator is often revealed to be less analogous to God than to an epistemologically compromised (not to mention potentially malevolent) being – 'a small-scale, prurient, menacing entity, more like a stalker than a deity' (116; 123). As Nicol demonstrates with reference to the numerous 'inconsistencies, gaps, and contradictions' that he encounters in the aforementioned novels, what emerges in Spark's fiction 'is a vision of the author as "loitering with intent"' in amongst the texts' various assemblages of characters and plotlines, 'rather than fulfilling any loftier ambition' (123).

Nicol's proposed model of the Sparkian narrator as a 'small-scale' and somewhat sinister loiterer, while certainly not applicable to all of her novels and short stories, invites the attentive reader to look for revelatory flaws in the author's supposedly 'crystalline' narratives, and to consider what meanings may lurk beneath. I am reminded here of the significance of Spark's 1962 essay, 'Edinburgh-Born', in which the author identifies the word 'nevertheless' (a word that she recalls overhearing amid the chatter of the Morningside tearooms she visited as a child) as 'the core of a thought-pattern' that she retained ever since. Spark proceeds to relate this 'thought-pattern' to Edinburgh's peculiar topography, perceiving the sheer incongruity of 'the primitive black crag' of the Castle Rock 'rising up in the middle of populated streets of commerce, stately squares and winding closes' as analogous to 'the statement of an unmitigated fact preceded by "nevertheless"' (1992d: 22). As Joseph Hynes asserts, this 'nevertheless principle' came to 'typif[y] [Spark's] life, her psychology, and her work', in that it demonstrates 'that any position taken or point made has another side' (1992: 2). The same is true of her narratives, in which displays of apparent omniscience and infallibility inevitably contain inconsistencies, blind spots, or obsessive, frustrated or malign motivations.

If Spark's fiction does not attempt to provide a singular, *sub specie aeternitatis* perspective of human life, then what might constitute or inform the author's way (or indeed manifold *ways*) of seeing? Brown and Nicol are each correct to identify varying degrees of fallibility and prurience in the narration of Spark's novels, which can be seen to exhibit a variety of modes of knowledge and perception. An obvious example is *The Comforters*, in which the ingenious conceit of a spectral typewriter (known to the protagonist as the Typing Ghost) replaces narrative omniscience with a model of telepathy wherein both narrator and protagonist strain to anticipate the other's thoughts and actions. Elsewhere, techniques derived from the object-oriented prose of the *nouveau roman* have the effect of limiting Spark's narrators to recording surface-level observations of people and things, without access to characters' thoughts and emotions. Even a seemingly unambiguous indicator of omniscience – an awareness of future events, for instance – can serve as a marker of epistemological *impotence* when paired with glaring gaps in the narrator's knowledge. Similarly, the flagrant displays of disregard for the ontological status of the narrated subject, evinced by the narrators of resolutely contemporary texts including *The Public Image* and *Not to Disturb*, may not be evidence of authorial indifference, but a more nuanced articulation of what Fredric Jameson famously conceptualised as the 'depthlessness' of postmodern experience (1992: 9–15). Each of these examples – the ghostly (or perhaps haunted) narrator; the detached observer; the frustrated voyeur; the postmodernist attention to surfaces over depths – is examined in this study as a valuable alternative to the familiar model of Sparkian omniscience. Before discussing these models in greater detail, it is necessary to consider the position my book occupies in relation to the evolving critical discourse on Spark.

Desegregating Spark: The 1970s to Now

By paying specific attention to her archival materials and lesser-known texts (including her early short stories, ostensibly 'minor' novels and her little-known stage play), and considering her fiction's longstanding engagement with the theories and techniques of the *nouveau roman*, as well as the applicability of diverse strands of literary theory to her writing, this book seeks to advance the belated attempts of critics to expand the terms on which Spark has predominantly been read. Indeed, such attempts did not begin in earnest until 1974, when Peter Kemp's monograph on the author's literary career thus far, entitled simply *Muriel Spark*, paid unprecedented attention to the influence of Robbe-Grillet on her then recent novels, *The Driver's Seat, Not to Disturb* and *The Hothouse by the East River* (115–55). Kemp's study, which elects to approach each of Spark's novels on its own terms, is thus unique among similar novel-by-novel accounts of the author's œuvre (all also entitled *Muriel Spark*) by Karl Malkoff (1968), Patricia Stubbs (1973), Allan Massie (1979), Velma Bourgeois Richmond (1984), Alan Bold (1986), Dorothea Walker (1988) and Norman Page (1990), as well as Ruth Whittaker's *The Faith and Fiction of Muriel Spark* (1982) and Rodney Stenning Edgecombe's *Vocation and Identity in the Fiction of Muriel Spark* (1990), which interpret her novels (to the exclusion of her short stories, poetry, stage play and radio dramas) as variations on the narrow, theologically informed myth outlined earlier. Elsewhere, attempts to broaden the existing discourse on Spark would suffer notable shortcomings. The approach taken in Judy Sproxton's *The Women of Muriel Spark* (1992), for example, ironically mirrors the various misogynistic and desubjectifying forces at play in the author's fiction by reducing each of her female characters to a narrowly defined 'type', without exploring their respective complexities or considering the vital connections that exist between them. Joseph Hynes's *The Art of the Real: Muriel Spark's Novels* (1988) is similarly hamstrung by its insistence on applying an inflexibly binaristic model of realism (and anti-realism) to Spark's diverse body of fiction.

The discussion of Spark's fiction in a number of ground-breaking studies of experimental and postmodern literature published between the mid-1980s and early 1990s, including Patricia Waugh's *Metafiction*, Brian McHale's *Postmodernist Fiction* (1987) and Gerardine Meaney's *(Un)Like Subjects: Women, Theory, Fiction* (1993), would expand the terms on which her literary innovations could be read. McHale, for example, interprets *The Comforters* not as a straightforward theological analogy, but rather as a 'postmodernist parodic version of Proust, tracing its heroine's apprenticeship to the point where she is literally able to write the very text in which she figures as a character' (122–3), while Meaney's uniquely feminist reading of *The Hothouse by the East River* draws upon the work of Julia Kristeva and Luce Irigaray to claim Spark's deathly protagonist, Elsa Hazlett, as a source of maternal abjection whose body 'impinges on representation' (161). The nuanced analyses of Spark in studies such as Regina Barreca's *Untamed and Unabashed: Essays on Women and Humour in British Literature* (1994), Judy Little's *Comedy and the Woman Writer: Woolf, Spark, and Feminism* (1983) and Elaine Showalter's 'Rethinking the Seventies: Women Writers and Violence' (1981), meanwhile, highlight the pointedly gendered implications of Sparkian satire. For Showalter, *The Driver's Seat*'s sinister tale of a woman's purposeful search for her male murderer offers a blackly comic perspective on female agency (or the lack thereof), in which 'Spark gives us the devastated postulates of feminine wisdom: that a woman creates her identity by choosing her clothes, that she creates her history by choosing her man' (164). Such studies offer a welcome counterpoint to Gayle Greene's critical overview of the history of feminist fiction, *Changing the Story* (1991), which elects to omit any detailed discussion of Spark on the unelaborated grounds that the author's 'metafictional devices – artist figures, speculations on fictionality or the function and morality of art' are not employed 'in a way that is related to gender', being 'uninformed by feminist consciousness' (25).

The most decisive shift in critical approaches to Spark arrived in 2001, with the publication of Martin McQuillan's edited collection, *Theorising Muriel Spark: Gender, Race, Deconstruction*. In his bold and often polemical introduction to the essays that follow, McQuillan asserts that 'the task of theorising Muriel Spark [. . .] is long overdue', before criticising the way in which the author is 'continually reduced by the power of English canonical criticism to the safe domain of the properly "Catholic"' (McQuillan 2001a: 8; 2–3). McQuillan contends that 'such divisive and rigid categorisation (which takes little account of Spark's Scottish Presbyterian upbringing and entirely overlooks her avowed Jewish cultural history) leads to doctrinal criticism', which entails 'read[ing] Spark's novels for moral and theological content' and thus 'reading her texts like the penny catechism' (2). Like the red scarf that pulled attention away from the author in her portrait, such 'rigid categorisation', argues McQuillan, causes 'everything which might be interesting' about Spark's fiction to be 'squeezed out [. . .] in the name of a Catholic doctrinal orthodoxy' (3). The collection's twelve chapters pay heed to McQuillan's concerns by utilising strands of literary, psychoanalytical and sociocultural theory to provide a more rounded view of Spark's fiction: Eleanor Byrne offers an incisive postcolonial reading of the author's early, African-set short stories, including 'The Curtain Blown by the Breeze' (1954) and 'The Go-Away Bird' (1958); Susan Sellers draws upon Kristeva's psychoanalytical study of love (1983's *Tales of Love*) to dissect the murky marriage at the centre of *The Public Image*; Nicholas Royle's ingenious interpretation of *Memento Mori* argues persuasively that 'Spark's work is pervaded by the telepathic', and that 'the uncanny transmission of thoughts' staged in this particular novel 'are bound up with the very nature of fictional narration' (2001: 192–3). That the content of Royle's chapter, which investigates telepathy as a conceptual alternative to narrative omniscience, would be developed at length in his acclaimed 2003 study, *The Uncanny*, underscores the purpose of *Theorising Muriel Spark*; released from the narrow '"realm of mythology"' that once contained them, the author's fictions are free to spark new ideas into life. 'Theory', surmises Willy Maley during a Derridean reading of *Not to Disturb*, 'has in fact much to learn from *Spark*', rather than the other way around (2001: 171).

The efforts of McQuillan et al. to effect the desegregation of Spark's art would be taken up afresh by David Herman in 2008. In his edited special issue of *Modern Fiction Studies* – later published as a book, *Muriel Spark: Twenty-First Century Perspectives* (2010), featuring additional essays by Patricia Waugh and Bran Nicol – Herman assembled a set of critical responses to Spark which further demythologised the author by recontextualising her fiction and widening the terms on which it can and should be read. Lisa Harrison's detailed study of Spark's relationship with *The New Yorker* (2010), for example, examines the author's contributions to the magazine (as well as her unpublished correspondence with its editors) in order to position her, in the words of Herman, 'as a major contributor to world literature' (Herman 2010: 7). Jonathan Kemp's analysis of *The Driver's Seat*, developed in dialogue with the writings of Irigaray, Gilles Deleuze and Félix Guattari, explores the novel's refusal to provide insight into the mind of its protagonist as reflective of its essential *queerness*; the novel is 'queer', asserts Kemp, because it 'buckl[es] commonsense notions of the self by excavating all psychology; queer, that is, in that it [. . .] posits the self as some form of discursive residue devoid of meaning or interpretable content' (2010: 545). In a reading which echoes Peter Robert Brown's analysis of *The Prime of Miss Jean Brodie*, Kemp questions the presumed omniscience of Spark's narrator by teasing meaning from the lacunae and ambiguities placed within the prose.

In the decade since the publication of the *Modern Fiction Studies* special issue, numerous articles have continued the task of disentangling Spark from the mythology with which she has long been associated. Bearing out Willy Maley's belief that 'theory has in fact much to learn from Spark', such studies have sought, through close textual analysis of Spark's fiction, to illuminate concepts drawn from realms as diverse as psychoanalysis, literary theory, and sociocultural and historical analysis. In '"Another world than this": Muriel Spark's Postwar Investigations' (2012), for example, Eluned Summers-Bremner examines how Spark's early novels *Robinson* (1958) and *Memento Mori* (minimised and pigeonholed in one overview of her fiction as 'witty theological parables' [Glavin 2000: 298]) artfully reflect the diminishment of postwar Britain's national imperial status. John Foxwell's 'Enacting Hallucinatory Experience in Fiction' (2016), meanwhile, draws upon research in the fields of cognitive literary studies and audionarratology to assess *The Comforters*' depictions of voice-hearing as accurately reflective of 'the phenomenological "reality" of abnormal psychological experience' (144), as opposed to a more abstract theological and/or metafictional 'truth' (Spark had been inspired to include such sequences, after all, following her own experience of psychosis, as I discuss in the following chapter). More recently, Cairns Craig's *Muriel Spark, Existentialism and the Art of Death* (2019) reads Spark in dialogue with Søren Kierkegaard, while relating her conceptualisation of death to a Scottish literary tradition that includes writings by James Hogg and J. M. Barrie.

While McQuillan's call for scholars to attend to the 'long overdue' task of 'theorising Muriel Spark' has certainly been heeded in the years since 2001, there remains significant work still to be done. Unlike contemporaries including Christine Brooke-Rose, John Fowles and B. S. Johnson, for example, Spark continues to be overlooked in much of the critical discourse surrounding experimental literature, and the reasons for this demand further scrutiny. Similarly, Spark's self-acknowledged interest in the *nouveau roman* has been explored predominantly in relation to a narrow selection of overtly experimental novels written by the author in the early 1970s, without consideration of earlier instances of engagement with the 'anti-novel'. Spark's unpublished drafts, manuscripts and research notes, meanwhile, offer an invaluable yet hitherto largely unexamined insight into the composition of some of her most innovative works, revealing in the process an author writing in active engagement with the techniques of literary postmodernism, and devising imaginative alternatives to narrative omniscience. By turning my attention to these and other aspects of Spark's fiction, I seek to advance the project of desegregating Spark from the modes of 'rigid categorisation' and 'doctrinal criticism' outlined by McQuillan (2001a: 2).

Muriel Spark's Early Fiction

It is my intention in this book to present Spark's fiction as less neatly contained and narrowly didactic than is often alleged to be the case, and to focus instead on its deceptively expansive and decidedly more equivocal qualities. Particular attention is paid throughout to formal and generic liminality, self-reflexivity and stylistic experimentation. In the chapters that follow, I also aim to reassess some of Spark's ostensibly minor fictions as deceptively major ones, to consider crucial convergences between what has been termed her one and only 'big novel' (*The Mandelbaum Gate*) and the 'witty' and 'laconic' phases of writing that lie on either side (Glavin 2000: 298), and to pay specific attention to her achievements as a playwright and short-story writer. I therefore resist taking the long view of the author's œuvre, as many other studies have, and concentrate instead on a narrower timeframe, spanning the mid-1950s (the earliest text discussed in detail is the 1953 short story, 'Harper and Wilton') to the publication of her bizarre anti-novel, *The Hothouse by the East River*, in 1973. I consider the latter text, which combines a number of the stylistic and conceptual innovations exhibited in the author's earlier works, to be the apex of Spark's literary experimentation, which fails at every turn to correspond with the enduring myth of its author. Following its publication, Spark would explore comparatively more conventional themes and structures; in the sociopolitical satires that followed immediately thereafter, *The Abbess of Crewe* and *The Takeover* (1976), she took playful aim at the Watergate scandal and the 1973 oil crisis respectively, while two later novels, 1996's *Reality and Dreams* and 2004's *The Finishing School*, would return to the interpersonal dynamics at play in the film industry and the classroom, the politics of which were investigated more inventively (and with sharper focus) in *The Public Image* and *The Prime of Miss Jean Brodie*.

Focusing on this twenty-year period not only affords an opportunity to trace formative instances in Spark's development of a mode of writing that sought to reconceptualise realism through a 'rediscovery of form' and a refinement of 'the arts of pretence and counterfeit', but also allows me to consider how her fiction came to intersect with newly emerging ideas concerning postmodernism, metafiction, metatheatre and the *nouveau roman*. I do not, however, attempt to offer highly detailed analyses of two of Spark's best-known and most highly regarded novels, *The Prime of Miss Jean Brodie* and *The Girls of Slender Means*, despite their publication within this timeframe. These novels have each attracted a wealth of critical commentary, often to the detriment of other works published within the same period. By contrast, the seven novels, five short stories and single stage play that form the focus of my book have been either under-represented in Spark scholarship, or examined predominantly in terms of the rigid theological approach delineated earlier. Although necessarily selective, it is my hope that these texts will provide a fresh insight into some of the more interesting and frequently neglected aspects of Spark's fiction.

This book is organised thematically for the purpose of best highlighting some of the most pertinent areas of interest for present and future Spark criticism. By taking a broadly chronological approach to the texts discussed within each chapter, it allows for both the continuities and the changes in Spark's fiction to be traced in a coherent manner. The discussion of Spark's relationship with the *nouveau roman* in Chapter Three, for example, analyses three of her novels in the order of their publication, and thus offers an account of the author's evolving engagement with the theories and narrative techniques associated with the so-called 'anti-novel'. The book as a whole, however, occasionally diverges from a chronological structure by grouping texts together based on the particular focus of each chapter. This allows for the productive, albeit unconventional, pairings of texts such as *Doctors of Philosophy* and *Not to Disturb* in Chapter Two, and *The Ballad of Peckham Rye* and *The Mandelbaum Gate* in Chapter Three. Accordingly, my study offers no monolithic conceptual perspective on Spark's fiction, choosing instead to explore a variety of theoretical and narratological approaches, and drawing upon a particular strand of theory when it most usefully illuminates either a specific text or the contrasts and convergences between texts. By taking this approach, I seek to establish a more complex language or framework for discussing Spark, which, rather than disregarding those features that appear anomalous when placed within the parameters of a single literary tradition, is better suited to accommodating and analysing the tensions and contradictions that may arise through the juxtaposition and interaction of multiple literary 'codes'.

Chapter One examines the manifestations of the supernatural depicted in Spark's debut novel, *The Comforters*, as well as in a selection of her early (and otherwise realistic) short stories. In so doing, it discusses some of Spark's earliest attempts to realise in narrative prose – to quote from her preceding study of John Masefield – 'how sharp and lucid fantasy can be when it is deliberately intagliated on the surface of realism' (1992b: 165). The first half of this chapter concerns what might be classified as the *textual* haunting, whereby the supernatural encounter is treated as an instance of metalepsis – a violation, that is, of the text's diegetic boundaries, which is in some way analogous to the ghost's traversal of ontological ones. Through a critical approach which combines detailed archival research with aspects of postmodern narrative theory, I examine how, by (re)constructing her nascent novel around a supernatural conceit, Spark developed a mode of writing which suited her existing ambition to write experimental, self-reflexive fiction. Focusing on Spark's belief in 'treat[ing] the supernatural as if it was part of natural history' (Brooker and Saá 2004: 1036), the chapter's second section examines the significance of the ghost story as a vital means of critiquing forms of patriarchal power, along with conventional gender roles and their attendant expectations. The respectively literal and figurative treatment of spectral phenomena in 1957's 'The Girl I Left Behind Me' and 1961's 'Bang-Bang You're Dead' come to articulate the female protagonists' slight and stifling existences. In 1958's 'The Portobello Road', meanwhile, a female murder victim reflects critically and authoritatively on her carefree yet curtailed life. Like *The Comforters*, each text emerges in dialogue with realist and self-reflexive tendencies, and thus constitutes a formative attempt, on the author's part, to cultivate a literary style located between both discourses.

In seeking to extend the preceding chapter's discussion of Spark's literary liminality, Chapter Two examines how the self-reflexive strategies employed in the author's writing work to facilitate moments of gendered social critique, while also interrogating the wider functioning of power and personal identity in the increasingly mediatised postmodern consumer culture in which they were written. I focus predominantly here on three of Spark's most formally and thematically experimental works: 1962's seldom discussed work of metatheatre, *Doctors of Philosophy*, 1968's slight and sparsely detailed *The Public Image*, and the elaborately metafictional *Not to Disturb*, published in 1971. In each case, I read Spark's literary innovations alongside her longstanding preoccupation with the tensions that exist between private selves and public performances, with bodies neatly inscribed within oppressive cultural narratives (and those deemed to be deviant for daring to exist outside of them), and with the sinister, violent negation of female subjectivity. Across each of the chapter's three sections, I pay particular attention to aspects of dialogue, narration, setting and characterisation which draw attention to the staged and stilted aspects of seemingly 'natural' existences, and which thus prompt readers to look askance at the narrow roles that Spark's female characters have come to inhabit. In the process, I seek to reassess Spark as not only a writer of experimental fiction, but a *woman* writer whose literary innovations have arguably energised the interrogations of female agency (or the lack thereof) that figure so prominently within her work.

Examining the development of her fiction during the decade spanning 1960 to 1970, Chapter Three traces the evolving relationship between Spark's novels and the style and ethos of the *nouveau roman*. I focus in particular on Spark's inventive appropriation of what she termed 'the drama of exact observation' (Toynbee 1971: 73), as derived from the meticulous, externalised narration characteristic of the work of one of the key practitioners of the *nouveau roman*, Alain Robbe-Grillet. Although critical analysis of Spark's relationship with the anti-novel has largely been restricted to discussions of the series of purportedly 'brief, brittle, [and] nasty' (Nye 1971: 9) novels written by the author during the early 1970s, I demonstrate that the *nouveau roman* also served as a crucial influence on earlier works, including 1960's subversive social satire, *The Ballad of Peckham Rye*, as well the uncharacteristically expansive sociopolitical novel, *The Mandelbaum Gate*, published in 1965. In my discussion of *Ballad*, I observe how Spark draws playfully upon the apparent depthlessness of Robbe-Grillet's prose to depict a community in thrall to the superficial and deadened by habit and convention. The relentless exteriority of Robbe-Grillet's narration, I argue, presented Spark with an ideal means of communicating a Bergsonian form of comedy – one which involves the supposedly vital individual appearing, to humorous or even unsettling degrees, as a mindless automaton or two-dimensional stock character. In the chapter's second section, I relate Spark's developing interest in the *nouveau roman* to her first-hand experience of the trial of the Holocaust administrator, Adolf Eichmann, in 1961. Examining the representation of the trial as a scene in *The Mandelbaum Gate*, I consider how Spark's inclusion of a reference to 'the anti-novelists' enabled her to evoke something of the 'repetition, boredom, [and] despair' induced by Eichmann's robotic speech and emotional disengagement from the human reality of death and suffering (1985: 177). Political reality, I assert, emerges in this novel as both the subject and the agent of Spark's literary practice; the *nouveau roman* offered Spark a means of exposing the artificiality of supposedly natural orders, pursuing the ethical, and evacuating the glass box represented by Eichmann and his horrifyingly detached worldview.

Concentrating solely on what Spark described as her 'best [. . .] and creepiest' novel (McQuillan 2001c: 229), Chapter Four offers a thorough reassessment of *The Driver's Seat*'s largely one-sided critical reception, as well as its nuanced approach to the inextricable relationship between gender, narrative perspective and epistemological power. I argue that the novel – which has been read predominantly as Spark's most starkly drawn, or 'crystalline', parable of human fallibility versus divine omniscience, as dictated by a pitiless authorial surrogate – is concerned instead with that which escapes and thus destabilises the exacting, investigative and emphatically *male* gaze of its narrator. Through a critical framework which combines commentary on the *nouveau roman*, previously unexamined archival material, studies of metaphysical detective fiction, and theory related to narrative point of view (including that derived from feminist film theory), my chapter shifts focus from existing readings of the protagonist, Lise, as the hopeless object of a God-like narrative viewpoint, and considers her instead as a captivating figure who, even after her death, confronts and commands the epistemologically limited perspective of her hopelessly fascinated narrator–voyeur. Spark's description of *The Driver's Seat* as 'a study, in a way, of self-destruction' (Gillham 1970: 412) can thus be seen to relate not only to Lise's determined drive to death, but to the subversive unravelling of the narrating 'self', tormented and undone by the novel's perennially unknowable subject. A concluding chapter offers an examination of Spark's most outlandish work of metafiction, *The Hothouse by the East River*, as a means of uniting the various, interrelated strands of literary experimentation, satire, subversion and social critique discussed over the course of the preceding chapters.

'A certain detachment', a phrase employed twice by Spark, acquired a special resonance during the writing of this book. The phrase makes its first appearance in the self-reflexive ghost story, 'The Portobello Road', whose spectral narrator, Needle, announces that her newfound ghostliness has enabled her to 'perceive and exploit' all that she encounters in the world 'with a certain detachment, since it suits with my condition of life' (2011: 499). This revelation, which disrupts the otherwise realistic nature of Needle's observations and recollections, enforces a powerful sense of estrangement between the reader and the diegetic world, allowing the cold realities of the protagonist's lived experience to emerge in sharper focus. Almost fifty years later, in one of her final interviews, Spark would return to these exact words when asked to reflect upon the influence of Robbe-Grillet on her fiction. 'All I have from him', she remarked, 'is a certain detachment' (Hosmer 2005: 135). Although Spark attempts here to minimise or even deny Robbe-Grillet's role as a source of literary inspiration, her comment provides an accurate description of the mode of defamiliarising dispassionateness that, adapted from Robbe-Grillet's prose, came to transform her writing and its uses of rhetoric. Taken together, the phrase's two uses capture something of the 'abiding doubleness' that defines Spark's writing. This book reads Spark's fiction as a sustained attempt to effect 'a certain detachment' between reader and text, and by extension between reader and world, for the purpose of achieving what Spark describes in 'The Desegregation of Art' as 'an environment of honesty and self-knowledge, a sense of the absurd and a general looking-lively to defend ourselves from the ridiculous oppressions of our time' (1992c: 36).

'Everything that wriggles': A Note on the Archives

I am a hoarder of two things: documents and trusted friends. The former outweigh the latter in terms of quantity.

Curriculum Vitae (208)

This book is the first non-biographical study to draw extensively upon Spark's two vast archives of personal correspondence, research materials, manuscripts and notebooks, which are held at the National Library of Scotland in Edinburgh and the McFarlin Library at the University of Tulsa. The only other text to make such thorough use of these resources is Martin Stannard's *Muriel Spark: The Biography* (2009), which, given its self-evident biographical focus, pays specific attention to archival material that pertains to the author's career and personal relationships, including letters to and from her friends and family, associates, editors and publishers. As a result, Stannard's book focuses rather less closely on those materials, including notebooks, loose fragments and manuscripts, through which developments in Spark's composition of narratives, plots and characters can be meticulously traced and intricately examined. Broadly speaking, the Edinburgh and Tulsa archives present two very different versions of the author, with the contents of the former revealing more about Spark's personal and professional life, and the materials in the latter relating to the research and writing of her novels, short stories, poetry and plays. Whereas the National Library of Scotland teems with letters, contracts, receipts (spanning everything from Spark's acquisition of a racehorse from the stables of Queen Elizabeth II to innumerable bills from her hairdressers), cheque stubs, appointment diaries and postcards, for example, the notebooks, research folders and manuscripts that fill the McFarlin Library offer a much more revealing insight into her *fiction*, and have thus been of far greater use in the writing of this book.

There are, of course, some notable exceptions to this broad distinction. Among the items listed above, the archive at the National Library of Scotland also holds research materials for novels such as *Memento Mori* and *Not to Disturb* (I consult the latter in detail in Chapter Three), as well as evidence of a number of unfinished creative projects, including drafts of her supernatural comic play, *Warrender Chase* (drafted in 1952, and detailed in Chapter One), and notes for an abandoned historical novel, *Watling Street*, concerning the recollections of a Roman army officer. In addition to this, further accessions from Spark's home in Tuscany, which include the manuscripts of her later works, as well as further items of personal correspondence, are currently in the process of being catalogued and prepared for public access. I would maintain, however, that the largely unexamined McFarlin Library archive is, by some distance, the more useful resource for scholars of Spark's fiction as opposed to her biography; its importance continues to be overlooked in favour of the materials housed at the National Library of Scotland, I wish to suggest, due in part to the significance of Edinburgh as the place of Spark's birth, the setting of her most famous novel, and the official site of recent celebrations to mark the centenary of her birth.

Perhaps surprisingly, this book rarely refers to the manuscripts of Spark's novels, and focuses instead on their corresponding notes and research materials. This is due to the uncanny, near-perfect resemblance that these manuscripts bear to their published counterparts, thus revealing very little about their own composition. A scholar consulting the manuscript of *The Prime of Miss Jean Brodie*, for example, will struggle to spot any significant differences between the words neatly handwritten on alternate lines of one of Spark's large, spiral-bound notebooks (always procured from the Edinburgh stationer, James Thin, no matter where in the world she was living) and those printed on the pages of the published text. 'I don't correct or rewrite', Spark remarked of her novelwriting process in a profile piece for *The New Yorker*, 'because I do all the correcting before I begin, getting it in my mind. And then when I pounce, I pounce' (Schiff 1993: 42). To 'pounce' with a perfect landing, it was essential for Spark to compile what she described as 'a bundle of notes' beforehand, to which she could refer while writing her novel:

> I need a sheet [of notes] for every character: what they say, what they wear, who knows what, who knows whom, and what they do – all cross-referenced. I have a place for everything that wriggles – human beings, dogs, ice cream. Then I can fit it all together. (Ibid.)

It is to these various 'bundle[s] of notes', contained for the most part in the McFarlin Library, that I return throughout the present study. In doing so, I tend to discuss what Spark chose either to omit from, or further develop in, the largely uncorrected manuscripts of her novels. Among the materials discussed over the course of this book, for example, is a paragraph-long fragment entitled 'The Parquet Floor', from which the full manuscript of *The Public Image* can be seen to have emerged, dialogue drafted for (yet, significantly, never used in) *The Driver's Seat*, and the numerous plot sketches which the explicitly metafictional *The*

Comforters would conjoin into a tangled skein of competing fictions. As I sifted through the heaps of plot outlines, character profiles, newspaper cuttings and scraps of plot and dialogue contained in Spark's files and boxes, I found the author's description of her various assortments of notes as 'bundle[s]' to be rather too generous; alongside each near-pristine manuscript are several folders and envelopes heavy with hundreds of loose and unnumbered scraps of paper. When referencing such materials, therefore, I can often refer only to the specific boxes and folders from which they have been found, along with a brief description of the item in question.

Chapter One

'Author's Ghosts': Manifestations of the Supernatural in Spark's Early Fiction

Spark knew her ghosts. Her novels, short stories, plays and poems abound with unquiet spirits, haunted settings, spectral narrators, and eerie encounters with supernatural phenomena and disembodied voices. These elements can be traced back to her earliest works; indeed, it was the ghost story, and tales of the uncanny and the unexpected more generally, that preoccupied Spark as she made her first forays into fiction-writing – first in the form of short stories and plays, and later in the development of her debut novel, *The Comforters*, published in 1957. Ghosts take a wide variety of forms in these early works. They appear, for example, as manifestations of fractured psyches and mental illnesses in 'The Leaf-Sweeper' (1952) and 'The Pearly Shadow' (1955). In the former, the supposedly sane ghost of a sectioned (and still alive) young man makes an annual visit to the home of his aunt for a slice of Christmas cake, while the titular phantom in the latter is the spirit of a psychiatrist whose skin has been rendered 'translucent and pearly' after an intentional overdose of barbiturates (301). The unsettling imbrication of mental deterioration and ghostly haunting also forms the focus of Spark's 1958 radio play, 'The Interview', in which conversations between the elderly Dame Lettice and her nephew, Roy, are revealed to be either paranormal interactions, senile delusions or an eerie combination of the two. The festivities of century-old partygoers disturb the sleep of a present-day bedsitter in 'The Party Through the Wall' (1957), a radio drama whose seemingly reliable narrator is revealed, ultimately, to be himself a malevolent spirit. Elsewhere, a plasterer's apprentice is hectored about his career ambitions by a sniffy apparition in an unfinished draft entitled 'The Ghost That Was a Terrible Snob' (c.1955). 'The House of the Famous Poet' (1952), meanwhile, is a surreal rumination on posthumous legacy and the anticipation of one's own death, its initially esoteric concerns with spectral soldiers and 'abstract funerals' (346) brought into sharp focus by its wartime setting. 'Fictional phantoms make for heady literature', claimed Spark in 'Ghosts', a short *Observer* article published in 1956, which concluded that ghosts 'have melodramatic scope', and can therefore 'be used to upset the reader satisfactorily' (7).[1]

Spark's notebooks from this period teem with research into, and imaginative musings on, matters of death and the afterlife. This is nowhere more apparent than in the drafts and working notes for her unfinished play, *Warrender Chase* (the title of which Spark would later assign to Fleur Talbot's novel-in-progress in 1981's eerily metafictional tale of life and literature, *Loitering with Intent*). Drafted in 1952, the play is a ludic and frequently absurd meditation on mortality, spectrality and the significance of one's life's work.[2] The surname of the eponymous protagonist, Spark writes in her notes for a supplementary *précis*, is itself meaningful: Chase is an author consumed with anxiety as he seeks with mounting desperation to bring innumerable creative endeavours to completion (NLS 1952a: 9). Death is at Chase's heels, however; his interactions are overseen by a figure named 'Apparition', who punctuates characters' dialogue with a recurrent '"Boo!"' (NLS 1952b). Prospective publishers were, unsurprisingly, baffled. Writing to Spark after reading the first of *Warrender Chase*'s three proposed Acts, for instance, Emmanuel Wax (an agent at ACTAC Theatrical and Cinematic Ltd) expressed his disbelief that Spark should describe the play to him as a 'tragedy' (NLS 1952c). Perhaps Chase's 'tragedy' is that death catches up with him before his work is done; Spark, like her protagonist, never finished the job, and the play remained uncompleted. In other notebooks, Spark is shown to take death rather more seriously. Her notes for 1959's *Memento Mori* (the members of whose elderly cast of characters are each stalked by a ghostly voice, which perhaps emanates from Death itself) comprise extensive research into aspects of physical and mental decline among geriatrics,[3] which is paired with quotations from sources as diverse as Shakespeare, Plato, Cicero and Russian folksong, each relating to matters of death, ageing and the hereafter.[4]

There is, as the above examples demonstrate, no shortage of angles from which to approach Spark's interest in, and treatment of, the possibilities presented by the ghost story.[5] The present chapter narrows its focus to two distinct (yet interrelated) manifestations of the supernatural in the author's early fiction. The first concerns what might be called the *textual* haunting, whereby the sight or sound of a ghost is treated as an instance of metalepsis – a violation, that is, of the text's diegetic boundaries, which is in some ways analogous to the ghost's traversal of ontological ones. I concentrate predominantly here on Spark's development of *The Comforters*, in which the protagonist's experience of ghost-hearing enables her to effect the metafictional unravelling of the text to which she belongs. It was by constructing her novel around this conceit, I argue, that Spark made productive use of her own troubling experiences with mental illness and visual hallucinations, and developed a mode of novel-writing which suited her ambition to write experimental, self-conscious fiction. This process of textual haunting can be seen to have been repeated, I proceed to observe, in Spark's drastic revisioning of her 1953 short story, 'Harper and Wilton', when it was rewritten and republished as a metafictional ghost story in 1996. The chapter's second part, 'Living Ghosts', examines Spark's unsettling and subversive explorations of the ghostly 'absent presence' of women living under patriarchy, and examines the author's use of the ghost story as a means of critiquing forms of patriarchal power, as well as conventional gender roles and their attendant expectations. Whereas, in 'The Girl I Left Behind Me' and 'Bang-Bang You're Dead', the respectively literal and figurative emergences of ghosts appear as unnerving extensions of female characters' curtailed and confining existences, 'The Portobello Road' resurrects the dissident voice of a female murder victim to speak from beyond the ending and at last assume a level of narrative autonomy.[6]

'If it is a wet Saturday I wander up and down the substantial lanes of Woolworth's as I did when I was young and visible,' announces Needle, the spectral narrator–protagonist of 'The Portobello Road'. 'There is a pleasurable spread of objects on the counters,' she adds, 'which I now perceive and exploit with a certain detachment, since it suits with my condition of life' (498–9). This 'certain detachment' characterises the shared effect of the literary hauntings examined in the present chapter. In each text, the ontological jolt effected by the ghostly arrival prompts characters and readers alike to look askance at the plots, narratives and social hierarchies presented therein. If this enforced estrangement produces a critical engagement with the dynamics and conventions of plot and characterisation in *The Comforters*, for example, it provokes the suspicious scrutiny of the violent, oppressive structures of patriarchal authority and colonial culture in 'Bang-Bang You're Dead'. In either case, seeing ghosts (or, indeed, seeing *as* ghosts) leads to radically altered perspectives, and thus to new ways of seeing.

'Author's Ghosts': Typing Spooks and Critical Fictions

In her 2004 poem, 'Author's Ghosts', Spark imagines authors as spectral beings who return 'nightly to haunt the sleeping shelves / And find the books they wrote', before making 'final, semi-final touches' to their old works (ll. 2–3). 'The author's very touch', notes the speaker at the poem's end,

> is here, there and there,
> Where it wasn't before, and
> What's more, something's missing –
> I could have sworn . . . (ll. 18–21)

Here, as it draws to a close, Spark's poem enacts the very haunting it earlier described. The ending at which its speaker expected to arrive has vanished, having 'been tampered with' by a meddlesome ghost writer on another narrative plane (l. 16). An abrupt shift in tone is detected in its penultimate line, where fanciful speculation gives way to wide-eyed bemusement as the speaker trails off, caught out by unforeseen changes to the text and now unable to proceed. What precedes this line is the poem as its speaker once knew it – something familiar, finished and seemingly self-contained. In unravelling in the manner that it does, 'Author's Ghosts' performs what Gérard Genette calls metalepsis: the traversal of the 'shifting but sacred frontier between two worlds, the world in which one tells [the extradiegetic]' and 'the world of which one tells [the diegetic]' (1980: 236). The titular ghosts, mistakenly assumed by the speaker to have been contained within the diegetic realm of the recitable poem, have lived up to their reputation by fostering a disorienting sense of ontological ambiguity. The reader is left to hover indeterminately between both narrative realms, displaced and disoriented by the ghostly textual intervention.

What is especially striking about 'Author's Ghosts', Spark's final published work before her death in 2006, is that its twinned themes of ghostly haunting and ontological disruption can be traced back to some of her earliest fictions, including her debut novel. *The Comforters*, to quote the playful description that Spark would offer to her interviewer, Frank Kermode, is 'a novel about writing a novel, about writing a novel sort of thing' (1963: 79). As she would later reflect in *Curriculum Vitae*, it had been necessary to write in such a way in order to determine her specific abilities as a novelist:

> I didn't feel like 'a novelist' and before I could square it with my literary con-
> science to write a novel, I had to work out a novel-writing process peculiar
> to myself, and moreover, perform this act within the very novel I proposed
> to write. (206)

The narratorial self-consciousness to which Spark alludes is achieved by way of metaleptic interruptions to the plot by a figure known as the Typing Ghost, whose narration of the novel's action (heralded by the noisy clanking of typewriter keys) is overheard at various intervals by the protagonist, Caroline Rose. Caroline experiences the 'haunting' of the Typing Ghost in moments of solitude and contemplation, the first instance of which proceeds as follows:

> Caroline thought, 'Well, he will ring in the morning.' [. . .] On the whole she did not think there would be any difficulty with Helena.
> Just then she heard the sound of a typewriter. [. . .] It stopped, and was immediately followed by a voice remarking her own thoughts. It said: *On the whole she did not think there would be any difficulty with Helena.*
> There seemed, then, to have been more than one voice: it was recitative, a chanting in unison. It was something like a concurrent series of echoes.
> [. . .]
> A typewriter and a chorus of voices. [. . .] [W]hat worried her were the words they had used, coinciding so exactly with her own thoughts. (34)

'[R]emarking', as it appears here, takes on a telling duality. Are the 'recitative' voices *remarking* Caroline's thoughts, and thus demonstrating an ability to dictate and determine the contents of her mind? Or, as indicated by their italicised repetition, are Caroline's '*own* thoughts' being re-*marked* – repositioned and repurposed, that is, as narrative content? If the first of these possibilities suggests the Typing Ghost's omniscience and creative power, the second points to Caroline as the unwitting source of an emerging text, experiencing her own narrative voice being played back to her. The latter option would make *Caroline* a Typing Ghost in the making, who transforms the content and structure of the novel she inhabits by altering it drastically from the inside out. The two possibilities are not, however, mutually exclusive, and a tussle between them plays out over the course of the novel; as the story progresses, Caroline comes to antagonise the voice by resisting the plot it dictates. '"I refuse to have my thoughts and actions controlled by some unknown, possibly sinister being"', she asserts defiantly (93). 'It is not easy to dispense with Caroline Rose', the Typing Ghost eventually concedes: 'Caroline among the sleepers turned her mind to the art of the novel, wondering and cogitating, those long hours, and exerting an undue, unreckoned, influence on the narrative from which she is supposed to be absent' (154). Unlike 'the sleepers' who comprise the novel's cast of stock characters, Caroline *Rose* is a restless character-turned-revenant, ascending from her storyworld to wrest authorial control from her creator by altering the fabric of the novel she occupies.

As a conceit, the metaleptic 'haunting' of Caroline (and Caroline's responsive 'haunting' of the text she inhabits) offered Spark the means of performing the 'novel-writing process peculiar to [her]self' that she had long been seeking, which radically transformed her plans for the novel as a consequence. As her archival materials reveal, one of the first of several working titles for *The Comforters* was *The Loving of Mrs. Hogg*, which refers to a character who would later become a secondary (and self-consciously insubstantial) figure in the published text. Under this earlier title, Spark sketched a number of details concerning the story that she intended to develop. Two intricate and intertwining plot strands were sketched out. The first (marked 'Sub-plot: diamond smuggling') is concerned with the elaborate attempts of Louisa Jepp, the grandmother of a budding detective, Laurence Manders, to sneak the jewels procured by her accomplices, Andrew and Mervyn Hogarth, into tins of pickled fish, which would then be delivered to another co-conspirator, Willi Stock (MFL c.1955a). The second revolved around a 'shuttlecock of blackmails' initiated by the villainous and self-righteous Georgina Hogg, into which the other characters would find themselves drawn (MFL c.1955b). A *précis* of the latter plot strand is quoted below:

> Mrs. Hogg married Mervyn Hogg unaware that he was her half-brother. On discovering the relationship he leaves Mrs Hogg, changes his name to Hogarth and marries Eleanor, committing bigamy.

> Mrs. Hogg obtains Laurence's letter to Caroline, revealing his grandmother's criminal activities [. . .]. On the strength of this she tyrannises the Manders by a sort of un-self-acknowledged blackmail. Eleanor's sister, Caroline Rose, is engaged to Laurence Manders.

> Caroline enters her 'psychotic' state. Discovers the situation, but refuses to act. (Ibid.)

Spark added to these notes a list of genres under which her nascent novel might fall: detective story, adventure, psychological novel, domestic tale, crime caper, romance, Gothic novel, social satire (Ibid.). Rather than her work being refined to fit more neatly within one or more of these categories, however, *The Comforters* ends up even more convoluted than its author's notebooks already indicate. The published text includes, for example, an additional, bizarre, plot strand concerning Willi Stock's obsession with the Black Mass, and fixates on Mervyn Hogarth's suspected status as a diabolist, able to transform at will into a black dog. 'The plot', wrote Evelyn Waugh in an admiring yet bemused early review, 'thickens to inspissation. [. . .] It is all rather absurd' (1957: 32).

By making Caroline conscious of the voice(s) of the Typing Ghost, and thus alert to the various machinations of the plots in progress, Spark cuts through the tangled skein of competing (or unconvincingly coalescing) storylines that she had earlier designed. Spark's notes already indicate Caroline's role as a disruptive force; there, her newly '"psychotic" state' appears to relate to, or even prompt, her 'refus[al] to act' in the ongoing blackmail saga. Following the intervention of the Typing Ghost in the published novel, Caroline's non-participation assumes a metafictional dimension. Having listened exasperatedly to Laurence's suspicions concerning the criminal activities of his grandmother, for example, she announces her intention '"to stand aside and see if the novel has any real form apart from this artificial plot"', before admonishing her fiancé for acting, '"under the suggestive power of some irresponsible writer"', as '"an amateur sleuth in a cheap mystery piece"' (92–3). This spells trouble for the so-called '"irresponsible writer"'. The novel's first chapter, which precedes the introduction of Caroline and her voice-hearing episodes, has worked hard to set its hokey plot in motion. Laurence, introduced by way of a rather convenient description of 'his reputation for being remarkably observant' (5), grows almost immediately wary of his grandmother; '"I may take up detective work one of these days,"' he announces, '"[i]t would be quite my sort of thing"' (11). As a literary scholar (she is mid-way through writing her monograph, *Form in the Modern Novel*), Caroline is more than capable of recognising such conventions when they appear: '"I haven't been studying the novel for three years without knowing some of the technical tricks,"' she remarks sniffily; '"[i]n this case it seems to me there's an attempt being made to organise our lives into a convenient slick plot. Is it likely that your grandmother is a gangster?"' (92).

In first sketching Caroline as '"psychotic"', and then developing her into a character who hears voices shortly after suffering a psychiatric episode (she has just left a retreat at the Pilgrim Centre of St Philumena in Liverpool, where she had been recuperating following 'a time when her brain was like a Guy Fawkes night, ideas cracking off in all directions, dark idiot-figures jumping round a fiery junk-heap in the centre' [34]), Spark drew directly upon her own distressing experiences of hallucinations and psychosis.[7] In *Curriculum Vitae*, Spark links this experience to her use of the amphetamine Dexedrine as an appetite suppressant, during an anxious period of intense work and financial precarity in the early months of 1954. The hallucinations, she remarks, first occurred as she attempted to complete a critical study of T. S. Eliot's play, *The Confidential Clerk* (1953):

> As I worked on the Eliot book one night the letters of the words I was reading became confused. They formed anagrams and crosswords. In a way, as long as this sensation lasted, I knew they were hallucinations. [. . .] It is difficult to convey how absolutely fascinating this involuntary word-game was. I thought at first that there was a code built into Eliot's work and tried

to decipher it. Next, I seemed to realise that this word-game went through other books by other authors.

[. . .]

My friends [. . .] were very sympathetic. I was aware of being surrounded by friends. (204)

Spark's hallucinations, according to Stannard, had left her 'unable to distinguish inside from outside, fact from fiction, which was at once terrifying and stimulating' (2009: 165). She was, in effect, living through her 'Author's Ghosts' poem half a century before writing it, and finding herself endlessly consumed by an 'involuntary word-game' which appeared to emanate from an ever-changing text. If these hallucinations were to inform (or, indeed, *transform*) *The Comforters*, however, Spark recognised that they must be amended to accommodate the reader: 'From the aspect of method, I could see that to create a character who suffered from verbal illusions on the printed page would be clumsy. So I made my character "hear" a typewriter with voices' (1992a: 207).

While Spark would eventually recognise her own delusions as just that, Caroline's auditory hallucinations reveal a profound metafictional *truth*: that her free will is illusory as long as she remains written into what Cairns Craig describes astutely as 'a typographic world of prede-termined types' (1999: 174). The sensation, then, is one of ontological reduction – a dawning realisation of lives that are, in fact, flimsy plots, and people who are merely characters or *types*. As she continued to work on the manuscript, Spark's changes to its title reflect the growing significance of such themes to her novel-in-progress. The title, as Stannard notes, was altered gradually from *The Loving of Mrs. Hogg* to '*Characters in a Novel*, then *Types and Shadows*, then *Shadow Play*' (2009: 169). The final choice of *The Comforters*, she told her editor at Macmillan, 'pins down my main theme' (qtd in Ibid.). The reason for the title's suitability can be deduced from the contents of the author's notebooks, which reveal that her work on the novel coincided with two detailed reviews of books about the Book of Job, written by Carl Jung and T. H. Robinson respectively. Spark's commitment to completing these reviews, of which only the former was published, was perhaps a way of compensating for her own failure to submit a monograph on the subject, which had been commissioned by the publishers Sheed & Ward in 1953 (Stannard 2009: 143). Both reviews fixate on the same theme: Job's intolerable *comforters*, whose solipsistic behaviour exacerbates their friend's present suffering. 'The harm Satan did to Job seems trivial in comparison with the crushing afflictions which we actually see in progress,' she wrote in the review of Jung's book. 'He appears sur-rounded', she continued, 'by a conspiracy of mediocrity' (1955: 7). The unpublished review of Robinson's study reiterates this point: while '*the comforters* express themselves on the theory of suffering', she observed, 'Job speaks as one who suffers, not only from his boils *but from them*'. Here, Spark places particular emphasis on the 'employ[ment] [of] irony to portray a situation where men speak in the same tongue but in a different sense'; the supposed comfort offered by Job's friends, she asserts, is simply inapplicable to the torment with which Satan tests him (NLS c.1955, emphases mine).

Job's peculiar malaise is mirrored in *The Comforters* by Caroline's psychological and ontological estrangement from her friends, who appear to be 'isolated', as Alan Bold observes, 'by their egocentric aberrations' as they 'obsessively pursue their own ends' in accordance with the rapidly thickening plot (1986: 39). Spark had herself recalled being 'surrounded by friends' as she retreated ever further into her own delusional 'word-game', and this experience perhaps informed her depiction of the 'crushing afflictions' endured by Caroline (1992a: 204). The 'conspiracy of mediocrity' to which Caroline is exposed takes the form of the novel's hackneyed detective and diamond-smuggling plots, as well as its assorted strands of bigamy, blackmail and diabolism, and the numerous contrivances that unite them; Caroline's 'sense of being written into the novel', the reader learns, 'was painful' (181). In a drafted passage, Spark has Caroline articulate this pain with a sense of clarity that is unmatched in the published text:

> Caroline: I have the feeling that someone is writing the story of our lives – some author on another plane of existence. Sometimes I think it's a man, sometimes a woman, but whoever he is, he haunts me. The author records everything that's important about us. A novel. Why do I come into it? I'm not a person of action. I'm an intellectual, a person of ideas. (MFL c.1955c)

Caroline 'come[s] into it', as she puts it, precisely *because* she is 'a person of ideas' as opposed to 'a person of action'. Her intellectual ability, creative imagination and intricate, scholarly understanding of narrative form afford her a supernatural insight into the workings of the plot, and this brings an attendant frustration when the perceptive powers of her friends fail to match her own. The sense of irony that Spark identified in the Book of Job is evident here, as the consolations of the comforters possess painful metafictional implications for Caroline. '"She is a charac-ter"' (46), says Baron Stock of Louisa Jepp, in an attempt to explain away her eccentricities and prevent the smuggling scheme from coming to light. '"She's not all there"' (167), remarks Laurence's mother, Helena, of Georgina Hogg, whom she suspects of being mentally unstable. For Caroline, such comments only confirm the ontological diminishment she already fears; Louisa, a wildly unconvincing gangster, *is* '"a charac-ter"', while Georgina, who 'simply disappear[s]' into thin air whenever left alone, owing to the fact she 'has no private life whatsoever' or any purpose other than that of villainous 'gargoyle', is ontologically insubstantial rather than mentally unwell (142). Once haunted by the otherworldly voice of her Typing Ghost, Caroline now begins to perceive her own life as a ghost world, stalked by flickering figures and thinly drawn caricatures.

Hogg, to draw upon the famous distinction between 'round' and 'flat' characters outlined in E. M. Forster's *Aspects of the Novel* (1927), undoubtedly falls into the latter category, 'constructed' as she is 'around a single idea or quality' (103). A repulsively dogmatic orthodox Catholic, she is known only for her 'chronic righteousness' and a 'fanatical moral intrusiveness, so near to an utterly primitive mania' (29; 105); like the characters of Beckett or Scheherazade, who speak to ward off their own extinction, she continues to tyrannise Caroline and her friends so as not to vanish for good. Clues to Hogg's insubstantiality are littered throughout the novel. Mervyn Hogarth is the first to notice this when, having 'mounted the stairs towards [the bedroom currently occupied by Hogg], he heard the swift scamper of mice, as if that part of the house was uninhabited' (140). Similarly, when Hogg visits Caroline at home, 'Caroline got the impression that nobody was there, but then she immediately saw the woman standing heavily in the doorway and recognised the indecent smile of Mrs Hogg' (118). Due to her insubstantiality as a character, Hogg assumes some of the characteristics often associated with the similarly insubstantial spectre (the ability to appear or disappear at will, for example). In this sense, however, she is something of an outlier. The other characters appear less like maniacal caricatures, who might evaporate if left alone, than beings still in the process of being absorbed, to varying degrees, into their respective roles and plots – and growing ever flatter as a result. Caroline has noticed this in Laurence's gradual transformation into an '"amateur sleuth"', for instance, and identifies similar distortions in her old friend, Eleanor Hogarth:

> it was impossible to distinguish between Eleanor and the personality which possessed her [. . .] as well as try to distinguish between the sea and the water in it. [. . .] Her assumed personalities were beginning to cling; soon one of them would stick, grotesque and ineradicable. (76)

Caroline's suspicions about Eleanor appear to be compounded when, in a nightclub, she 'caught her view of Eleanor's head, *described* against one of the black squares of velvet in the background, just like a framed portrait, indistinct, in need of some touching-up' (73, emphasis mine). Few images could better illustrate Forster's idea of a 'flat' character.

One of the novel's most arresting examples of this 'grotesque and ineradicable' human flattening is encountered in the figure of Baron Willi Stock, a bookseller whose fanatical obsession with researching and discussing diabolism has transformed him into a rather *barren, stock* character, devoid of any other aspects of personality or temperament. In a passage that Spark chose not to include in the published text – intended to appear when Caroline seeks refuge at the Baron's home, following her first encounter with the voice of the Typing Ghost – the protagonist watches in bemusement as her old friend grows increasingly insubstantial:

> He seemed hardly human. He was, for that moment, nothing more than the books he had read, so that in citing them, he turned over the pages of himself. He was an egg that hatched an egg; a system of thought about a system of thought; or, at the most eloquent, a fermented grape that had got itself drunk.
>
> Caroline regretted that she was not in the mood to get some private fun out of the performance; it was the only way in which a human person could possibly benefit by it. (MFL c.1955c)

In this extraordinary sequence, the Baron becomes so preoccupied with his outlandish theories that he sinks into them without trace. The metaphors of the drunken grape and the egg-hatching egg point to infinite regress – a vertiginous proliferation of further fictions and delusions, which in turn indicates that any 'original' or 'authentic' self has been buried in the shuffle of pages. The sequence thus complicates longstanding readings of *The Comforters*, which 'has typically been described', notes Michael Gardiner, rather too simply 'as a story of a heroine "trapped within a novel"' (2006: 46). In place of any clear distinction between reality/fiction, life/role or person/character, however, examples including the extract quoted above suggest an ontological diminishment (or 'flattening') *by degrees*; indeed, the respective behaviours of the Baron, Laurence and Eleanor indicate a gradual descent *into* fiction, whereas Caroline's critical awareness of both the conventions of storytelling and the voice of the Typing Ghost suggests a steady *ascent* towards ontological richness – an aspect emphasised by Spark's tautological reference to her as a 'human person'. Caroline's recent exposure to the Typing Ghost has, presumably, prompted her to perceive the Baron in this newly suspicious light: '"Is the world a lunatic asylum"', she asks him, '"are we all courteous maniacs discreetly making allowances for everyone else's derangement?"' (44). To be seduced by obsession or dogma, or to entertain or participate in the '"derangement[s]"' of others, Caroline's words suggest, is to risk descending into a state of ontological instability, which finds its limit in the '"not all there"' Georgina Hogg. It is for this reason that Caroline believes she might still salvage her relationship with Laurence, if he could only be persuaded to abandon his sleuthing and concede instead to her suspicious '"logic"':

> 'Will you be able to make an occasional concession to the logic of my madness?' she asked him. 'Because that will be necessary between us. Otherwise, we shall be really separated.' She was terrified of being entirely separated from Laurence.
>   'Haven't I always tried to enter your world?'
>   'Yes, but this is a very remote world I'm in now.' (85)

In his analysis of *The Comforters'* self-reflexive treatment of authorial power, ontological levels, and the dynamics and tyrannies of plot and character, Bran Nicol contends that, far from exposing Caroline's insignificance in relation to the plot dictated by her God-like author, the novel in fact 'contributes to the diminishing of the aura of the novelist, a key effect of the work of metafictional writers in the postwar period' (2010: 123). More specifically, Nicol identifies Spark's 'deflationary conception of authorship' as 'unmistakably the product of what Nathalie Sarraute once called the "age of suspicion"', in that it emerges from 'the cultural moment when the traditional realist forms of writing became regarded incredulously by both reader and writer, following the lessons they had absorbed about the complexity of human psychology from Freud and modernist writers like Proust, Kafka and Joyce'. As a result, the 'automatic investment of faith in the realist writer that typifies the nineteenth-century novel' shifts to a dynamic whereby 'author and reader establish a more productive relationship based on mutual suspicion', and in which 'the reader is reminded of the constructed, artificial quality of the text' (126). Nicol is referring specifically to the title essay of Sarraute's 1963 collection, *The Age of Suspicion*, which claims as outmoded (and, crucially, *mistrusted*), the over-determined and elaborate plot typically encountered in the nineteenth-century novel, 'which winds itself around the character like wrappings', and thus affects her or him with a 'mummy-like stiffness'. Without the faith of either their author or reader, 'which permitted them to stand upright with the burden of the entire story resting on their broad shoulders', characters 'may now seem to vacillate and fall apart' (Sarraute 1963: 61).

With its depiction of plots that coalesce and coagulate until they become absurd and implausible, a villain who disappears without trace when her services to the story are no longer required, and other characters who allow themselves to ossify gradually into rigid and reductive roles,

The Comforters appears to encapsulate Sarraute's claims for the novel's new age. Indeed, Caroline's announcement that work on her monograph has stalled due to her '"difficulty with the chapter on realism"' (57) even evokes Sarraute's later description of the realist novel as 'a faith that is waning' (55). The reader, too, comes to share this Sarrautean suspicion. Like Caroline, who casts a wary eye over aspects of dialogue and plot that she has already overheard in the form of utterances from the Typing Ghost, the reader is placed at arm's length from the diegetic world, having been made privy to its inner workings:

[Laurence's] mother told him repeatedly, 'I've told you repeatedly.' (5)

Sir Edwin Manders had been in retreat for two weeks.
  'Edwin has been in retreat for two weeks,' said Helena. (134)

In instances such as these, the reader becomes not only wary but also profoundly *weary* of the diegetic world, where speech and story appear to lumber artlessly onwards. This weariness evokes a text with which *The Comforters* shares an even greater affinity, perhaps, than it does with 'The Age of Suspicion': John Barth's 1967 essay, 'The Literature of Exhaustion'. Barth suggests that conventional means of literary representation have reached a critical point of 'used-upness', and cites Jorge Luis Borges, Vladimir Nabokov and Samuel Beckett as examples of authors whose works, through their self-reflexive playfulness, offer welcome renewal (64). Barth describes Borges's short story, 'Pierre Menard, Author of the *Quixote*' (1939), in which the hero comes to compose 'a number of pages which coincided – word for word and line for line' with those of Miguel de Cervantes's novel (Borges 1939: 37), as a text which 'confronts an intellectual dead end and employs it against itself to accomplish new human work' (Barth 1984: 69–70). Borges, writes Barth, has written 'a remarkable and original work of literature, the implicit theme of which is the difficulty [. . .] of writing original works of literature' (69).

As with the texts praised by Barth, *The Comforters* both thematises and transcends its own 'used-upness'. Spark achieves this primarily through Caroline's transformation from struggling literary critic into an accomplished novelist in her own right (the implication being, of course, that her scholarly awareness of hackneyed plots and 'intellectual dead end[s]' will lead her to produce the kind of revivifying 'new human work' described by Barth). 'Now I feel released from a very real bondage & can make use of the experience' Spark wrote in 1954 to her then partner, Derek Stanford, after her period of Dexedrine-influenced psychosis (qtd in Stannard 2009: 157). Similarly, as *The Comforters* draws to a close, a now reposeful Caroline begins to ruminate both critically and creatively on all that she has experienced:

> Caroline had been reflecting recently on the case of Laurence and his fantastic belief that his grandmother had for years been the leader of a gang of diamond-smugglers. She had considered, also, the case of the Baron and his fantastic belief in the magical powers of Mervyn Hogarth. [. . .] [S]he was impatient for the story to come to an end, knowing that the narrative could never become coherent to her until she was at last outside it, and at the same time consummately inside it. (165–6)

Shortly thereafter, Caroline announces to her friends that she will soon depart to write a novel about '"characters in a novel"' (186). Her notes are later discovered by 'the character called Laurence Manders', who proceeds to berate her in a letter for 'misrepresent[ing] all of us', before changing his mind, tearing up the paper and throwing its tattered remains into the wind. The novel ends, however, with the paradoxical revelation that Laurence 'did not then foresee his later wonder, with a curious rejoicing, how the letter had got into the book' (187–8). How has the destroyed letter been read? And why would Laurence rejoice at seeing his accusatory words revived and reprinted? This paradox can be interpreted in terms of Caroline and Laurence's transition between ontological realms – or, to return to Genette, from 'the world of which one tells' to 'the world in which one tells'. Caroline has persuaded Laurence, over the course of the novel, to abandon his subscription to the phony detective plot in order to enter what she calls her own '"very remote world"', and thus to develop from comforter to *confidant*. The ending indicates that Laurence has finally and successfully done so; while '*the character* called Laurence Manders' cannot abide the truths encountered in Caroline's notes, the mention of his '*later* wonder' suggests a newly altered state, which is not simply emotional, but ontological. Similarly, the contents of his old letter, despite being destroyed, have nevertheless been accessed and *re-marked* by Caroline, now the author of a novel about '"characters in a novel"'.

'It is always a joyful thing when a novelist breaks the obvious rules of fiction and gets away with it,' wrote Spark in an *Observer* article, two years after the publication of *The Comforters* (1959: 18). Spark's gradual development of that novel – from the details sketched under 'Sub-plot: diamond smuggling' and 'The Loving of Mrs. Hogg', to the metafictional unravelling of the plots and characters outlined therein – can itself be read as a sustained exercise in rule-breaking, in which the event of haunting acts as a central component. Such a reading conflicts with the longstanding interpretation of *The Comforters* as a text which, according to Randall Stevenson, 'uses[s] artistic control as a figuration of irresistible divine will' (100), by suggesting instead that the authorial figure is more ghostly than godly, and as capable of *being* haunted as haunting others. The relationship between spectral haunting and the ontological instability and self-reflexivity often encountered in, and frequently associated with, postmodern literature is examined at length in Allan Lloyd Smith's 1996 essay, 'Postmodernism/Gothicism'. 'The quality of indeterminacy which [. . .] is the stock in trade of the Gothic mode', writes Smith, 'is surely the very *raison d'être* of the postmodern':

> In the Gothic, indeterminism is a narrative necessity, providing the essential properties of mystery and suspense [. . .]. For the postmodern, indetermin-ism is an intellectual inevitability, following from the working through of modernist aesthetics towards a valorising of partial orders in opposition to comprehensive structures and orderings, and the oft-diagnosed breakdown of metanarratives. [. . .] In both [models] we confront the embattled, decon-structed self, without [. . .] any coherent psychology of the kind observable in both the Enlightenment or modernist traditions. (7)

Spark would arrive upon a similar connection when, having been asked by Martin McQuillan to articulate what she took postmodernism to mean, she responded: 'I think that it means that there is another dimen-sion which is a bit creepy, supernatural, [. . .] not necessarily consequen-tial. I always think that causality is not chronology' (McQuillan 2001c: 216). Spark's answer – while far from a definite, or indeed definitive, description of postmodernism – doubles as a description of the ghost story, which, much like postmodern literature, can be said to be charac-terised by a deconstructive (and consequently 'creepy' or 'supernatural') disruption of temporal linearity and ontological stability.

If, as I have argued, Spark's development of *The Comforters* entailed the suspicious 'haunting' of her own novel-in-progress (as opposed to the author's development of a fiction informed by God-like omniscience or 'irresistible divine will'), then a similar process can be identified in her drastic revisioning of her 1953 short story, 'Harper and Wilton', as a disorientingly metafictional ghost story when it was republished in 1996. In its original form, 'Harper and Wilton' is an anaemic, farcical tale of an eponymous pair of Edwardian Suffragettes, and the lecherous, cross-eyed young man who stares incessantly into the adjacent windows of their boarding-house bedrooms. Thrown by the stranger's lustful squint, each woman suspects the other of being the complicit object of his desire, with Wilton accusing Harper of '"encouraging the advances of a strange man"' and Harper complaining to the Secretary of the Suffrage Committee that Wilton has '"lately behaved in a manner preju-dicial to our Cause"' (248).[8] Wilton, now intent on incriminating her former friend in retaliation, leaves the man a letter written on Harper's headed notepaper, inviting him to Harper's room later that night. When the young man climbs a drainpipe to reach Harper's window, a chaotic fight ensues. Harper and Wilton – squabbling loudly and continuing to blame one another for the stranger's advances – are arrested for disturbing the peace and each sentenced to a month's imprisonment. As such details demonstrate, 'Harper and Wilton' is contrived and cartoonish, its protagonists crudely drawn and its resolution hurried and unsatisfying; the stranger's unnerving advances go unchallenged and unpunished, while the women's noisy dispute only confirms the prejudices of the arresting constable, who is left sighing (as much to the intended reader as to himself, perhaps), '"Suffragettes, eh?"' (249).

Over forty years later, Spark would resurrect 'Harper and Wilton' to stage the metaleptic haunting of its dramatised author by her disgruntled creations. Published in a limited edition run by Colophon Press in 1996, and later anthologised in the 2011 *Complete Short Stories* collection, the modified version includes the original story in its entirety in the form of an embedded narrative, which the author finds herself compelled to revisit when the Suffragettes return to accost her. In its revised (and indeed *revived*) form, therefore, 'Harper and Wilton' takes on the form of a ghost story. Its narrator, now attempting to complete a novel while residing temporarily at a house in Hampshire, finds herself troubled by a 'feeling of chilling weirdness', and a sensation of 'oddness around the house' (244). She attributes this to the behaviour of Joe, the resident gardener, who spends his days staring cross-eyed at the bedroom windows of the house. Unable to determine which of these rooms so intrigues Joe, or why he should be fixated on either one in the first place, the narrator returns to her work only to be unsettled by distant female voices, before being approached by two women, 'dressed in Edwardian-type long skirts and shawls, with their hair knotted up severely' (245). Wilton announces that she and Harper have returned to their author because she had '"cast [their] story away"' without providing a satisfactory ending; '"Now you've got to give us substance"', she threatens, '"otherwise we'll haunt you"' (246). The pair's lack of '"substance"' functions punningly here, with the word referring simultaneously to the women's flimsy characterisation and their consequent presence as ghostly tormentors.

As far as the narrator is concerned, 'Harper and Wilton' was an inconsequential draft from 'many, many years ago, some time in the 1950s', whose characters she 'had certainly had some fun with' (246), but has not since thought of. She is, then, the kind of '"irresponsible writer"' identified by Caroline Rose, whose cognisant creations are left to endure the misery of existing in a mediocre work of fiction.

The implications here are rather more sinister than in *The Comforters*, however. The young man, says Wilton, '"has given us no peace"' ever since his author created him: '"[he] follows us everywhere. Don't you know this is a crime?"' Harper concurs that the man '"is molesting us"' and that '"it was he who should have gone to prison, not us"' (251). Given his unnerving fixation on the bedroom windows of the Hampshire residence, the revelation that the man to whom Harper and Wilton refer is, in fact, Joe is hardly surprising. The narrator has, to her presumed horror, created a sexual harasser as a component in a feather-weight comedy of errors, who has terrorised both women ever since. In their quest for '"substance"', Harper and Wilton demand that their author take their plight seriously by elevating their story beyond the level of farce, rewriting it 'in the light of current correctness' so that they 'were vindicated and it was the squint-eyed student who was taken to the police'. When their creator complies, Harper and Wilton, 'evidently satisfied', announce their departure, while Joe is at last arrested (251).

In its revised form, 'Harper and Wilton' draws upon conventions familiar to the ghost story – including an eerie house, a procession of strange noises and the appearance of vengeful revenants – to reflect critically and self-consciously on the short story's previous, unsatisfactory, incarnation, as well as the possibility of its productive rejuvenation. In so doing, Spark stages the haunting of *herself* as author–narrator by old characters who now double as suspicious readers, critical of their creator's past work and keen for it to be amended. More intriguing still is the author–narrator's role as revenant; it is *she*, after all, who has come to reside at a house so similar to the one she once imagined (an environment she shares with Joe, who also turns out to be her fictional creation). Instead of presenting a singular metaleptic crossing from its embedded story to the realm occupied by its narrator, 'Harper and Wilton' thus depicts a pattern of mutual metaleptic pursuit, whereby characters 'ascend' to haunt their creator, who herself 'descends', albeit unwittingly, to revisit and revivify the storyworld she created and abandoned long ago.[9] We might interpret this unusual dynamic in terms of Barth's work on literatures of exhaustion and replenishment. What Spark dramatises in 'Harper and Wilton', that is, is her own attempt to return to 'confron[t] an intellectual dead end' by allowing previously flattened, closed-off caricatures a right to return and reply (Barth 1984: 69–70). She does so by 'break[ing] the obvious rules of fiction', as she puts it, by way of metaleptic intrusions that are presented as ghostly, yet entirely enlivening, visitations. It is not incidental, then, that 'Harper and Wilton' should end with a description of Joe, having returned from the police station, '[getting] on with his weeding of the garden' (251).

Similarly, the revised short story performs a clearing out of dead matter to make space for itself as a worthy addition to Spark's (haunted) house of fiction.

'Everyday apparitions': Narrative Agency and Ghostly Realism

In both *The Comforters* and the revised 'Harper and Wilton', Spark forges a crucial link between the metaleptic traversal of what Genette terms the 'sacred frontier' between diegetic and extradiegetic levels, and the eerily indeterminate position of ghosts, who cross the threshold between life and the afterlife. In his seminal critical study, *Postmodernist Fiction* (1987), Brian McHale identifies this same sense of deathliness as an inherent feature of the 'self-reflective, self-conscious texts' that he associates with postmodernism:

> Insofar as postmodernist fiction foregrounds ontological themes and onto-logical structure, we might say that it is *always* about death. [. . .] In a sense, every ontological boundary is an analogue or metaphor for death; so foregrounding ontological boundaries is a means of foregrounding death, of making death, the unthinkable, available to the imagination if only in a displaced way. [. . .] Texts about themselves, self-reflective, self-conscious texts, are also, as if inevitably, about death, precisely because they are about ontological boundaries and the transgression of ontological boundaries. (231)

If, as McHale asserts, any text which foregrounds the traversal of ontological boundaries inevitably evokes death, then a text which deals directly with death and the afterlife – one which features a posthumous narrator, for example – is ideally suited to techniques associated with textual self-consciousness. For such narrators, who were once living characters occupying the diegetic realm of the story ('the world of which one tells'), the journey to the afterlife constitutes a metaleptic crossing to an extradiegetic level ('the world in which one tells'), from which the world of the living can be observed and narrated with a simultaneous sense of intimacy and estrangement.

This interplay between intimacy and estrangement is a characteristic feature of 1958's 'The Portobello Road'. The short story is narrated by Needle, the ghost of a murdered young woman, who announces early on in the text that she 'departed this life nearly five years ago' but 'did not altogether depart this world. There were those odd things to be done which one's executors can never do properly. Papers to be looked over' (498). Occupying a liminal position 'not altogether' rooted in the diegetic realm of the living, Needle can review her life as though it were a completed text to be 'looked over' and narrated as she sees fit: 'I did not live to write about life as I wanted to do', she explains, 'possibly that is why I am inspired to do so now in these peculiar circumstances' (501). Like the revenant versions of Harper and Wilton, now intent on transcending their shared status as petty-minded caricatures by articulating the disturbing truth of their victimisation, Needle seeks not only to confront her killer, but to dictate the terms on which her story is told – an act which will emancipate her from the narratives that defined her in both life and death. Needle's talk of '[p]apers to be looked over' holds a secondary, literal meaning, however; in the five years since her death, she has come to be remembered as the victim of what the newspapers named 'The Haystack Murder' (520), after the place from which her corpse was eventually retrieved. The grim fate suffered by Needle, who acquired her nickname after pricking her thumb on a needle 'one day in [her] young youth at high summer, lolling with [. . .] companions upon a haystack' (495), has since become fertile ground for bad jokes: 'when my body was found,' she recalls disdainfully, 'the evening papers said, "Needle is found: in haystack!"' (520).

'The Portobello Road' is thus a short story *about* a short story, concerning as it does a life cut short, a sense of potential remaining unfulfilled, and a reputation reduced to a tiresome punchline. Its narrator's longstanding belief that she is somehow 'set apart from the common run' (495), a suspicion apparently confirmed by her chance discovery of the needle in her 'young youth', comes to bolster her 'ambition [. . .] to write about life, which first [she] had to see' (500). This formative instance exists in uneasy tension, however, with the stifling (and increasingly sinister) influence of her friend, George. While Needle believes that her extraordinary find 'attested the fact [of her uniqueness and independence] to [her] whole public: George, Kathleen and Skinny' (495), George responds by gathering the four friends for a photograph. This seemingly innocent gesture comes to define the terms of George's relationship to the group, and to Needle specifically; 'desperately afraid of neglect', he proceeds to supply each of the friends with a copy of the image, announcing that they '"must stick together"' as they leave Scotland to embark upon their respective careers (500). Consequently, the 'small red river' that Needle interprets as thrilling, conclusive evidence of her 'difference from the rest' (495; 524) is reconfigured, in George's photograph, as a blood oath that will forever bind her to her peers. For Susan Sontag (whose work I discuss in greater detail in the following chapter), photography constitutes 'a way of imprisoning reality, understood as recalcitrant, inaccessible; of making it stand still', so that while 'one can't possess reality, one can possess (and be possessed by) images' (1977: 163).

George is equally possessive of and 'possessed *by*' his idealised image of the group, and is thus incensed when Needle, who threads whimsically between careers and continents in the years that follow, fails to adhere to her assigned role as his faithful friend. '"You aren't bound by anyone,"' he will complain to her years later, while unhappily (and secretly) married in South Africa: '"You come and go as you please. Something always turns up for you. You're free, and you don't know your luck"' (507–8). His disclosure of the marriage only to her, Needle realises, constitutes an attempt to 'enforce some sort of bond' of secrecy between the pair (511), which is tested when he proposes to Kathleen some years later. When Needle insists that she will bring his bigamy to light, George proceeds to kill her in a manner that symbolises a chilling reversal of the moment at which she became aware of both her individuality and her narrative agency:

> He looked as if he would murder me and he did. He stuffed hay into my mouth until it could hold no more, kneeling on my body to keep it still, holding both my wrists tight in his huge left hand. I saw the red full lines of his mouth and the white slit of his teeth last thing on earth. Not another soul passed by as he pressed my body into the stack, as he made a deep nest for me, tearing up the hay to make a groove the length of my corpse, and finally pulling the warm dry stuff in a mound over the concealment, so natural-looking in a broken haystack. (520)

By suffocating and silencing Needle, George attempts to eradicate the dissident female voice and thus uphold an oppressive 'master' narrative that is designed to ensnare Kathleen within a deceitful marriage plot. In burying his victim, George's use of Needle's corpse as a means of penetrating the haystack is connotative of an act of rape, in which the dead female body is appropriated, horrifyingly, as a phallic instrument to be 'pressed' forcefully 'into the stack'. Needle's nickname, which once signified her uniqueness and free will, now suggests the violent, phallic mastery (and subsequent erasure) of a woman judged dangerous and deviant for being 'set apart' from the dominant order. We might read the murder as an unnerving extension of George's practice of photography. In both cases, what is 'recalcitrant, inaccessible' is forcibly made to 'stand still'.

Were 'The Portobello Road' to have recounted Needle's short life without including her posthumous narration, it might well have read as a cautionary and deeply conservative tale, warning women of the dangers of speaking freely and straying too far from their place among 'the common run'. Instead, the existence of a narrative afterlife offers Needle a second chance to fulfil her authorial ambition by allowing her to ascend to a diegetic plane from which her voice can at last be heard. The unique narrative capabilities of a posthumous narrator are explored at length in Alice Bennett's 2012 study, *Afterlife and Narrative in Contemporary Fiction*. The posthumous perspective, Bennett observes, poses a distinct challenge to the binaristic model of narrative possibilities proposed in studies including Richard Walsh's 'Who is the Narrator?' (1997), which contends that 'the narrator is always either a character who narrates, or the author', leaving 'no indeterminate position' between the two: 'The author of a fiction can adopt one of two strategies: to narrate a representation or to represent a narration' (Walsh 1997: 505). As Bennett argues, 'narration from the afterlife forces this categorisation to the surface by combining the characteristics of authorial omniscience with those of a fictional character narrator, as well as affecting the relationship between the levels of diegesis within the text' (128). These dual possibilities are afforded to Needle, who is able to recount her lived experience as a character narrator might, while also witnessing, as if omnisciently, a number of subsequent events including her own post-mortem and the imprisonment of a young man falsely convicted of killing her.

Needle is not only a posthumous narrator, however, but a *revenant* one, and is thus eager to return to play an active role in the diegetic realm from which she was expelled. It is perhaps fitting, then, that she should choose to greet George during his and Kathleen's visit to the Portobello Road market, appearing from among the displays of second-hand 'combs and hankies, cotton gloves, flimsy flowering scarves, writing-paper and crayons' (499) that make up the detritus of past lives, and thus presenting herself as a remainder and *reminder* of the woman he killed. 'As I spoke,' Needle notes, 'a degree of visibility set in' (500), allowing her to be seen by her murderer and consequently undoing the violent erasure that she suffered at his hands; 'the voices of the dead', as Bennett asserts, 'de-sacralise closure and its revelations by adding supplementary time beyond the end and refusing to keep silent about what could fall outside any given plot' (2009: 471). Indeed, it is now *George* who is plunged into a state of deathly silence. Needle's seemingly offhand remark that George's 'new bristly maize-coloured beard and moustache' causes him to look 'as if he had a mouthful of hay' (522) is therefore far from incidental; by describing her newly silent murderer with reference to the material he used to suffocate *her*, she gleefully acknowledges the reversal of agency effected by her return.[10] Tormented by the ghostly encounter, George returns obsessively to the market, confesses to his crime and, taken to be psychotic and delusional, is persuaded to emigrate in order to recuperate. 'George has recovered somewhere in Canada,' remarks Needle with characteristic detachment at the story's conclusion, 'but of course he will never be the old George again' (524). Needle's narrative afterlife has allowed her to return to prick her killer's conscience and at last enjoy a measure of retribution.

As evinced by Needle's defiant enjoyment of her new-found narrative agency, as well as the recalcitrant return of Harper and Wilton, the ghost trope is no mere metafictional stunt, but a valuable means of reinstating a dissident voice that has been unjustly silenced. The dynamics of the ghost story, recognised by Nickianne Moody as a mode of writing 'particularly concerned with *injustice*', which 'actively reverses patriarchally preferred interpretations of events and hierarchies of knowledge' when adopted by women writers in particular, can thus be seen to have provided Spark with an effective means of subverting supposedly stable structures of patriarchal authority (1996: 78). This is perhaps unsurprising; as Moody discusses, the ghost story has historically presented women writers with the freedom to formulate inventive critiques of patriarchal oppression and the stifling rigidity of gender roles, as exemplified in texts such as Charlotte Perkins Gilman's *The Yellow Wallpaper* (1892), Clothilde Graves's 'The Spirit Elopement' (1915), Ellen Glasgow's 'The Shadowy Third' (1923) and Edith Wharton's 'Miss Mary Pask' (1925), along with more recent examples including Jeanette Winterson's *Written on the Body* (1992), Margaret Atwood's *The Robber Bride* (1993) and Ali Smith's 'The Hanging Girl' (1999). Far from being a fanciful addition to an otherwise realistic tale, the supernatural manifestation announces itself as a disruptive countertext to an oppressive reality, and an entirely necessary means of conveying truths that could not have otherwise been spoken. 'I treat the supernatural as if it was part of natural history,' Spark remarked in 2004. 'If I write a ghost story it wouldn't come under the heading of a ghost story necessarily because I treat it as if it was a natural thing' (Brooker and Saá 2004: 1036).

Spark's 'natural' treatment of the ghost story is nowhere more apparent than in 'The Girl I Left Behind Me', first published in a 1957 issue of *Ellery Queen's Mystery Magazine*. Its narrator, an unnamed office worker who appears to have been lifted from a work of kitchen-sink realism, recounts the end of a wearisome yet seemingly uneventful day at work, including apparently inconsequential details regarding her bus journey home, the grievances of her manager, Mr Mark Letter, and the banal goings-on at her boarding-house lodgings. Her mood is one of despondency as she recalls feeling 'particularly anonymous among the homegoers' on having boarded the bus, 'depressed' when another passenger 'looked away' from her 'without response', and later 'desolate' after being ignored by her landlady (278–9). Her thoughts turn frequently to Mr Letter, whom she had last witnessed in a trance-like state, clutching his necktie and whistling the folk tune with which the story shares its title. It is only when she returns to the office, convinced of there being something 'left unfinished' to which she must urgently attend, that the narrator discovers her own body, 'lying strangled on the floor' (280; 283). The 'trick' played by Spark, then, is to reveal her narrator's seemingly unimportant observations as vital clues to her murder and present spectrality, which appear to account for her sense of isolation and invisibility, as well as the unsettling behaviour of Mr Letter.

It is perhaps because of this shocking yet seemingly neat resolution that 'The Girl I Left Behind Me' is cited by Alice Bennett as an example of a text in which 'the dead narrator is essentially a punchline', whose posthumous presence 'shuts down possibilities rather than opening them up' (2012: 18–19). Rather than eliminate possibilities, however, the 'punchline' revelation of the narrator's death raises further questions concerning her silent, passive presence while still alive. Indeed, what is perhaps even more unsettling than the narrator's murder is her subsequent failure to recognise that it happened. 'No one [. . .] took any notice of me', she remarks of her commute from work, 'of course, why should they?' (278). The implication produced here is that the narrator's present, spectral, state is not entirely unlike her past, living, one. The story is thus an example of what Aviva Briefel, in her study of films including Herk Harvey's *Carnival of Souls* (1962), Adrian Lyne's *Jacob's Ladder* (1990) and Alejandro Amenábar's *The Others* (2001), terms 'spectral incognisance' – a ghost story 'subgenre' which 'represents death as an event that can be overlooked'. Such narratives, Briefel argues, 'are predicated on the idea that dying is not only a corporeal failure, but also a cognitive act: those who overlook their deaths are not really dead. Instead, they lead a liminal existence scattered with clues signalling their passing', and 'can only transition into real death once they have interpreted these clues properly' (2009: 96–7). Spark's narrator manages to overlook *her* death not because it is too traumatic to recall (as is the case for the once murderous and suicidal ghostly mother in *The Others*, or the still-traumatised Vietnam veteran/fatality in *Jacob's Ladder*, for example), but rather because, having grown so radically detached from her body over a prolonged period of time, the violence inflicted upon it merely fails to register.

'The Girl I Left Behind Me' can thus be read as a ghost story, regardless of its protagonist's death and present spectrality, suggesting as it does a slow and sinister process of self-alienation which was set in place long before her murder. Quite how this came to be is never made explicit over the course of the story (one of Spark's shortest at only five pages in length), yet the narrator's recollection of her interactions with Mr Letter acquire an unnerving resonance when read in light of the ending. Read retroactively, for example, what the narrator had described as Letter's frequent 'dreamy states' and 'lapses into lassitude' (278) reveal themselves to be periods of murderous contemplation, while his incessant whistling of the story's eponymous folk tune takes on a similarly chilling sense of foreboding. These and other habitual practices, including fits of anxiety-inducing mania in the workplace, leave the protagonist perennially apprehensive and timorously silent, her mood and behaviour manipulated to such an extent that she becomes a stranger to herself and those around her. As his name alone indicates, Mark Letter occupies a position of patriarchal authority and representational control. He is the Letter of the law, whose overbearing influence haunts the narrator's existence ('when his tune barrelled round my head long after I had left the office', she remarks of his habitual whistling, 'it was like taking Mr Letter home' [278]), and whose deliberate attempts to overwhelm his employee with swathes of dead letters in the form of endless 'needless telegrams', dictated 'by fits' through 'his chattering mouth' of rotten teeth (279), deny her the opportunity to write, or indeed think, outside of his control. Only this can account for the narrator's overwhelming sense of joy upon discovering her strangled corpse at the end of the story, which she 'embraced [. . .] like a lover' (283). While Spark's story ends at this point, one senses that the titular 'Girl' has only just begun to speak for herself.

'Again and again, with almost shocking repetitiveness', writes Jennifer Uglow in her introduction to *The Virago Book of Victorian Ghost Stories* (1988), ghost stories written by women have 'attack[ed] the symbolic and actual domination of the father, the husband, the lover, the doctor, the cruel emperor – the men of power' (xii).[11] 'The Girl I Left Behind Me' can be seen to continue this tradition by employing the ghost trope to make plain the abuses of Mr Letter and to depict what Diana Wallace describes as 'the "ghosting" of women within patriarchy' (2004: 60). The ghost story, Wallace asserts, 'has allowed women writers special kinds of freedom, not only to include the fantastic and the supernatural, but also to offer critiques of male power and sexuality which are often more radical than those in more realist genres' (57). Rather than being summoned from the dead by séances or spells (or haunting the text via metaleptic border-crossings, as explored earlier), Spark's *living ghosts* are characters whose sense of vitality and free will has been occluded by manipulative relationships, deadening routines and inhibitive social conventions.

Such is the theme of 'Bang-Bang You're Dead', perhaps Spark's most personal short story, in which the prospect of becoming one's own ghost lurks as an ever-present threat. The story was inspired in part by an incident that occurred during Spark's life in Southern Rhodesia in the late 1930s, in which her former schoolfriend and fellow expatriate, Nita McEwan, was murdered by her jealous and controlling husband. As Spark recalled, the incident became all the more unsettling due to the uncanny resemblance the two women shared:

> I was staying at the same place as the girl when I heard two screams, a bang and then another bang. In the morning I was told my friend had been killed by her husband. He shot her and then himself. The next morning when I entered the communal dining room, a woman screamed and fainted, thinking I was a ghost, because I looked so similar to the shot girl. There were quite a lot of shooting affairs at that time. It was quite savage. (Greig 1996: 9)

For Spark, who had also been suffering for some time in an abusive marriage, Nita's murder appeared to foreshadow her own – a feeling compounded by the friends' physical similarities and Spark's consequent, ghostly appearance to the fainting woman.[12] The presageful incident became the starting point for the story of Sybil Greeves, whose long and fraught relationship with her own near-double, Désirée Weston, plays out as a series of simulated, symbolic and literal deaths, and finally as a ghostly interaction.

'Bang-Bang You're Dead' employs as a framing device a social gathering attended by Sybil, who entertains her host and fellow guests by showing home movies of her life in South Africa eighteen years earlier. The films, which paint a rosy picture of colonial life, including footage depicting Sybil's apparent friendship with Désirée, an old acquaintance to whom she shares a distinct physical resemblance, are placed in uneasy juxtaposition with flashbacks revealing the reality of their relationship in both childhood and early adulthood. As children in 1920s England, one such flashback reveals, the girls would stage imaginary gunfights, or 'shooting games', during which (and 'contrary to the rules') 'Désirée continually shot Sybil dead [. . .] whenever she felt like it'. Despite disapproving of her friend's unruly conduct, the nine-year-old Sybil 'obediently' plays along, endlessly 'resurrect[ing] herself' to endure a 'repeated daily massacre' in uneasy compliance with Désirée's newly invented rules (88–9). The games, though seemingly innocent, set an eerie pattern for Sybil's later life and her continued, submissive relationship to Désirée when the pair are reunited in South Africa years later. Against her better judgement, Sybil goes 'in obedience' to the home of Désirée and her husband, Barry Weston, where she feels compelled to participate in 'a game for three players', in which, 'according to the rules, she was to be in love, unconsciously, with Barry, and tortured by the contemplation of Désirée's married bliss' (106). Much like her compulsion to participate in the 'shooting games' as a child, the adult Sybil is drawn repeatedly, as if by a 'magnetic field' (101), to occupy a role intended to silence, tame and humiliate her.

In keeping with her name, Désirée stands as a patriarchal construct, a depthless object of male desire designed to torment Sybil by goading her into complying with a heteronormative script of gender and sexuality. This 'script' is imbued with the particular expectations placed upon the white woman settler; 'in the colony', Spark recalls in *Curriculum Vitae*, 'there was one white woman to three white men, which led to violent situations – sometimes to murder' (126). This gender imbalance, Spark explains, produced a hostile environment of febrile suspicion and deadly violence, within which men were killed by their sexual competitors, while women were killed by paranoid partners or jealous admirers. A similar imbalance exists in the colony depicted in Spark's short story, and contributes toward what Eleanor Byrne describes as a rigid and dangerous 'framework of desire and disavowal', within which 'the white woman's body has a forceful ideological role to play' (2001: 118). The logic of such a framework becomes as deranged as the skewed rules of Désirée's childhood 'shooting game', as Sybil's obligatory performance of desire becomes a 'repeated daily massacre' in its own right (86). Despite possessing a 'superior' intellect to her companions, and a 'brain [. . .] like a blade' (87), Sybil remains hopelessly drawn to the commanding influence of her double, restlessly pursuing passionless affairs with a variety of men, including one David Carter (ironically, the manager of a passionfruit plantation). Treating the affairs as an 'attempt [. . .] to do the right thing', Sybil 'worked herself as in a frenzy of self-discipline, into a state of carnal excitement' over each new encounter, which she achieved 'only by an effortful sealing-off of all her critical faculties'. As if in an act of protest, however, her body succumbs to a bout of tropical flu, leaving her suffering a 'twilight of the senses' on a bed 'overhung with a white mosquito net like something bridal' (97–8). With its conflated imagery of marital customs and abject horror – the honeymoon suite and the sickbed; the bridal veil and the ghostly white sheet; the virgin bride and the vulnerable, feverish body – the period of illness becomes a grim omen for Sybil's fate, should she bow to convention and pursue marriage. To do so, her sick body warns her, would be an act of self-destruction, a deadly *ghosting* of her real self from which there is no way back. Sybil's sickness thus appears as an initial stage in the sinister process of woman's corporeal estrangement within patriarchy (and, specifically, colonial life), which reaches its chilling completion in 'The Girl I Left Behind Me'.

As in the Freudian model of the uncanny, where the double operates as 'the uncanny harbinger of death' (Freud 1955: 235), Désirée represents the imminent, ghostly future that awaits Sybil, should she go against her better judgement and adhere to what Byrne describes as 'the overbearing sexual logic of the colony' (2001: 119). Possessing a suitably sibylline awareness of such a fate, Sybil attempts to repudiate the twisted 'logic' of colonial life by refusing to marry David, and in doing so initiates a sequence of events that culminate in her double's death. Incensed at Sybil's rejection of his proposal ('"it's your duty to me as a man"', he angrily insists [114]), David forces his way into the Westons' home and, mistaking Désirée for his former lover in the dim light, shoots her dead before killing himself. The scene rests, finally, on Sybil, who 'rose from Désirée's body' (118) like a spirit might from a corpse. The impression produced here is disturbingly ambiguous, suggesting on the one hand that Sybil has finally rid herself of the ties that bind her to her double, yet on the other that she will live on as *Désirée*'s ghost, condemned to exist forever in her image. The reality, in fact, lies somewhere in between; as she entertains the gathering of party guests many years later, Sybil is shown to be caught once again in a tired performance of female subservience, offering tactful half-truths about her life in South Africa, while agreeing politely to replay the film reels despite the discomfort they evidently bring her. 'Am I a woman', she asks herself at the story's close, 'or an intellectual monster?' (120). Sybil's question, which betrays her unflattering estimation of either possibility (and her treatment of the two as though they are mutually exclusive), reveals Désirée's lasting influence. In an earlier scene, Désirée remarks sourly that '"Sybil's too intellectual, that's her trouble"' and that she '"should either marry or enter a convent"', and later balks at Sybil's suggestion that she shouldn't have to '"fit into a tidy category"' of womanhood (104). As Sybil obligingly replaces the reel and allows Désirée's spectral projected image to flood into the present and once again obscure her own, it becomes unclear as to which woman is dead and which is alive.

Seeing (as) Ghosts

'I have often found', noted Spark in a brief *pensée* written in 2003, 'that the supernatural is a good factor for intensifying the vision of a story. It gives an extra dimension' (2014a: 161). Given the preceding analysis of the disorienting (and, in the latter examples, deeply disturbing) manifestations of the supernatural in Spark's early fiction, the author's comment seems almost comical in its understatement. The 'extra dimension' to which Spark refers constitutes, in fact, a radically different way of perceiving plots, characters, patterns of behaviour and structures of power. In *The Comforters*, Caroline's uncanny awareness of the Typing Ghost comes to alter drastically her relation to, and participation in, the plot that threatens to minimise and envelop her; in a similar way, Spark's decision to introduce the supernatural and metafictional voice of the Typing Ghost would transform her own novel-in-progress by bringing it closer to the novel-about-a-novel that she wished to create. As the revised 'Harper and Wilton' demonstrates, the effects of such a haunting can be highly subversive; the revenant characters, doubling as critical readers, transform the original text from the inside out by demanding that their voices are heard and that their victimiser is punished.

Matters of retribution and self-expression form the twin focus of 'The Portobello Road', whose narrator – rather like the returning Harper and Wilton – is intent on dictating the terms on which her story is told, while effecting change within the diegetic world (an ability that is unique, as I have argued, to the revenant narrator, who straddles diegetic realms as well as ontological ones). Such a quality can be seen to complicate the influential description of Spark, proposed by Malcolm Bradbury, as a writer of 'end-directed' fictions, from which 'the beginning, which creates expectation and freedom, and the middle, which substantiates and qualifies it, seem absent', so that characters 'arise at the last, *from* the last; what has withered is a world of motive, purpose, aspiration' (1992: 189–90). While it is true that Spark's fictions often foreground their own conclusions (be it through proleptic revelations of the end, or a ghost's narration of the story of a life already lived), this does not negate motive but rather *enhances* it by 'adding supplementary time beyond the end', as Alice Bennett writes of the spectral narrator, during which further action can be taken (2009: 471).

Spark's ghosts, observes Susan Owens in *The Ghost: A Cultural History* (2017), 'are not showy or macabre; neither are they deep elemental forces, nor comforting historical presences. They are everyday apparitions' (248). They serve the purpose, as Spark notes above, 'of intensifying the vision of a story'. Like the bellowing 'Apparition' in the unfinished *Warrender Chase*, whose presence heightens the protagonist's panicked need to complete his ongoing work and thus emphasises the play's dominant themes of mortality, productivity and posthumous legacy, Spark's 'everyday apparitions' are often introduced in service of their texts' pre-existing concerns. That the narrator of 'The Girl I Left Behind Me' is speaking posthumously only underscores her antecedent estrangement and alienation; indeed, she is so inured to Mr Letter's recurrent aggressions as to be incognisant of her eventual murder at his hands. Similarly, Sybil's struggle to adapt to the gendered expectations of colonial life in 'Bang-Bang You're Dead' is intensified by the unsettling presence of Désirée – herself an eerie doppelgänger, whose every interaction with the protagonist comes loaded with the threat of death (be it physical, social or intellectual), and who continues to haunt Sybil as a ghostly, flickering projection many years later. In both stories, gendered divisions are reconceptualised in relation to the supernatural, so that ghostliness is presented as the consequence of curtailed freedoms and limited lives.

When asked in a 2003 interview whether her interest in writing ghost stories reflected a personal belief in the supernatural, Spark responded with a measure of caution:

> Yes, I do [believe in ghosts]. But not in the sense that one could possibly describe it. I have never seen a ghost. I have never had a real psychic experience that I felt a ghost in the room [. . .]. Ghosts exist and we are haunted, whether we like it or not in the sense that it can only be expressed by a physical presence, or a ghost [. . .]. I don't see any other way in which you can express this actuality, and I can't deny the actuality simply because there is no other way to express it. (Devoize and Valette 2003: 247)

For Spark, then, the distinct 'physical presence' of the ghost serves as a necessary means of articulating the otherwise inexpressible, undeniable 'actuality' of being haunted. The present chapter has sought to examine various examples of these hauntings – from texts that reflect warily upon their own claustrophobic contrivances, to characters who are prompted to scan the contours of their similarly stifling existences with mounting suspicion. The estrangement effected by the ghostly arrival would come to characterise Spark's unique mode of metafiction, where, as the following chapter proceeds to discuss, the surprising and often surreal effects of metaleptic frame-breaking allow the author to examine similar curtailments to the lives and freedoms of her female characters.

Chapter Two

'The role in which you've cast me': Reassessing the Myth of Spark

W. Gordon Smith: There is something very theatrical about your treatment of characters, your assembly of them.
    Muriel Spark: Yes, I like to get them all on stage and moving.

(Smith 1971: n.p.)

Leonora: I have a definite sense of being *watched*. [...] A definite sense of being observed and listened to by an audience. [...] An invisible audience. Somewhere outside. Looking at all of us and waiting to see what's going to happen.
    Annie: Leonora, this is thrilling. All my life I've had a feeling of being looked at by an audience. That's why I always take care to be suitably dressed.

Doctors of Philosophy (63)

Paring Her Fingernails: Spark and Her Critics

For all its metafictional leanings and its self-reflexive treatment of plot, character and narration, Spark's fiction occupies a vexed position in relation to the existing critical discourse on experimental writing. Although her novels have been discussed in a number of ground-breaking literary studies, including Patricia Waugh's *Metafiction*, Gerardine Meaney's *(Un)Like Subjects* and Brian McHale's *Postmodernist Fiction*, she is still all too often excluded from critical overviews of experimental fiction – including that written specifically by women. Unlike a number of her contemporaries, such as Christine Brooke-Rose, Alain Robbe-Grillet, Marguerite Duras, John Fowles, John Barth and B. S. Johnson, Spark goes entirely unmentioned in the recent *Routledge Companion to Experimental Literature* (2012), for example, despite the text's inclusion of detailed sections on metafiction, metalepsis and postmodernism, into which discussions of her fiction would fit comfortably. The *Routledge Companion* also contains a single and all too brief chapter on experimental literature written by women, in which Ellen G. Friedman is tasked with covering *l'écriture féminine*, modernist women's writing and the work of contemporary feminist authors in little more than ten pages. Much of Friedman's chapter stems from the content of her co-edited collection (with Miriam Fuchs), *Breaking the Sequence: Women's Experimental Fiction* (1989), an expansive and highly important volume of essays committed to 'outlining [. . .] three generations and eight decades of the tradition of women's experimental fiction' (41), in which, however, Spark's name is nowhere to be found. Despite the efforts of both collections to outline, evaluate and historicise modes of experimental writing (including, for Friedman and Fuchs, the largely undervalued work of women), the apparent ease with which Spark's contributions can be neglected is doubly significant. Why is Spark so often overlooked and underestimated, not only as a writer of complex, experimental fiction, but as a *woman* writer whose literary innovations have arguably energised the interrogations of female agency (or the lack thereof) that figure so prominently within her work?

The answer to both questions, as I suggested in my Introduction, lies at least in part with the outdated yet abiding notion of Spark as an author engaging in a cruel and capricious God-game with an assemblage of anaemic caricatures. This was the idea proposed persuasively in Malcolm Bradbury's influential 1972 essay, 'Muriel Spark's Fingernails', in which Spark finds herself grouped among the 'Catholic novelists of detachment, like Joyce, whose godlike writer is indifferent to creation, paring his fingernails' above his handiwork (187).[1] If Spark's narrator stands as a surrogate God, Bradbury's reading implies, it is the vengeful, violent God encountered in the Old Testament. Although a number of critics have since contested Bradbury's reductive characterisation of Spark (observing that, despite self-identifying as Catholic, her fictions do not gesture unequivocally toward a Judeo-Christian or specifically Catholic interpretive framework), the dominant perception of her authorial identity as being akin to that of an indifferent, 'godlike' manipulator has proved difficult to dislodge.[2] A relatively recent example of Bradbury's lasting influence is encountered in Ian Gregson's chapter, 'Muriel Spark's Puppets of Thwarted Authority', from his 2006 study, *Character and Satire in Postwar Fiction*. Without referring directly to Bradbury, Gregson adopts a near-identical critical stance, by drawing upon Spark's Catholicism to liken the author to a master puppeteer who remains entirely apathetic to the fates of the lifeless marionettes at her disposal:

[Spark's] satire arises from the calculated contempt with which she displays her subject-matter. [. . .] Spark's satirical vision is directed not so much at specific targets but at human beings as a species. From her Catholic perspective the merely human and worldly is inevitably flat and two-dimensional because the richest and most complex truths lie elsewhere. (102)

Paring her fingernails dispassionately above a 'flat and two-dimensional' world populated by similarly paper-thin figures, Spark is accused of toying mercilessly with a cast of 'authorial puppets', who 'evoke, not the branching roads of the humanist self, but the cul-de-sac of caricature' (Ibid.: 104; 107). Adopting a binaristic approach not unlike that proposed by Ihab Hassan, who equates modernism with 'form (conjunctive, closed)' and postmodernism with 'antiform (disjunctive, open)' (1987: 91–2), Gregson affirms that 'what is unpostmodern about [Spark's] novels [. . .] is their refusal of open-endedness, their compact definitiveness' (2006: 105). In this hermetically sealed, 'unpostmodern' world of caricatures, it is the Sparkian woman who fares worst of all; in *The Public Image*, for example, Gregson contends that the narrative's 'caricatural effects' come to 'evoke its heroine's complete emptiness' by exposing and ridiculing her for being 'all lustrous surface' and nothing more. 'There is no grieving over any [. . .] loss of ontological richness', he argues, as 'the protagonist is remorselessly revealed to be entirely shallow' (Ibid.). The young women in *The Girls of Slender Means* and the schoolgirls in *The Prime of Miss Jean Brodie* do little better, with Gregson comparing each group to a set of vapid ventriloquist's dummies, spouting endless streams of 'mechanically repeated phrases' without any evidence of independent thought (107). Such a reading is hardly unique. References to characters as puppets, dolls and dummies abound throughout Spark criticism, both old and new: Peter Kemp compares Jean Brodie's pupils to 'marionettes, devoid of free will and individual value' (1974: 81); Graham Hough likens the characters in *Loitering with Intent* to 'mere gesticulating puppets' (1981: 14); Michiko Kakutani refers to the cast of *Reality and Dreams* as a pack of 'cardboard crackpots, pulled hither and thither like puppets by their serenely tyrannical creator' (1997: 29); Allan Massie describes *The Bachelors*' titular protagonists as 'no more than wax dolls' (1979: 41); Parul Sehgal, more recently, compares Spark's characters to a set of 'poor puppets' who find themselves 'torture[d] [. . .] voluptuously' at every turn (2014: n.p.). Gregson's special focus on the vapidity of female characters is even used to support a claim for Spark as 'the least feminist of women writers' (107), who treats her women as literary dolls – that is, as hollow, lifeless and endlessly expendable.

Although Gregson's stance is perhaps an extreme one, the longstanding critical conception of Spark as a purely satirical writer of closed-off, caricature-filled fictions, whose authorial cruelty is especially evident in her (mis)treatment of female characters, might go some way towards explaining her recurrent omission from various discourses on experimental writing (and particularly that authored by women). By returning continuously to the familiar analogy between the author and God as the ultimate hinterland of interpretation, such criticism precludes considerations of how Spark's literary innovations might facilitate more nuanced instances of gendered social critique, or interrogate the functioning of power and personal identity in the increasingly mediatised postmodern consumer culture in which they were written. Indeed, what such criticism so often overlooks is Spark's concern with how real lives – and specifically *women's* lives – can play out as dull or even deadly fictions, and how human vitality and personal autonomy might be diminished or destroyed entirely by oppressive relationships and tightly scripted public performances; Annabel Christopher in *The Public Image*, a famous film star whose scriptwriter husband (along with a coterie of directors, press agents, photographers and journalists) has manipulated numerous aspects of her image, identity and reputation, can be described as 'all lustrous surface' precisely because this is all that she has been allowed to be. Similarly, the 'mechanically repeated phrases' that reverberate throughout the communal settings depicted in *The Prime of Miss Jean Brodie*, *The Girls of Slender Means* and *The Abbess of Crewe* come to reflect the often sinister structures of control and conformity at play within each text. One need only think, for example, of Selina Redwood's repeated recitation, in *The Girls of Slender Means*, of the components necessary for 'the maintenance of poise in the working woman', which echoes along the hallways and landings of the May of Teck Club like a code of conduct for its exclusively female residents: '*Poise is perfect balance, an equanimity of body and mind, complete composure whatever the social scene. Elegant dress, immaculate grooming, and perfect deportment all contribute to the attainment of self-confidence*' (57). Spark thus finds herself unjustly excluded from Gregson's incisive wider discussion of 'the significance of caricatural effects in [postwar] fiction' as they pertain to matters of gender and sexuality, institutional control, and 'postmodern conceptions of the self' (3), despite the appropriateness of each of these subjects to her fiction. Gregson's detailed reading of the 'powerful male manipulativeness' (95) at play in Joyce Carol Oates's fictional account of the life and death of Marilyn Monroe, *Blonde* (2000), for example, is equally relevant to the mediatised commodification of Annabel Christopher, while his analysis of the 'institutions [. . .] responsible for turning what might have been individuals into two-dimensional characters, in fact into caricatures' (31) in the allegorical fictions of

Joseph Heller could also have been applied to the cloistered communities governed by Jean Brodie or Abbess Alexandra.

Seeking to resolve this oversight, the present chapter offers detailed readings of a selection of Spark's most formally and thematically experimental works: her rarely discussed work of metatheatre, *Doctors of Philosophy*, the sparsely detailed and seemingly superficial *The Public Image*, and the outlandishly metafictional and pointedly postmodern *Not to Disturb*. Alongside these texts, I also discuss 'A Dangerous Situation on the Stairs', a short story discovered in the author's archive at the McFarlin Library in Tulsa. In each case, Spark's literary innovations are read alongside her longstanding preoccupation with the tensions that exist between private selves and public performances, with bodies neatly inscribed within oppressive cultural narratives (and those deemed to be deviant for daring to exist outside of them), and with the violent, sinister erasure of female subjectivity. As evinced by the 'realist' approach to the ghost story adopted in 'Bang-Bang You're Dead' and 'The Girl I Left Behind Me', Spark's fictional experiments have the propensity to articulate her longstanding concern with what Adam Piette describes, with reference to the limitations placed upon the respective freedoms of *The Mandelbaum Gate*'s Barbara Vaughan and *The Prime of Miss Jean Brodie*'s Sandy Stranger, as 'the confinement of a scripted identity' (2010: 56). In the texts that I have chosen to discuss, Spark makes this especially evident through aspects of dialogue, narration, setting and plot which draw attention to the staged and stilted aspects of seemingly 'natural' existences. Through my analysis of these examples, I propose that perceiving characters such as Annabel not as lifeless puppets but rather as living *performers*, who forgo personal freedom to enact fictions in life (whether consciously, unwittingly or even unwillingly), might enable a valuable reconsideration of Spark's experimental fiction and its inventive approach to matters of gender, identity and free will.

Making a Scene: Theatrical Self-(Un)Awareness and 'Flimsy' Realism in *Doctors of Philosophy* and 'A Dangerous Situation on the Stairs'

Paraphrasing Jean-François Lyotard's famous definition of the postmodern,[3] Bran Nicol characterises much postwar writing as being 'shaped in some way by an incredulity towards realism – a state of mind [. . .] convinced that the act of representation cannot be performed as unselfconsciously and wholeheartedly as it was in the nineteenth century' (2009: 19). Spark, as the previous chapter discussed, came to share this sense of incredulity, even having Caroline Rose overhear her own author's typewriter while struggling to complete a chapter of literary criticism on realism in the modern novel. As evinced by her aforementioned disdain for the attacks made upon experimental fiction by the likes of C. P. Snow, William Cooper and Kingsley Amis during the 1950s and 1960s, Spark was keen to draw away from the standardised, myopic and stable conceptions of realism (and thus reality) endorsed by such self-proclaimed realists. Instead, she wished to gesture toward a model of reality that is relative and unsettled, and which carries the ever-present possibility of achieving, to quote the title of Sandy Stranger's famous treatise, a radical 'Transfiguration of the Commonplace' (Spark 1972: 143).

Few narrative techniques better communicate this literary and existential possibility than metalepsis – a process, as outlined earlier with reference to Genette, which involves the violation of a text's diegetic boundaries, and which dramatises by extension the obfuscation of the border between reality and fiction. However playful or outlandish the effects of metalepsis might appear, studies including Debra Malina's *Breaking the Frame* (2002) have recognised the device's potential to articulate serious truths about our own construction as subjects and the fictions we come to live by. Malina observes how, 'because it traverses an ontological hierarchy, metalepsis has the power to endow subjects with greater or lesser degrees of "reality" – in effect, to promote them into subjectivity and demote them from it' (4). This, in turn, 'bears a *mimetic* relation to subject-construction processes in our own world, and [. . .] may be made to reach through the final frontier, the boundary between fictional text and extratextual reader, that effect *our* construction as subjects' (9). 'Paradoxically', observes Adam Katz of the relationship of metalepsis to mimesis, 'the rigorous enactment and exploration of the artificiality of narrative boundaries is closer to experience than traditional, "realistic" narration', because '"experience" is nothing more than ongoing constitution, probing, testing, transgression and reconstitution of the boundaries separating and relating subjects to one another and their common world' (2005: 190).

The ability of metalepsis either to 'promote' or to 'demote' a character's ontological status, and thus to reproduce mimetically the processes of subject construction and desubjectification operating in the world *outside* of the text, is especially relevant to Spark's fiction and its own particular 'incredulity towards realism'. In her play *Doctors of Philosophy*, Spark stages and deconstructs the shared, insular reality of Charlie Delfont, a leading economist, and his wife Catherine, herself a once brilliant scholar of Assyrian palaeography who has since sacrificed an academic career for marriage and motherhood. Visiting their London home during the university vacation is Catherine's cousin, Dr Leonora Chase, a successful academic and the Fellow of an Oxford college. The women had been friends while studying for their doctorates some years earlier, but Catherine has since grown resentful of Leonora's career and dismissive of women who prioritise their own intellectual development over marital subservience. 'I like to please men', she announces proudly to her cousin, 'do you think it pleases a man when he looks into a woman's eyes and sees a reflection of the British Museum Reading Room?' (15). For Spark, who described *Doctors of Philosophy* specifically as a 'woman's play' (Frankel 1987: 448), this was to be no disengaged puppet show, but rather a sustained exploration of 'women's problems, whether they got married or didn't get married – the problems [of] being intellectual and not being married and being married and intellectual, and [then] what do you do with your intellect?' (Smith 1998: 213).

Although dismissed by theatre critics during its short-lived London run, and largely neglected by critical studies of the author – overlooked, perhaps, as a frivolous digression written between two of her best-known novels, *The Prime of Miss Jean Brodie* and *The Girls of Slender Means*, which was entirely at odds with a London theatre scene in thrall to Angry Young Men – *Doctors of Philosophy* offers a valuable model of Sparkian metalepsis that can be applied to, and traced across, the author's prose. The play begins in the Delfonts' living room, where Charlie and Catherine are discussing Leonora's decision to retire early to bed rather than admire their home's prized view of the Regent's Canal. 'I thought she might like to look at the water as it isn't term-time', Catherine complains to Charlie, 'I quite see that during term a thing like the Regent's Canal would be an idea to Leonora, it would be a geographical and historical and sociological idea, but during vacation I do think Leonora ought to take a look at reality' (1). Catherine's apparently sincere belief that offering Leonora a rare 'look at reality' outside of the academic term constitutes an altruistic act is, from the audience's extradiegetic perspective, rich in dramatic irony. From the stage set that comprises their plush surroundings to the imaginary canal that they gaze upon each evening, the stage-managed lives of Charlie and Catherine – whose surname is likely a sly reference to the renowned theatrical impresario, Lord Bernard Delfont – could hardly be further from the 'reality' in which they believe and to which they wish to expose Leonora.

That the Delfonts exist within a realm of pure artifice is foregrounded by the presence of their '*daily help*' (v), a housekeeper tellingly named Mrs S. Here Spark places her authorial surrogate within a long theatrical tradition of the knowing yet peripheral servant, from the sagacious butlers of Wildean social comedies to then recent examples such as Miss Bennett in Agatha Christie's *The Unexpected Guest* (1958) and Crestwell in Noël Coward's *Relative Values* (1951). As an authorial presence within the play, as well as an agent of metalepsis – occupying the liminal space between audience and stage, Mrs S. can be witnessed shaking, dismantling and rearranging the various fixtures and fittings of the set, playfully interrogating the narrow margins of the Delfonts' reality in the process. In a manner plainly at odds with Ian Gregson's conception of Spark's characters as 'authorial puppets' placed at the mercy of their creator, Charlie and Catherine are shown to have narrowed their *own* horizons by retreating ever further into a life of smug solipsism. Mrs S. mocks them for this without them ever realising, even reading aloud from a feature on Catherine published in a local lifestyle magazine, *Life and Looks*, to underscore her pride and delusion:

> Mrs S: This is the home, situated near Regent's Park, of the celebrated economist, Charles Delfont and his charming wife [. . .]. Mrs Delfont, before her marriage a scholar in her own right, told *Life and Looks* that she has found it perfectly easy to reconcile her capacity for intellectualism with the duties of wife and mother. 'After all,' she said with a serene smile, 'higher education broadens the horizons.' (21)

Life and Looks could well serve as an alternative title for *Doctors of Philosophy*, concerned as it is with real lives subsumed beneath layers of pretension and artifice in a dangerous hothouse of fictions. The play was staged only a year before the publication of Lionel Abel's seminal collection of essays, *Metatheatre: A New View of Dramatic Form* (1963), which introduced 'metatheatre' as a concept relating to 'theatre pieces about life seen as already theatricalised' (60). Whereas Abel associates such 'theatricalised' existences with the individual's dawning self-awareness – arguing that 'the persons appearing on stage [. . .] knew they were dramatic before the playwright took note of them. What dramatised them originally? Myth, legend, past literature, *they themselves*' (Ibid.) – Spark's play suggests the opposite, presenting characters such as Leonora, who appear to drift unconsciously into predetermined dramatic roles. The audience is first introduced to Leonora when she appears before Charlie in a seemingly somnambulant state, communicating solely through a litany of repetitive demands (as if, in consonance with the metatheatrical premise of the play, reciting lines from a script) as she begs him to impregnate her: 'Charlie, give me a child', 'a child, I want a child', 'I wish to conceive a child', 'I want a child, before it's too late' (3). For Charlie, who captures the bizarre demands on a tape-recorder, this behaviour serves as necessary confirmation of Leonora's jealousy of his and Catherine's carefully cultivated façade of marital and domestic contentment, a piece of irrefutable proof that her academic career has failed to compensate for the absence of a husband and child. Away from Charlie, however, Catherine confesses to Leonora that it is *she* who has long been dissatisfied with her role as 'charming wife'; 'Can you imagine what it has felt like', she asks her cousin, 'as a scholar, to be the mere chattel of another scholar for all these years?' (18). Has Catherine, too, become an unwitting performer in what might be described – to borrow from Spark's earlier review of Jung's *Answer to Job* – as 'a conspiracy of mediocrity' (Spark 1955: 7), devised by her husband? Her desperate outburst certainly suggests so. A full decade before Ira Levin's famous satire of social conformity and domestic entrapment, *The Stepford Wives* (1972), which critiqued pervasive gender roles through its memorable presentation of female characters as artificial replicants devoid of bodily autonomy, *Doctors of Philosophy* interrogated similar themes of male manipulativeness and female subservience through comparable scenes of mindless play-acting.

Despite its arch tone and absurdist leanings, *Doctors of Philosophy*'s central preoccupation with the limitations placed upon the lives and self-perceptions of its two female protagonists comes to reveal an unequivocally feminist agenda, committed to radically undermining the circumstances that have reduced Catherine to the meagre role of her husband's 'chattel' and Leonora to that of a jealous, desperate spinster. Act II, Scene ii begins not within the familiar confines of the Delfonts' living room, but upon a bare stage which, according to the directions, '*is empty and without scenery except for various pulleys and switches*' (46). Catching Mrs S. as she goes about dusting and polishing the numerous exposed contraptions responsible for staging the Delfonts' daily existence, Leonora reacts with horror:

> Leonora: The wall, the room! Where is it? What's happened?
> Mrs S: I told you, Leonora, I'm getting the place ready. Have patience. I've got to work in my own time-space.
> Leonora: Mrs S., I'm frightened. [. . .] I just can't bear the sight of it.
> Mrs S: Are you interested in the nature of reality, Leonora, or are you too frightened?
> Leonora: I'm interested. (47–8)

By affording Leonora a privileged insight into 'the nature of reality' (something altogether different from the 'look at reality' offered by Catherine earlier in the play) from the vantage point of her own extradiegetic 'time-space', Mrs S. enables her to determine the part she has come to play for the satisfaction of the Delfonts. Confronting her tormentors, Leonora declares that she has been desubjectified by sleepwalking – quite literally – into a 'dramatic role' against which Charlie and Catherine can measure their own contentment (60), thus upholding the elaborate illusion upon which their lives are built:

> Leonora: I have occupied the role in which you've cast me. At times of low spirits when one is tired one behaves largely as people expect one to behave. It has been expected of me that I should be envious of you, Catherine, and I should want Charlie to give me a child. I've instinctively played the part in your minds of Leonora the barren virgin. (61)

In an effort to convince Leonora that she is in the throes of a mental breakdown, Charlie attempts to bully her into receiving psychoanalysis in order to restore her to a perceived 'normality' (63). Leonora refuses, insisting: 'My condition isn't in the least distressing. It's most interesting. Exhilarating. I feel like the first woman who's ever been born. I feel I've discovered the world' (64). This 'exhilarating' awakening proves to be somewhat contagious, and soon Catherine, too, is transformed; her new-found sense of instability, provoked by Leonora's outburst, makes her so attractive to her daughter's boyfriend (who is also named Charlie)[4] that the pair kiss passionately. Catherine finds her characteristic equanimity suddenly 'blown to hell', a sensation that she claims repeatedly to find 'thrilling' (65). From this point onwards, the play has great fun with dialogue and set pieces pertaining to stasis and change, dramatic roles and drastic epiphanies, and closed sets and exploded fourth walls. Leonora retaliates against the dismissive charge that 'scholars are not realists', for example, when she *'reaches out and gives the wall a push'*, before replying that 'realism is very flimsy' (97–8), while a third cousin, Annie, declares triumphantly that 'the women of this household always engage in a high level of conversation among themselves; very high' (94). This 'high level' points to the women's acquirement of a new-found ontological richness, and a dawning awareness of a world beyond the confines of the stage (and the dull Charlies who stand upon it).

Doctors of Philosophy met with a lukewarm critical response when it opened at London's New Arts Theatre Club in October 1962. 'Miss Spark's assaults on the technical canons of stagecraft were grandiose', complained Tom Stoppard, who argued that the play would work 'better as a straightforward and literate comedy' (1962: 91). Kenneth Tynan called the play 'one of the most baffling I have ever witnessed. No doubt it has a shape and even, perhaps, a purpose; let me discretely say that they are not evident and may never be' (1962: 26). 'Still, it's cheerful' (1962: 5), offered Philip Hope-Wallace, following a brief but similarly bemused review. What each of these early reviews neglects to consider is how Spark's play operates, in fact, as a defamiliarised interrogation of two polarised, crudely drawn and patriarchally inflected stereotypes of the contemporary woman, to which the various 'assaults on [. . .] stagecraft' criticised by Stoppard prove essential. With Brechtian anti-illusionism and playful self-referentiality, such 'assaults' expose the roles occupied by Leonora and Catherine as precisely that, so that the play enacts the metatheatrical deconstruction of the mutually exclusive extremes presented at the end of 'Bang-Bang You're Dead', when Sybil asks herself mournfully: 'Am I a woman [. . .] or an intellectual monster?' (120).

What is significant about *Doctors of Philosophy*, then, is not Spark's treatment of her characters as inert puppets, but rather the ease with which these characters are shown to ensnare themselves, and one another, within various narrow, preconstructed dramatic parts, to be enacted upon a stage of their own making. Before the play has even begun, Leonora's words imply, the Delfonts have worn her down to such an extent that she can only submit to the dead-eyed and depthless stereotype to whom the audience is first introduced. In dismantling the roles of Leonora as 'barren virgin' and (albeit to a lesser extent) Catherine as submissive 'chattel', Sparkian metalepsis can thus be read as a feminist strategy, committed to exposing and subverting the processes by which patriarchy constructs its subjects (and, in turn, its passive objects). As Malina argues, 'although metalepsis may infiltrate narratological taxonomies camouflaged as just another element of narrative structure, it harbours the potential to undermine the whole elaborate construction'. As a 'dynamic force rather than a static element', the purpose of metalepsis 'is precisely to *undo*, at least temporarily, stable levels and definite boundaries' (2002: 132). By having her authorial surrogate disassemble and thus ridicule the Delfonts' fixed reality, Spark articulates her own resistance to conventional modes of realism which only reproduce, rather than question or subvert, dominant ideologies and structures of power. 'Are you interested in the nature of reality?', Leonora enquires of Mrs S. as she goes about her daily housekeeping duties. 'Very', Mrs S. replies, 'I'm trying to give it a polish as you can see' (47). The task of Mrs S. is much like that of her authorial namesake; Sparkian metalepsis here works away at the dull surface of reality until it gleams with new meaning.

'I see the absurd in a great many things, but I think that we learn from absurdity', Spark remarked in a 2001 BBC radio interview. 'The fact that things strike us as absurd', she added, 'makes us stop and think. I'm quite sure of that. I like to ridicule where I think ridicule is due' (Gilbert 2001: n.p.). In this respect, the figure of the housekeeper serves not only as an ideal authorial stand-in – existing at a comfortable remove from the other characters, yet closely attuned to their various secrets, habits, foibles and distorted realities – but a model ridiculer, who is able to cast a wry eye over proceedings from her or his unique vantage point: 'I've learned to preserve my detachment and scholarly calm', announces Mrs S., 'on the other side of the door' (9).

Mrs S. is not the only sagacious housekeeper to appear in Spark's fiction, however. The archival research undertaken for this book has led to the discovery of a previously unseen short story entitled 'A Dangerous Situation on the Stairs'. The story, which is contained within a folder of handwritten notes for the novel that would become *The Prime of Miss Jean Brodie* (and which can therefore be dated approximately to 1960), depicts – in an elliptical, fragmented fashion – a series of romantic encounters between its protagonist, Sarah, and her unnamed lover during a six-month period spanning autumn to the following spring. The story begins *in media res*: '"You know your way up,"' the housekeeper tells Sarah, as she sweeps a heap of dead leaves from the front step, before disappearing into darkness behind a silent, swinging door of green beige (MFL c.1960–1). Is this an innocuous greeting, Sarah begins to wonder, or a veiled criticism of the frequency of her visits? Has the affair left her paranoid, or is she being judged from the shadows beyond the swinging door?

Sarah, the reader soon learns, is indeed familiar with the journey upstairs, having visited the townhouse on several prior occasions. She appears to insist, however, on treating each visit as though it were her first. By doing so, she hopes that she may continue to recreate what she has come to regard fondly as 'the bannister scene': a set of actions which involve Sarah waiting in the hallway as her lover gazes down from the landing, before he beckons her upstairs to join him. The pair proceed to conduct their relationship as though they are a pair of dedicated performers, repeatedly play-acting the same, pleasurable scene before the watchful eyes of the housekeeper. While the interior of the townhouse becomes a static 'scene', life outside carries on as usual: the narrator describes how fallen leaves continue to accumulate beyond the front door between October and December, while the winter air thickens steadily with fog and influenza. The housekeeper repeats her nagging welcome on each of Sarah's visits. A chasm widens, meanwhile, between Sarah and her friends. Perturbed by their reservations about her lover, she resolves to end the affair, yet finds herself seduced by her role in the still-unfolding drama:

> She was aware as she climbed, head down, that they were distinguished lovers. And yet, people would giggle, she supposed, if they knew. She kept her head down so that she could, at the bend in the stairs, delight herself with his leaning over the bannister. We are both, she said to herself, verging on the dangerous years for men and women, he fifty, I forty.

What a refinement of pleasure, she said, is this self-consciousness, seeing the affair from without and feeling it from within. We are abundantly favoured. I will put an end to it now, to-day, because it will never last. Our love must disintegrate after this; to-day is so perfect, so ripe in my awareness. I will not wait till March. [. . .] It will never come to anything, it will only be danger. (Ibid.)

The 'danger' that Sarah fears, and which she later grows to accept and even welcome, relates to her concern that the pair's 'distinction' will be tarnished, should their relationship become widely known. There lurks a greater 'danger', however, to which the short story's title appears to allude; in first attempting to preserve their 'solitary gifts' by conducting their affair in private, Sarah and her lover have settled into a strange and self-alienating charade of romance, in which she plays the subservient role of the swooning romantic heroine, climbing the stairs only when beckoned to do so. Spark's repeated use of 'scene' encourages the suspicious reader to perceive these interactions as unnatural – less like stages in an organically evolving relationship, that is, than a staged sequence of romantic set pieces modelled on hackneyed gender roles. We might return, then, to the certain insight and foreknowledge that is implicit in the housekeeper's greeting, '"You know your way up,"' which recurs throughout the story like an ominous refrain (Spark's handwritten draft reveals that a crossed-out 'The Way Up' was its original title). The housekeeper's words suggest an acute awareness of Sarah's overfamiliarity with 'the bannister scene', and thus her gradual descent into a delusory romantic ideal. As in *Doctors of Philosophy*, Spark appears to endow the figure of the housekeeper with *a certain detachment*, with which she observes characters as they drift deeper into dramatic roles.

The seeming unreality of the courtship can be further surmised by reading the story against a memorable, and notably similar, passage from *The Prime of Miss Jean Brodie*, in which two of Brodie's teenage pupils, Sandy Stranger and Jenny Gray, construct an imaginary love letter from their teacher to the school's singing master, Gordon Lowther. The letter reads, as Alan Bold observes, as a 'gloriously comic' reproduction of aspects of 'romantic pulp fiction' (1986: 68), which betrays the schoolgirls' naivety concerning love and sex – matters which, writes Katherine Dalsimer, are here 'obscured by a romantic haze' (1986: 38):

My Own Delightful Gordon,
Your letter has moved me deeply, as you may imagine. But alas, I must ever decline to be Mrs. Lowther. [. . .] But I was proud of giving myself to you when you came and took me in the bracken on Arthur's Seat while the storm raged about us. [. . .] I may permit misconduct to occur again from time to time as an outlet because I am in my Prime. [. . .]

I wish to inform you that your housekeeper fills me with anxiety [. . .]. Pray ask her not to say "You know your way up" when I call at your house in Cramond.

[. . .]

Allow me, in conclusion, to congratulate you warmly upon your sexual intercourse, as well as your singing.

> With fondest joy,
> Jean Brodie
> (73–4)

It remains unclear as to whether Spark composed the girls' love letter before or after she completed 'A Dangerous Situation on the Stairs', and thus whether the contents of Sandy and Jenny's concocted romance came to influence the nature of Sarah's indulgent self-image, or *vice versa*. Whatever the case may be, the likeness shared between both texts (their inclusion, in particular, of elaborate romantic set pieces, as well as a housekeeper who utters the potentially incisive words, '"You know your way up"') casts Sarah's relationship in a decidedly unflattering light. Despite her professed 'self-consciousness', we can now discern, Sarah perceives both herself and her lover through the same 'romantic haze' that clouds the vision of Brodie's inexperienced schoolgirls. Spark's 'dangerous situation' thus articulates the peril of losing touch with reality, of slipping unwittingly into a delusory, static fiction while the leaves pile up outside.

Similarly 'dangerous situation[s]' can be seen to recur throughout Spark's early fiction, from the enervating 'game for three players' which Sybil endures while in the company of Désirée and Barry Weston in 'Bang-Bang You're Dead' (106), to the drab and increasingly deadly 'play far advanced', into which Merle Coverdale finds herself hopelessly ensnared in *The Ballad of Peckham Rye* (53: as discussed in the following chapter). While the interactions between Sarah and her lover are certainly less sinister and life-threatening than those outlined above, they nevertheless point towards a sense of steadily increasing isolation, stasis and absurdity, which Spark views as detrimental (if not entirely disastrous) to human development and self-awareness. What distinguishes each of these texts from *Doctors of Philosophy* is the absence of a metaleptic frame-break; instead, real lives are shown to ossify gradually into stagnant and stifling roles, while characters' familiar environments come to close in around them like constrictive stage sets. Although it has been considered as something of an oddity in Spark's œuvre (being the author's only stage play, and a little-known and poorly received one at that), *Doctors of Philosophy* should thus be understood as the outlandish, metatheatrical extension of its author's pre-existing concerns, in which an oppressive reality is explosively revealed, as Leonora discovers to her shock and delight, to be 'very flimsy' indeed.

'Living parts' and Hidden Depths in *The Public Image*

In his 2017 article, 'Muriel Spark's Camp Metafiction', Len Gutkin observes how, following *The Comforters'* explicitly metafictional treatment of 'authorial mind reading and plotting', Spark's subsequent fictions 'would go on to engage these interests less directly, by translating Caroline's hallucinated typewriter into subtler medial analogies for narrative omniscience and plot construction' (60) in novels including *The Abbess of Crewe*, where electronic surveillance methods such as wiretapping and bugging come to replace overtly self-reflexive representations of authorial omniscience. A similar observation could be made of the novels that emerged during the decade after *Doctors of Philosophy*, in which Leonora's extradiegetic alertness to the restrictive role that she has played before what she describes as an off-stage 'invisible audience' (63) is transposed to a media-saturated contemporary landscape, where tabloid prurience and the prospect of becoming a media spectacle can instil within the subject a heightened (and yet entirely plausible) dramatic self-consciousness. 'I love the glossies and the newspapers and film mags', remarked Spark in 1971, on being asked about her recent fiction's preoccupation with celebrity, scandal and technologies of mass reproduction, 'and that's where I find a lot of my material' (Toynbee 1971: 73). Bryan Cheyette chooses 'machine made' as the most fitting description for these novels, borrowing the phrase from Angus Wilson's review of *The Mandelbaum Gate* (owing to its numerous references to modes of modern technology and mass media communication [1965: 28]). As Cheyette suggests, however, the phrase is far better suited to the fictions that followed immediately after that novel – *The Public Image, The Driver's Seat* and *Not to Disturb* – which 'are dominated by machines of all kinds such as [. . .] cameras, tape-recorders, [and] telephones', as well as 'sophisticated [. . .] propaganda equipment' (2000: 72). Drawing upon the experimental narrative techniques encountered in the *nouveau roman*, in which (as the following chapter examines in detail) the meticulous surveillance of outward appearances took precedence over articulations of emotional depth, Spark reduces the publicity-crazed settings of such novels to an affectless landscape of flattened images. The author, as Cheyette surmises, 'has shown that the themes of her novels dictate their form and there is a crucial link here between her heartless "machine made" tone and her highly mechanised creations' (Ibid.).

Given that it was the first entry in Spark's trilogy of 'heartless "machine made"' fictions, the brevity and detachment of *The Public Image*'s spare prose and spiky plot caught some critics unaware: this ostensibly 'unwritten novel', wrote Saul Maloff, 'is both banal and thin-to-vanishing' (1968: 108); '*The Public Image* is a blown-up short story rather than a novel', claimed Francis Hope, who added that 'what was crisp' in Spark's previous work 'has become tense, what was sharp has become vinegary – and worst of all, what was devastatingly particular has become diffusely general' (1968: 24); 'Characters', complained Richard Holmes, 'are merely touched in', while the setting of Rome 'is lost in the anonymity of Annabel's unfurnished apartment, room after room of sunlit parquet' (1968: 21). Conjuring a disquieting sense of sparseness and anonymity was precisely Spark's aim, however. Indeed, the idea of reducing a city as distinctive as Rome to a featureless parquet landscape was her starting point for the novel, which began life as a paragraph-long fragment entitled 'The Parquet Floor', quoted in full below:

> The gold-brown shines new on the parquet floor of the flat that somehow she has come to. There is no furniture to be seen. There is a feeling that the rent is high and that no difficulty exists in paying it. The baby is laid on the floor by the wall, he is sleeping peacefully on a white little pillow tucked in with sheets. She is wondering where her husband is, he has been away a long time, that is the only worry. Suddenly his friend from Belfast is there, eating at a table in large smiling mouthfuls, his hair and eyes are shining. He is Bill. She says, 'Have you seen Frederick? I don't know where Frederick can be. He hasn't been home.' (MFL: 1966)

Possessing the hazy, impressionistic quality of the dream from which it is said to have emerged,[5] 'The Parquet Floor' reads like a condensed version of *The Public Image*'s first chapter, and exhibits the bare bones of themes and plot elements which would be developed over the course of the completed novel. At the opening of the published text, the unnamed 'she' is Annabel Christopher, a successful film star who has taken it upon herself to procure the parquet-floored flat as a home in which to live with her husband, Frederick, and their newborn son, Carl. For Annabel, whose 'world of people had been full of mutual assistance on all practical matters', the purchase represents a decisive bid for privacy and personal autonomy – an attempt, that is, to bridge the 'distance from life that occurred at the same time as the close-ups on the screen', after which she 'became fixed in the public imagination as the English Tiger-Lady' (37; 38; 22). With its bare, sun-dappled floor, the empty flat functions in Annabel's consciousness as a *tabula rasa* – a gleaming blank slate, far removed from the prying eyes and whirring lenses of the public and paparazzi – upon which she might at last cultivate and project an authentic sense of self, and, in doing so, nurture and protect her relationship with her child:

> The baby, Carl, was the only reality in her life. His existence gave her a sense of being permanently secured to the world which she had not experienced since her own childhood had passed. [. . .] She felt a curious fear of display where the baby was concerned, as if this deep and complete satisfaction might be disfigured or melted away by some public image. (35)

Annabel's perception of the empty flat differs, however, from those of its unwelcome visitors, who take it upon themselves to enter at will. 'Until the furniture had arrived and been put in place', she realises, 'everyone felt they could come and go, like the workmen and removal men, without permission', as well as the 'neighbours [who] had already toured the flat, smiling and exclaiming' (6). This treatment of the private space as a public arena is underscored by the unannounced arrival of Billy O'Brien (who appears in 'The Parquet Floor' as Bill, defined by his unnerving act of eating 'in large smiling mouthfuls'), whose accusatory question to Annabel, '"is this all in aid of your public image?"' (7), betrays his belief that the flat constitutes a superficial extension of the glamorous life of her dramatic persona. These numerous, minor interactions with Annabel's empty home dramatise in miniature the competing claims on her identity and privacy, which have come to define her existence ever since she found fame. Whereas Annabel might consider herself to be walking freely across the sunlit parquet into a long-yearned-for private life, to those around her she is still treading the boards, fixed in a permanent performance for her amassed spectators.

Annabel has been partially complicit in cultivating the public image for which she has become renowned, however, and Spark's narrative flits repeatedly from the parquet-floored present to detail the history of the English Tiger-Lady's elaborate construction. Working closely alongside a film director, Luigi Leopardi,[6] as well as a press secretary whose 'commission [was] to build up Annabel', Annabel develops the Tiger-Lady from a role that she had played in an otherwise unremarkable film scripted by her husband, in which she won plaudits for her on-screen aura of 'terrifying serenity [. . .] with a tiger in her soul' (23; 20). She was, announces her narrator, 'entirely aware of the image-making process in every phase', yet 'did not expect this personal image to last long in the public mind, for she intended to play other parts than that of the suppressed tiger' (27). Unwittingly, then, Annabel has allowed her identity to ossify into that of the Tiger-Lady – a composite, or palimpsest, of the fantasies of Frederick and Luigi – to the extent that even 'her face had changed, as if by action of many famous cameras, into a mould of her public figuration' (35). Her 'instinctive method of acting', which entails 'simply [. . .] playing herself in a series of poses for the camera, just as if she were getting her photograph taken for private purposes', causes distinctions between reality and fiction to blur disquietingly (10). As a consequence, Annabel constantly finds herself accused by those around her of affecting a façade, and of transforming private scenes into public spectacles: '"Oh, stop posing," Billy said. She was standing on the carpet, one hand on a side-table [. . .] as if playing a middle-aged part. "I'm not posing," she said' (14).

Annabel's public image comes to inform all aspects of her private life, including her relationship with Frederick. As Susan Sellers notes, the publicity-minded machinations of Luigi's press team have 'turn[ed] Frederick and Annabel's marriage into a legend, with fixed characters and an unvarying plot', so that, while 'Annabel gains in confidence through the images of their ideal marriage in the press, she becomes paradoxically dependent on Frederick's acquiescence' (2001: 38). Despite the well-publicised 'tiger in her soul', Annabel is thus shown to be remarkably tame, enduring an unhappy and unfaithful marriage for the sake of the status and livelihood afforded by her public identity as the Tiger-Lady. 'So deeply is each partner implicated in this "public image" of Annabel as Tiger', remarks Robert Ostermann in an early review of the novel, 'that together they are trapped, held together like a photograph of perfection permanently sealed in plastic, to be forever admired but untouched' (1968: 7). Ostermann's analysis acquires a literal resonance when read against a scene in which the couple are encouraged to pose for a series of highly stylised yet apparently 'candid' publicity shots upon an artfully 'disarranged' bed (26). In these images, Frederick poses 'on the edge of the bed, in a Liberty dressing-gown, smoking', while 'sweet but unsmiling' Annabel, wearing only a 'night-dress, [with] one shoulder-band slipping down her arm' and extending a teapot 'with a gracious hand' before her husband's outstretched cup, communicates an idealised mixture of wifely servitude and barely con-cealed desire (27). So effective are the photographs, reveals the narrator, that 'wives began to romp in bed far beyond the call of their husbands, or the capacities of their years, or any of the realities of the situation' (28). The images' wild influence and air of unreality thus evoke Susan Sontag's reflections on the 'virtually unlimited authority in modern society' of 'photographic images' as a 'means of shaping reality' (1977: 153). For Sontag, photographs are 'not so much an instrument of memory as an invention of it or a replacement' (165), and therefore 'as much an interpretation of the world as paintings or drawings are' (6);

the photograph, she writes, 'sets up a chronic voyeuristic relation to the world' (11).

That *The Public Image*'s public images are every bit as contrived and ideologically informed as the product of any other creative endeavour is hardly surprising; Spark's narrator has guided the reader through each stage in 'the image-making process', from the careful creasing of bed linen to the employment of intricate post-production techniques including 'the best colour methods of the cinema', which alter Annabel's ordinarily 'sickly-eyed' expression to something 'fiery and [. . .] marvellous' (16). Of greater significance is the diminished, distorted and severely compromised nature of the life of the photographed subject. Indeed, to accept Sontag's belief that 'to photograph is to appropriate the thing photographed' (1977: 4) is to perceive the subject as similarly contained, 'appropriate[d]' and 'thing'-like. 'The camera', remarks Sontag, 'may presume, intrude, trespass, distort, [and] exploit' its subject matter (13), and Annabel's private life is similarly encroached upon by what her narrator has slyly termed 'the *mould* of her public figuration', to the extent that she often 'took fright at the whole mythology that had vapoured so thickly about her' (30, emphasis mine). Similarly, for all his desire to abandon the unhappy marriage, Frederick finds himself, as a consequence of the publicity photos, 'rooted deeply and with serious interest in a living part such as many multitudes believe exist: a cultured man without temperament, studious, sportsmanlike, aristocratic, [. . .] Annabel's husband' (27). Having fooled the watching world with expertly crafted scenes from their marriage, Annabel and Frederick have themselves become seduced by the alluring unreality of their public personae.

The oxymoronic 'living part[s]' occupied by the husband and wife thus come to evoke *Doctors of Philosophy*'s stilted and self-reflexively staged gender roles, as captured in the Delfonts' idyllic *Life and Looks* profile. Without a benevolent Mrs S. on hand to offer the pair a welcome glimpse into 'the nature of reality' (48), however, resentment builds over each party's absorption within a world of images and artifice. 'It is the deep core of stupidity', remarks the narrator (in an aside which could have left the lips of Mrs S. herself), 'that it thrives on the absence of a looking-glass' (9); despite their increasing vanity, Annabel and Frederick lack such a 'looking-glass', and instead reflect hostilities towards one another's exasperating public images. Annabel, announces Frederick in a letter to his wife, has grown to resemble *'a beautiful shell, like something washed up on the sea-shore, a collector's item, perfectly formed, a pearly shell – but empty, devoid of the life it once held'* (92). Frederick's decision to kill himself, by leaping from a scaffold at the Church of St

John and St Paul, can thus be read, perversely, as a vengeful bid for posthumous *substance* rather than self-destruction. By selecting the site of the martyrdom of St Paul as his suicide location, Frederick strives to excoriate Annabel for her intolerable emptiness by emphasising the pain that it has inflicted upon *his* contrastingly delicate soul and unfailing morality. The accompaniments to Frederick's final act – a series of incriminating suicide letters addressed to an invented mother, detailing his wife's alleged participation in 'outrageous orgies of the most licentious nature', and the arrangement of a debauched party in her new flat – are intended, Annabel realises, 'to be blood on her hands, blood on her public image' (85; 58).

When Spark's narrative returns to the parquet-floored present, Frederick's 'intolerable party' is in full swing and the once gleaming surfaces of Annabel's flat are stained with wine and vomit, while an empty beer bottle lies next to her sleeping child (58). As details of her husband's suicide and anguished letters begin to filter through to the public and press, Annabel, learning that her home is now the intended site of her downfall, arranges a swift scene-change. The cleaned-up flat becomes the setting for a press conference, where the protagonist draws upon her dramatic training and innate sense of stagecraft to alter the course of events decisively:

> Annabel sat down on the chair left vacant for her. The neighbours, with their instinct for ceremony and spectacle, had arranged those chairs which they had brought from their own best rooms in two semi-circles which flanked the best chair of all; this was upholstered in red velvet, and its arms were antiquely carved. With equal instinct, Annabel sat on this best chair and adjusted the baby. The press would soon arrive. (67)

Here, as in the film roles for which she became famous, Annabel's dramatic 'instinct' corresponds harmoniously with the demands of her audience (the cameras of the paparazzi, as if in happy participation with this merry dance, 'were plucked like guitars and whirled like barrel organs' [71]). While Frederick had intended to stage-manage a scene of incriminating debauchery – not dissimilar, perhaps, to the wild orgy that occurs at the end of Federico Fellini's then recent tale of infamy, aristocratic decadence and media sensation in affluent Rome, *La Dolce Vita* (1960) – Annabel has other ideas. With her child raised before her 'like a triumphant shield', and with her newly sympathetic neighbours amassed on either side, she allows the unfolding scene to assume the grandeur of 'some vast portrayal of a family and household by Holbein' (68). The apparent ease with which Annabel's empty home can shift between competing spectacles of depravity and defiant dignity (all consumed unquestioningly by an 'on-stage' audience of voracious neighbours, lambasting or applauding each new scene with unflagging enthusiasm) speaks to what Guy Debord, only a year before the publication of *The Public Image*, had termed *The Society of the Spectacle* (1967). 'In societies where modern conditions of production prevail', Debord's polemic asserts, 'all of life presents itself as an immense accumulation of *spectacles*', so that 'everything that was directly lived has moved away into a representation' (1983: 2), leading to a disorienting, socially alienating dissimulation of reality. The spectacle, therefore, 'is not something *added* to the real world', but rather 'the very heart of society's real unreality. In all its specific manifestations – news or propaganda, advertising or the actual consumption of entertainment – the spectacle epitomises the prevailing model of social life' (13, emphasis in original). Contemporary Rome, referred to in *The Public Image* as 'the Motherland of Sensation' (24), is presented in Spark's novel as a prime example of a society in which all social interaction has been mediated into a spectacular unreality, so that life becomes indistinguishable from the posed and preened images circulated in 'the glossies'. As one of the focal points of the public and media gaze, Annabel must – to follow Debord's thesis – surrender her subjectivity to exist solely as a depthless spectacle:

> The individual who in the service of the spectacle is placed in stardom's spotlight is in fact the opposite of an individual, and as clearly the enemy of the individual in himself as of the individual in others. In entering the spectacle as a model to be identified with, he renounces all autonomy in order himself to identify with the general law of obedience to the course of things. (1983: 39)

In keeping with Debord's bleak prognosis of the spectacularised subject, Annabel's panicked need to retain her position 'in stardom's spotlight' leads to an alarming psychic schism. In her desperation to protect her reputation as the English Tiger-Lady from destruction following the release of Frederick's letters, she finds herself defensively unable to break role, and consequently adrift from reality. While travelling home from the hospital where she has identified Frederick's body, she wonders suddenly 'how the film would end', and imagines that a 'camera [had] swung round' to capture her movements through Rome's twisting hyways (60). Here, for the first time in Spark's detached, 'machine made' novel, Rome appears intensely cinematic rather than anodyne and anonymous. Its 'dark intertwining streets', containing 'narrow streets within narrower', recall the labyrinthine, disjointed vision of the city as depicted in Vittorio de Sica's *Bicycle Thieves* (1948), for example, while Annabel's delirious, irrational sense of there being a predatory 'poisoner' lurking 'behind the black window-square', or 'a man flattened against the wall with the daggers ready' (60), evokes Rome's appearance as a site of deadly violence and febrile paranoia in contemporary Italian *giallo* cinema, including Mario Bava's *The Girl Who Knew Too Much* (1963). Readers of the novel thus come to share Annabel's cinematic self-consciousness, encountering her world as an immersive, protean sequence of flickering celluloid spectacles – fleeting, fragmented and unreal.

In this state of heightened self-consciousness, Annabel comes to alienate even the most expert mythmakers in her company. Luigi, who responds to the majority of her image-protecting endeavours with banal, sycophantic praise ("you were *wonderful*," he repeatedly tells her, his words resembling those of a fawning critic [104; 112]), eventually bristles at her manner of "directing [Frederick's] inquest like a movie" (117). It is for a similar reason that Hélène Cixous, writing shortly after the novel's publication, described the protagonist witheringly as 'an ice-cold little vampire', who engages in a 'hollow' art of 'blind female vitality' in order to survive the scandal with her career in tact (2001b: 208). It could be argued, however, that Annabel's feverish practice of 'female vitality' is not especially monstrous, but rather an amplified version of the psychic splitting which, according to John Berger in *Ways of Seeing* (1972), is bound to have characterised her entire existence (and hard-won *survival*) as a woman:

> A woman must continually watch herself. She is almost continually accompanied by her own image of herself. Whilst she is walking across a room or whilst she is weeping at the death of her father, she can scarcely avoid watching herself walking or weeping. From earliest childhood she has been taught and persuaded to survey herself continually. And so she comes to consider the surveyor and the surveyed within her as two constituent yet always distinct elements of her identity as a woman. She has to survey everything she is and everything she does because how she appears to others, and ultimately how she appears to men, is of crucial importance for what is normally thought of as the success of her life. Her own sense of being in herself is supplanted by a sense of being appreciated as herself by another. (46–7)

Berger's analysis, which forms part of a larger set of Lacan-influenced, feminist interrogations of the visual field published in the 1970s (including, perhaps most notably, Laura Mulvey's seminal 1975 text, 'Visual Pleasure and Narrative Cinema', with which I engage in detail in Chapter Four's discussion of *The Driver's Seat*), is incorporated into Elaine Showalter's feminist study of psychiatry, *The Female Malady* (1985). Showalter argues that schizophrenia – which, after 1930, replaced hysteria as the predominant diagnosis ascribed to female patients – includes 'symptoms of passivity, depersonalisation, disembodiment, and fragmentation', which 'have parallels in the social situation of women' (213), as articulated by Berger. Analysing the narrative recollections of female asylum patients, Showalter pays particular attention to the

> repeated motif in the schizophrenic women's sense of themselves as *unoccupied bodies*. Feeling that they have no secure identities, the women look to external appearances for confirmation that they exist. Thus they continually look at their faces in the mirror, but out of desperation rather than narcissism. (212)

For Showalter, 'the abyss that opens between the schizophrenic's body and mind [. . .] can be seen as an exaggeration of women's "normal" state', which she defines in terms of a 'lack of confidence, dependency on external, often masculine, definitions of the self, split between the body as sexual object and the mind as a subject, and vulnerability to conflicting social messages about femininity' (211; 212).

Annabel's status, in the eyes of her husband, as nothing more than an 'empty [. . .], beautiful shell' – or, in the words of the novel's critics, a 'lustrous surface' (Gregson 2006: 105) or an 'image [. . .] without a heart' (Cixous 2001b: 209) – might thus be read as an extreme, deranged manifestation of the depersonalisation, disembodiment and self-surveillance that Berger and Showalter each associate with 'women's "normal" state'. Annabel has, after all, lacked 'a sense of being permanently secured to the world', and thus secure in her sense of self, since the point at which 'her own childhood had passed', which precedes her acting career by many years (35). Given the meticulous commodification of her image by numerous agents, publicists and 'famous cameras' within a spectacularised society, and her later desperation to salvage this constructed persona following Frederick's attempted sabotage, Annabel comes to experience the double bind of female identity more sharply than most, to the extent that, while intent on currying public favour in the panicked aftermath of her husband's suicide, she disappears altogether into a gendered spectacle, constructed for public consumption. Her newly acquired, sun-dappled flat, which once signified her privacy and personal autonomy, as well as her carefully guarded relationship with her child, now becomes the spot-lit stage upon which the English Tiger-Lady will perform without pause. Indeed, despite her former 'fear of display where the baby was concerned', Annabel now no longer hesitates to 'adjus[t] the baby', as though he is a jointed doll or puppet to be posed and manipulated before the media glare (35; 67).

Were *The Public Image* to have concluded at this juncture, with Annabel choosing to salvage her career by eviscerating her inconvenient inner life from its pristine public 'shell', the novel might better reflect the interpretations offered by Cixous and Gregson, while also supporting the latter's wider claim for Spark as an author of 'flat and two-dimensional' fictions that evoke only 'the cul-de-sac of caricature' (Gregson 2006: 102; 107). What both readings fail to acknowledge, however, is the curious instance of *anagnorisis* that arrives in the novel's final chapter, during a conversation between Annabel and her lawyer, Tom. While negotiating the arrangement of a payment to prevent a further batch of Frederick's incriminating letters from being shown at his inquest, Tom expounds his theory that babies '"understand more than you might think"' because of their apparently innate ability to '"record noises [which] they sort of remember afterwards"', to which Annabel replies unhesitatingly that she '"won't buy the letters"' (121). Annabel's unexpected response appears to have been prompted by her sudden recognition (or, indeed, remembrance) of her child as a conscious being rather than an image-enhancing prop. Making reference to Tom's hypothesis, she announces her desire '"to be free like my baby. I hope he's recording this noise"' (123). For Annabel, the baby now supplants the various other recording devices employed to propagate the myth of the Tiger-Lady (a persona brought to life after Luigi, on first meeting Annabel, perceived only 'her recordable image, eyes that would change with the screen's texture, something sheerly given in the face, like a gift that could be exercised' [93]). Only this can account for the protagonist's impulsive decision to 'slip away in the heat of the day', out of Frederick's ongoing inquest and decisively out of role, and to head purposefully to the airport (124). Once there, she and her child will leave Italy to begin a new life:

> Waiting for the order to board, she felt both free and unfree. [. . .] [S]he felt as if she was still, curiously, pregnant with the baby, but not pregnant in fact. She was pale as a shell. She did not wear her dark glasses. Nobody recognised her as she stood, having moved the baby to rest on her hip, conscious also of the baby in a sense weightlessly and perpetually within her, as an empty shell contains, by its very structure, the echo and harking image of former and former seas. (125)

This final image of Annabel, anonymous and alone but for her baby, invites comparisons with the ending of *Doctors of Philosophy*, where Leonora's awareness of the part she has played before her on- and off-stage audiences prompts her (along with several other characters) to break role, leave the stage and seek out new possibilities. Unlike in Spark's play, *The Public Image* presents no absolute distinction between reality and fiction; in abstracting herself from Rome's media circus, that is, Annabel does not traverse a diegetic boundary and become any more or less ontologically 'real' in the process. The effect is much the same, however. As she stands among the other passengers at the airport, Annabel appears, to all intents and purposes, to have abandoned her status as a shallow spectacle and taken a defiant first step into a fully rounded reality. Although she chooses not to obscure her 'newly-televised face' with her dark glasses, she still goes entirely unrecognised, as if the fiction of the Tiger-Lady has now evaporated just as quickly as it once 'vapoured so thickly about her' (124; 30). To reflect this, Spark subverts Frederick's dismissive assessment of the protagonist by endowing his cruel metaphor of the empty shell with redemptive meaning. Annabel's face, which now appears as 'pale as a shell' when seen without 'the best colour methods of the cinema' (16), has been blanched, liberatingly, of its previous associations. Similarly, the echoing interior of Annabel's once spectacularised shell-like self no longer suggests vacuity, but vital inner life. In this final sentence – criticised in a damning early review for its 'use of grandiose language [that] is sudden and uncommon' (Anon. 1968: 612) in comparison with the spare and monotonous preceding prose – *The Public Image* installs within its alienated, image-saturated universe the hopeful prospect of history, intimacy and hidden depths.

This remains a cautiously optimistic ending, however. The 'echo and harking image of former and former seas', I would suggest, imply the return of the protagonist's long lost 'sense of being permanently secured to the world' (35), brought about not only through her relationship to her child, but by a re-established connection, perhaps, to a matriarchal lineage of 'former and former' mothers. Indeed, almost no information concerning Annabel's family and background is provided in the novel, so that, aside from minor details concerning her favourite childhood pastime (writing and posting letters to her grandfather) and her place of birth (Wakefield, in West Yorkshire), the protagonist appears oddly lacking in personal history, and thus less like a human being than a flickering celluloid image. On the other hand, these distant and perhaps sirenic echoes might threaten to lure Annabel towards iconography more ancient, grandiose and seductive than the weightless contemporary construction of the 'English Tiger-Lady'. The empty shell, notes Vassiliki Kolocotroni, 'recall[s] the emergence from the sea of Botticelli's Venus', while Annabel, waiting with Carl to board her flight, 'seems unself-consciously to have struck a Madonna and child pose' (2010: 21–2). Who does Annabel think she is now? Her sensation of being 'both free and unfree' could allude at once to the liberating demise of her old role and the dangerous pull of new ones. In a spectacularised contemporary world, Spark appears to warn, the prospect of losing oneself to a public image looms as an ever-present threat.

What the Butler Foresaw: *Not to Disturb*'s 'insubstantial bodies'

By the end of *The Public Image*, Annabel appears to have escaped not only the constraints of her scripted identity, but the trajectory of its inevitable ruin; the 'happy launchings' of public images such as hers, remarks her narrator, 'were inevitably presented with the optimism of Act I, but bearing within them all the potentials of Act III and its doomed revelations, sooner or later' (24). That 'the sunny glossies of Italy' portray a world populated purely by 'sheer villains' and 'utter innocents', in which the 'most complicated celebrities have been cast anew in these simple roles' (23), suggests something of the distorted and eminently vulnerable nature of a public image, which is permanently poised to be shattered by whatever 'doomed revelations' are bound to lie in wait. The notion that a subject's public image, however celebrated or unsullied, necessarily precedes his or her eminently consumable tragic *dénouement* (a downfall which plays out with all the familiarity of a well-thumbed script) lies at the heart of *Not to Disturb*. In this novel – the final, and most detached and dehumanised instalment in Spark's 'machine made' trilogy – a team of domestic servants, headed by an enterprising and media-savvy butler named Lister, plot to capitalise on the predicted deaths of their (in)famous masters by arranging the lucrative sale of a salacious 'inside story' to the highest bidder. Drawing upon the contemporary, publicity-saturated environments depicted in her two previous novels (*The Public Image* and *The Driver's Seat*), along with *Doctors of Philosophy*'s twin concern with staged, seemingly artificial existences and the sagacity of household servants, *Not to Disturb* conjures a degraded, thoroughly mediatised consumer society, in which an impending human tragedy is detected with chilly indifference and then expertly exploited.

My archival research has determined that *Not to Disturb* was inspired by the circumstances surrounding – and the subsequent, highly sensationalised tabloid coverage of – a then recent murder–suicide committed by an Italian nobleman upon his wife and the man she loved. According to one of several reports from newspapers and 'glossies' preserved among Spark's notebooks and manuscripts, the *crime passionnel* occurred after Anna Fallarino, having long been coerced into performing in the orgies, pornographic films and sexual role-play scenarios devised by her abusive and domineering husband, the Marquis Camillo Casati Stampa, 'fell in love with one of the sex-game partners' procured for *his* voyeuristic gratification (Anon. 1970: 47, in NLS 1970c). It was by breaking from the role enforced upon her and acting with 'genuine love' for another person, the report implies, that Anna had made herself conspicuous, provoking the rage of her 'insanely jealous' husband, who proceeded to shoot both her and her partner before turning the gun – 'a hunting rifle' – on himself (Ibid.). Spark had underlined the choice of murder weapon, along with the report's concluding sentences:

> After a time the couple's sex games became common knowledge, destroying their carefully built up image as happily married and oh-so respectable members of Rome's high society. Their wild sex life was even known to staff in a city centre boutique where she was a free-spending customer. (Ibid.)

Confined to the numerous narrow roles carved out for her, Anna had long existed beneath a palimpsest of public images – defined at first by her perceived marital contentment, respectability and 'free-spending' wealth, and later by the 'wild' sexual identity dictated by her husband. For Spark, Anna's suffering would probably have represented an extreme, real-life example of the aforementioned 'dangerous situation[s]' that had formed the thematic focus of her previous fictions; indeed, the tarnishing of the female victim's 'carefully built up image', at the hands of her controlling husband, through her alleged association with orgies bears an immediate, uncanny resemblance to the ordeal of Annabel Christopher, which Spark had devised four years earlier. Anna's abuse did not end with her violent murder, however. In this uniquely modern scandal, excerpts from her private letters and journals – items seized by members of her staff and sold swiftly to the press – were published in the form of tawdry, mass-produced mock diaries, their pages interspersed with reprints of the pornographic photographs taken by her husband. In a mediatised modern society, Anna's seemingly inevitable demise became a profitable source of mass entertainment.

That Anna, even in death, could not escape the role in which she had been cast evidently held a certain fascination for Spark, who kept two such diaries in a folder of notes and research material for her novel.[7] Within one of these books, she included a brief handwritten note: 'Servants etc. watching to find a habit pattern in order to exploit it; as animal hunters, mothers, robbers and military tacticians do' (NLS 1970b). This expert familiarity with the 'habit pattern[s]' of others points not to divine or supernatural omniscience, but rather to the epistemological advantage that might be gained from the careful, studied scrutiny of human or animal behaviour. Indeed, each of the examples that Spark includes alongside the servant can be identified in her fiction: *The Driver's Seat* includes a detailed section of dialogue regarding tactics for 'big game' hunting, based on knowledge of the prey's typical

hunting habits (88); Freddy Hamilton in *The Mandelbaum Gate* learns
that his mother has artfully controlled the lives of others through a
'long-sustained tyranny' involving 'long-condoned lies' (60); *Memento
Mori*'s Dame Lettie Colston is beaten to death by a burglar who targets
her home after overhearing gossip concerning her self-imposed isolation;
the spectral Paul and Elsa Hazlett in *The Hothouse by the East River*,
having worked in 'black propaganda and psychological warfare' while
alive during the Second World War, now deceive, spy on and terrorise
one another in the afterlife (50). In a 1971 BBC television interview
conducted by her acquaintance, the playwright W. Gordon Smith, Spark
confirmed that a *human* propensity to exploit the habits of others was
central to *Not to Disturb*'s premise:

> I wanted to make a novel with a character who somehow or other knew what
> was going to happen in the future, not through any supernatural means but
> just because it was inevitable that people should act as they do, and that he
> should exploit it. And that was the butler, Lister, that character, who induced
> all the other servants to completely believe him. (Smith 1971: n.p.)

Transferring the elements of the Casati scandal to contemporary
Switzerland, *Not to Disturb* takes place during a single night at the
Château Klopstock, where the resident Baron and Baroness, Cecil and
Kathy, have retreated to their library along with Kathy's lover, Victor,
having instructed their staff that they are not to be disturbed under any
circumstance. Lister's intimate knowledge of the private lives and public
images of his masters leads him to predict correctly that none of the trio
will remain alive by dawn. The effect is that the Klopstocks and their
guest, while still alive, are thought of as though they are already dead:
'"They haunt the house"', Lister remarks sourly as he impatiently awaits
the morning, '"like insubstantial bodies"' (23). The servants' certainty
of this outcome produces a disorienting temporal effect; with the events
of the following day already apparently set in place, the characters'
conception of time becomes oddly flattened and spatialised, so that past,
present and future are treated as ontologically equivalent – as if already
set out in the various Acts of a prewritten script. Or, to put it in Lister's
terms, '"what's done is about to be done and the future has come to
pass"' (9). At various intervals throughout the evening, Lister advises
his colleagues not to '"split hairs [. . .] between the past, present and
future tenses"', nor to '"strain after vulgar chronology"', because '"to
all intents and purposes [the Klopstocks] are already dead although as
a matter of banal fact, the night's business has yet to accomplish itself"'
(6; 43; 12). An additional, comically grotesque exchange between Lister
and his colleague, Eleanor, concerning their masters' imminent, inevita-

ble deaths, and the pressing need to remain discreet about their plans, was drafted by Spark:

> "He was . . ."
> "Be careful, he'll hear you."
> "He is –" she says in a loud voice, "a very fine person."
> "A pity he got that dentist's leer from his new dental bridge. Not that it matters now."
> "They always compose the features at the mortuary, that is before rigor mortis sets in, as in this case. His dentures don't show. He lay peaceful as—"
> "Don't let him hear you. Was that the car downstairs?" (MFL 1970)

While Lister exhibits some of the hallmarks of authorial omniscience (he possesses a detailed knowledge of the future, for example, as well as an awareness of the behaviour and precise whereabouts of each the other characters), he has acquired this understanding *without* the use of what Spark described to W. Gordon Smith as 'supernatural means'. My interpretation of Lister as an expert manipulator of the 'habit pattern[s]' of other human beings is therefore markedly different to the divine and supernatural ones proposed in numerous readings of the novel. For Robert Hosmer, for example, Lister is *Not to Disturb*'s omniscient 'archmagician', a 'clever and consummate [. . .] *auteur*' who encourages the novel's 'demonic cast into *following his script*' (2012: 208, emphasis mine).[8] Lister is instead an exceptionally attentive – and deeply exploitative – version of the servant as described by Mikhail Bakhtin. 'Servants', Bakhtin asserts, are 'the most privileged witnesses to private life' because, as they are 'called upon to participate in all intimate aspects of personal life', they possess a 'distinctive, embodied point of view on the world of private life without which a literature treating private life could not manage' (1981: 124–5). But unlike similarly 'privileged witnesses' such as Mrs S., or the unnamed housekeeper in 'A Dangerous Situation on the Stairs', Lister does far more than remark sagely from the sidelines. Having attuned himself closely to a 'habit pattern' that, he realises, will inevitably and imminently lead to a profitable murder–suicide, he schedules the evening with precision timekeeping befitting of the novel's Swiss setting – a fact underscored, with macabre comedy, when he times the preparation of the evening meal around the expected deaths: '"fifteen more minutes for the casserole. [. . .] We sit down at seven if we're lucky and they don't decide to dine before they die"' (14). Elsewhere, Lister and his colleagues are seen to converge unsettlingly with the technological apparatus at their disposal ('Lister raises a finger and the discs of the [tape-recorder] begin to spin. [. . .] Lister raises a finger and the machine stops' [46]), which often appear more alive than their human operators (the house telephone 'wheezes' and 'hisses [. . .] through its wind-pipe', for example, while the tape-recorder 'emits [. . .] long, dramatic sighs' even before replaying a recorded voice [14; 43]). Lister's boastful remark concerning his colleagues' extraordinary proficiency with these devices, '"we're all computerised these days"', thus gestures towards a cold, eerily inhuman present, wherein what he calls '"the human touch"' has been subsumed by a detached, technological functionality (50).

Exhibiting morbid humour, an absurdist (or indeed disdainful) treatment of human vitality and mortality, and frequent, casual allusions to a grim yet inconsequential future that lies inevitably in wait, *Not to Disturb* could well appear as a prime example of the 'calculated contempt' that Spark, 'from her Catholic perspective', supposedly reserves for 'human beings as a species' (Gregson 2006: 102). Early reviews of the novel supported such a reading, and claimed to find Spark's increasing aloofness towards the suffering of her characters to be disquieting. Any 'residual warmth' that *The Public Image* or *The Driver's Seat* might have retained from Spark's preceding novels, complained Claire Tomalin, is entirely absent from *Not to Disturb*'s 'vision of hell, where all [characters] are pimps, bawds, madmen or corpses, those who batten and those who traffic in flesh living or dead'. The mortal world that Spark conjures is thus seen as an unnervingly 'inhuman' one, full of 'monsters dancing with monsters in the borders of a bestiary; grotesque and nasty, but remote' (1971: 33). Spark, remarked Robert Nye in a similarly unflattering review, 'has seemed for some books now to be engaged in a very peculiar game of her own devising. [. . .] Brief, brittle, [and] nasty in an arch sort of way, each new text appears almost consciously devised to dismay.' Referring to the acerbic and aptly nicknamed Gloria Deploresyeux (or Deplores You, to the ears), a character from Spark's 1958 short story, 'Come Along, Marjorie', Nye asserts that 'when the ghostly ghastly Gloria appears as a character [. . .] in Mrs Spark's fiction, the outcome is often very good. But when she stays outside the creation and assumes the role of *creator* it is horrid.' This, he argues, makes *Not to Disturb* an unpalatable novel that could best be described as 'life-deploring', in that its narrative tone and management of plot and character appear to have become infected by a growing authorial indifference to human life (1971: 9, emphasis in original).

Tomalin and Nye were, of course, correct to detect something of a 'life-deploring' chill in the pages of *Not to Disturb*, but to associate this with Spark's apparently contemptuous Catholicism, as Gregson and Bradbury are quick to do, is to overlook how the novel relates specifically to a postmodern, late capitalist and media-saturated consumer society, famously characterised in Fredric Jameson's *Postmodernism, or, The Cultural Logic of Late Capitalism* (1992) by 'the emergence of a new kind of flatness or depthlessness, a new kind of superficiality in the most literal sense', which is expressed 'in a whole new culture of the image or the simulacrum' (1992: 9; 6). Jameson, returning to Debord's 'remarkable formulation' of a spectacularised society in which all relationships are mediated by visual signifiers without a concrete referent (235), describes this 'depthlessness' as a certain 'waning of affect', linked to

> the liberation [. . .] from the older anomie of the centered subject [which] may also mean not merely a liberation from anxiety but a liberation from every other kind of feeling, since there is no longer a self present to do the feeling. (15)

This 'waning of affect' joins a host of other postmodern negations, including 'the waning of our historicity, of our lived possibility of experiencing history', and 'a radical eclipse of Nature itself' (21; 34). The result is a deathly flattening of human experience, so that previous – and precapitalist – oppositions between 'essence and appearance', 'latent and manifest', 'authenticity and inauthenticity' and 'signifier and signified' are each 'replaced by surface, or by multiple surfaces' (12). Modernist affect is thus displaced by a postmodern sheen, which signals 'the end [. . .] of the unique and the personal' and the arrival of 'a whole new type of emotional ground tone' that is distinguished by apathy, superficiality and 'schizophrenia' (15; 29). The 'joyful intensities' of this schizophrenic 'ground tone', Jameson believes, constitute an empty 'pastiche' of emotional experience, which contrasts sharply with the more radical practice of 'parody':

> Pastiche is, like parody, the imitation of a peculiar mask, speech in a dead language: but it is a neutral practice of such mimicry, without any of parody's ulterior motives, amputated of the satiric impulse, devoid of laughter [. . .]. Pastiche is thus blank parody, a statue with blind eyeballs. (17)

To articulate a sense of the distinctive 'depthlessness' that comes to define the postmodern era, Jameson juxtaposes descriptions of two emblematic artworks: Vincent Van Gogh's painting, *A Pair of Boots* (1887), and Andy Warhol's silkscreen reproduction, *Diamond Dust Shoes* (1980). Whereas the battered, dirt-encrusted boots depicted in the former evince something of the life, hardship and history of the peasant to whom they presumably belonged, Jameson argues, the one-dimensional assemblage of free-floating, glittering high-heeled shoes displayed in the latter are seemingly abstracted from any social context, and thus communicate only 'a new kind of superficiality in the most literal sense, perhaps the supreme formal feature of all the postmodernisms'

(9). Simon Malpas notes the following of the contrasting artworks' significance to Jameson's theorisation of the postmodern:

> [W]hat Jameson is [. . .] identify[ing] is the transformation of experience in postmodernity. The objects around us that we might once have experienced in terms of their use values are commodified to such an extent that exchange value, in fact the infinite exchangeability of all commodities, has come to account for the entirety of our experience of the world. Warhol's shoes are infinitely reproducible, interchangeable, superficial, and contextless, just one commodity from a potentially endless collection in which use value has become entirely irrelevant. (2004: 119)

What effect might such a 'contextless', simulacral culture of commodities and commodification – in which, Jameson asserts, the world 'comes before the subject with heightened intensity [. . .] here described in the negative terms of anxiety and loss of reality, but which one could just as well imagine in the positive terms of euphoria, a high, an intoxicatory or hallucinogenic intensity' (Jameson 1992: 27–8) – have on the form and content of the fiction produced within it? As Gregson suggests, much postmodern fiction has responded to a culture 'so influenced by the technological media that any sense of the real is lost' by 'draw[ing] attention away from the subjective interior, and [. . .] flatten[ing] characters in a process of ontological reduction in which they are rendered static and mechanical' (2006: 3). Postmodern affectlessness and commodification, Gregson later concludes, 'is precisely what leads to the prevalence of caricature' in much contemporary fiction, 'in which characters are portrayed by mere surfaces' (162).

With its glassy-eyed perspective on death and violence, and its cast of flattened, affectless caricatures and non-entities, whose bodies and minds are shown to merge seamlessly with the technologies of communication and mass-reproduction that they have to hand, *Not to Disturb* sits comfortably alongside other 'depthless' postmodern fictions, including J. G. Ballard's techno-dystopian *Crash* (1973) and Alain Robbe-Grillet's sinisterly denatured erotic fantasy, *Project for a Revolution in New York* (1970). The rigorously desubjectified Baroness Klopstock, whose '"insubstantial bod[y]"' is reduced to a sexualised surface by her husband, and then commodified relentlessly by her employees, appears as both emblem and victim of the postmodern era that Jameson describes. Indeed, it is the Baroness's development of something resembling genuine affection for her prearranged lover, Victor, that marks her out as deviant and doomed to those around her. '"The Baroness hasn't been playing the game,"' remarks Theo, the Klopstocks' chauffeur. '"She used to keep her hair frosted or blond-streaked,"' replies his wife, Clara: '"She shouldn't have let go her shape. Why did she suddenly start to go natural? She must have started to be sincere with someone"' (35). References to '"frosted"' hair and a carefully preserved '"shape"' attest to the importance placed upon a fixed and flattened identity from which the self must not dare deviate. As with Anna Fallarino, Baroness Klopstock's attempts to break from her assigned role (to transition, that is, from object to subject, from depthless commodity to rounded humanity) are met with both fatal physical violence and the similarly brutal reinscription of her enforced identity within narratives dictated by others. That Spark does not narrate the murder of Baroness Klopstock but only the ensuing media frenzy is itself meaningful; premeditated by her husband and feverishly anticipated by the rest of the household, her death is rendered abstract and devoid of human significance, serving only as a source of financial gain, media content, and the necessary restoration of the novel's elaborately scripted order. With an ending that invokes and yet refuses tragic catharsis, the novel rests, finally, upon the surface image of a policeman at the crime scene, nearing the end of his shift and 'waiting' in vain 'for the relief man to come' (96).

Despite its unwavering mood of crazed unreality and its numerous outrageous and eccentric set pieces (including, with more than a hint of dark comedy and Gothic pastiche, a chaotic sham wedding between a pregnant chambermaid and a madman clanking his chains in the attic, while a deadly thunderstorm rages outside), what lies at the heart of *Not to Disturb* is the insidious degradation of the private life and public image of Baroness Klopstock, which was set in motion long before the point at which the novel begins. Indeed, the obvious artificiality of the storyworld reads as a deeply unnerving extension of the dangerous fiction first cultivated by the Baron, within which the Baroness finds herself ensnared. Like the Marquis Casati Stampa, Baron Klopstock comes to be associated chiefly with his reputation as a lascivious and domineering amateur pornographer: he is '"obsessed with sex"', according to Eleanor, and '"a pornophile"', in the words of Lister (13; 76). 'There is the suggestion', Peter Kemp infers from the servants' gossip, 'that [the Baron's] fantasies and simulations [. . .] have taken on a merciless momentum of their own', so that 'the fictional stereotypes [the Klopstocks] have perversely toyed with close in vengefully around them' (1974: 135). This is a convincing interpretation, but one which tells only half of the story. As with the salacious commodification of Anna Fallarino's murder as a scandalous (and highly saleable) tragedy by her domestic staff, the circumstances surrounding the anticipated death of Baroness Klopstock are further embellished by Lister and his cohorts until any trace of the 'real' woman is obscured entirely. By offering snatches of the servants' backstairs whispers, the novel – like

The Public Image before it – expresses something of the inextricable connection between a late capitalist, mediatised culture of simulated and commodified identities, and a scopophilic, sexually imbalanced one of the devouring male gaze.

It is in this respect that *Not to Disturb* ought to be read as a stranger and far more sinister counterpart to *Doctors of Philosophy*, which is heavily inflected by a depthless postmodern present and the voracious commodification of life, sex and death. The metatheatrical aspects of Spark's stage play, I earlier argued, come to articulate the rigid limitations placed upon the identity and free will of Leonora while she languishes in the inhibiting company of the Delfonts, with dialogue that is often presented self-reflexively as lines from a prewritten script, and scenery that is designed to appear as deliberately artificial and constrictive. The form and content of *Not to Disturb* achieve something similar. The novel is replete, as Willy Maley notes, 'with metaphors of staging, screening, casting, corpsing, directing, producing, spinning, and setting' (2001: 172). In their efforts to exploit the anticipated deaths of their masters, the servants pose for staged photographs, record false testimonials before the murders have even taken place, and arrange to sell the rights to a future film adaptation of the night's events. As the servants go about their business, the once imposing Château Klopstock comes to resemble a cobbled-together stage set; with something of the wall-wobbling shock effected by Mrs S., Eleanor gleefully dislodges the scenery by upending the building's parquet flooring (repurposed, perhaps, from Annabel Christopher's stage-like flat or the Delfonts' disintegrating living room) with her nail file. Similarly, the plot is organised neatly into five chapters or 'acts', so that its overall structure complies with Gustav Freytag's well-known model of the five stages of the unified dramatic plot (1895: 114–40). The effect is rhetorical, in that it suggests that the servants' spatialised sense of chronology and expert familiarity with their masters' fixed public images and well-worn 'habit pattern' have enabled them to conceptualise and commodify the evening ahead as a predetermined 'script', which Lister has learned by heart. The novel is punctuated, as Peter Kemp observes, by the butler's 'resounding curtain-lines' (1974: 132), including his ominous, recurrent call to the others: '"Let's proceed"' (44). By encountering the novel as a depthless drama, the reader comes to share the servants' viewpoint, perceiving the assorted victims and villains as similarly '"insubstantial"' – 'little more than ciphers', or 'refugees from Cluedo', as Maley puts it (2001: 174).

For Spark, however, the overt theatricality or *textuality* of *Not to Disturb*'s flattened and denatured storyworld does not signify a complete absence of realism *per se*, but serves instead as an accurate (if satirically heightened) reflection of real people whose identities and interactions are distorted severely in a time of rampant consumerism and celebrity-obsessed culture. In the unpublished transcript of her 1970 interview with Ian Gillham (conducted while she was still at work on *Not to Disturb*, and edited for publication in *The Listener*), Spark spoke of feeling acutely aware, while living in Rome, of the power of the sensationalist press in Italy. Owing to the pervasive influence of 'the glossies', she felt, daily life in the city had come to assume a vividly dramatic quality, having become permeated with a febrile mixture of jealousy, anger and betrayal comparable to a Renaissance play (NLS 1970a). Spark's comment probably accounts for the intentionally heavy-handed reference to English Renaissance drama with which the novel begins: '"Their life" says Lister, "a general mist of error. Their death, a hideous storm of terror. – I quote from *The Duchess of Malfi* by John Webster, an English dramatist of old"' (1). The impression produced is of a deliberate dramatic disfigurement, on the part of the servants (and the wider culture that they inhabit), of an already lurid scenario, from which the febrile fictionality of the storyworld can be seen to have emerged. As the novel progresses, dialogue among the servants becomes increasingly overburdened by further references to a widening range of novels, poetry and plays (including Andrew Marvell's *To His Coy Mistress* [1681] and D. H. Lawrence's *Lady Chatterley's Lover* [1928]), which occur so frequently that any evocative or referential power that they might have once possessed is deliberately dulled. Indeed, the impression produced is not that the imminent deaths of the Klopstocks constitute a tragedy comparable with those encountered in English Renaissance drama, for example, but that, from the perspective of the servants, they might at least be marketed as such. In this sense, *Not to Disturb*'s literary references are every bit as 'infinitely reproducible, interchangeable, superficial, and contextless' (Malpas 2004: 119) as any other feature of its depthless postmodern storyworld, including the portraits that adorn the walls of the Château Klopstock (mere photocopies of distant originals) and the building itself (bathetically revealed to be an eleven-year-old construction, comprised of clumsily curated antiquities). Perhaps to underscore the vacuity of the servants' bookish gossip, the only room to which they and the narrator lack access in the château is the library, where the Klopstocks and Victor are sequestered. '"The books"', remarks Lister of the undisturbed space, '"are silent"' (44).

If, in *Doctors of Philosophy*, what I earlier termed 'Sparkian metalepsis' works to dismantle the Delfonts' elaborate and oppressive fiction from the inside out, in *Not to Disturb* it produces the opposite effect, by foregrounding both the artificiality and the extreme insularity of its diegetic world, and thus emphasising the hopelessly irreversible entrapment of the Baroness within the plots of others, and in the role in which she has been cast. In one memorable sequence, which arrives towards the end of the novel, the night's proceedings appear to be threatened by the unexpected arrival of two visitors, Anne and Alex, who demand entry to the Klopstocks' home in the hope of saving the lives of Kathy and Victor. Their attempted disturbance is thwarted, however, by an extraordinary *deus ex machina*:

> Meanwhile the lightning, which strikes the clump of elms so that the two friends huddled there are killed instantly without pain, zig-zags across the lawns, illuminating the lilypond and the sunken rose garden like a self-stricken flashphotographer, and like a zipfastener ripped from its garment by a sexual maniac, [. . .] skim[s] the rooftops of the house, leaving intact, however, the well-insulated telephone wires which Lister [. . .] has rather feared might break down. (86–7)

By summarily dispatching the pair of disturbers in a subordinate clause, the metaleptic, precision-engineered lightning bolt keeps the progress of the *crime passionnel* firmly on course, while ensuring that the closed-off 'set' of the Château Klopstock remains as conveniently 'well-insulated' as its telephone wires. This could be Old Testament Spark at her most cruel and flagrantly tyrannical, flexing her omnipotent muscles by demonstrating her effortless ability to remove any wrinkle from the smooth running of her expertly organised plot. The peculiar metaphors of the violent 'sexual maniac' and the 'self-stricken flashphotographer' suggest something rather different, however. Taken together, these images speak to the respective forces at play in cultivating *Not to Disturb*'s oppressive unreality (the abuses of the '"pornophile"' Baron, and the publicity-minded motivations of Lister and company), which have coalesced to brew what Lister describes via John Webster as a perfect "storm of terror". The sequence's heavily underscored 'compact definitiveness' and stark 'refusal of open-endedness', which Gregson identifies as the defining feature of Spark's distinctly 'unpostmodern' œuvre (2006: 105), gestures in fact to the postmodern death of affect; if Lister and his coterie of media-savvy and tech-obsessed vampires are to be understood as the collective embodiment of an affectless, posthuman future, then the lightning's metaleptic intrusion presents inescapable, inconsequential annihilation as the only possible outcome.

In a 2004 interview broadcast on BBC Radio Four's *Front Row*, Spark recalled *Not to Disturb* rather ambiguously as her 'complete breakdown and build-up book' (Lawson 2004: n.p.). While her comment might be interpreted most readily in terms of Lister et al.'s attempts to reconstruct and repurpose the lives and deaths of their masters as a lucrative commodity, it serves as an equally fitting description of the novel itself – a work which, as Stannard's biography has shown, was built from the ruins of real tragedy, and which employs deliberate artifice and metafictional pyrotechnics in order to reflect something of the heightened, unreal nature of its source material. Intriguingly, the author's archival material reveals that her elaborate fictionalisation of the Casati Stampa scandal was intended to extend far beyond a single novel; even while writing *Not to Disturb*, Spark was actively considering its suitability for both stage and screen. At Spark's request, the playwrights W. Gordon Smith, Brian de Breffny and Christopher Holme (all personal acquaintances of the author) each contributed scripts for a proposed theatrical adaptation. Adhering closely to the content of an earlier draft of the novel, the scripts pay close attention to the servants' calculated anticipation of the precise moment of their masters' deaths, and thus bear a remarkable similarity to one another – most strikingly in their recommendations for the set design. Smith specifies that a huge moon-faced wall clock is to appear prominently on stage throughout the performance, counting down ominously to the moment of murder (NLS 1971a), while de Breffny also includes a large brightly coloured electric clock, bearing enormous hands and fluorescent numbers, as part of his proposed stage set (NLS 1971b). Holme's script, meanwhile, stipulates that a series of similarly large clocks in the servants' quarters are to bear the design influences of Andy Warhol and David Hockney, while those in the main part of the château ought to appear old, grand and gloomy (NLS 1971c). The visual contrast between both spaces, he takes pains to note, would emphasise a series of contrasts: upstairs and downstairs; agility and obsolescence; forethought and obliviousness; liveliness and death (NLS 1971c).

While there is no evidence to suggest that any of these adaptations came to inform the content of *Not to Disturb* as Spark readied her novel for publication, it is fascinating, nevertheless, that each of the dramatic 'treatments' solicited by the author (and those submitted by de Breffny and Holme, in particular) should choose to depict the servants' activities and environment by way of direct references to the vibrant sheen of pop art. Associated as it is with the commodification of *already commodified* images (including those prevalent in mass culture, from pre-existing photographs of film stars to consumer goods as banal as tinned soup) via technologies of endless reproduction, the artistic movement serves as an ideal representation of the collective mindset of Lister and his colleagues. From what Holme calls their 'place of life' (NLS 1971c), the servants circle the unfolding tragedy like vultures, armed with the tools and imagination necessary to profit from the Klopstocks' already diminished and degraded public images by transforming them into further, increasingly distorted, reproductions. 'Warhol's human subjects [. . .] like Marilyn Monroe', notes Jameson, were 'themselves commodified and transformed into their own images' long before they fell under the artist's gaze (1992: 11). Like predatory pop artists, Lister and company seize upon lives that appear to have morphed already into what *The Public Image* termed their crude 'public figuration[s]' (35), and which have thus become, to return to Jameson's description of the postmodernist significance of *Diamond Dust Shoes*, 'shorn of their earlier life world' and consequently ripe for repurposing (1992: 8). '"They have placed themselves, unfortunately, within the realm of predestination"' (37), remarks the butler of his masters, his words referring less to Calvinist theology than to the prison of a profitable public image.

Private Lives, 'public figuration[s]' and the Myth of Spark

Rather like the policemen who attend the final scene of *Not to Disturb* to count the bodies and apportion the blame, Spark's critics have tended to survey the violence, misogyny, death and dehumanisation compressed into her characteristically concise narratives and treat this as incriminating evidence of authorial cruelty. For critics including Gregson, Bradbury, Tomalin and Nye, *Not to Disturb* may well reflect Spark at the height (or rather the most decadent depths) of her creative powers, self-consciously staging a murder that appears inevitable to everyone involved in the story except for its two oblivious victims, Kathy and Victor. What the author achieves in this novel is something much more inventive, however. Indeed, what might appear to be flaws or limitations in Spark's management of plot, characterisation and narrative perspective announce themselves instead as radical aesthetic and postmodern strategies. Instead of paring her fingernails above a puppet show, Spark depicts the insidious erosion of a character's sense of self by those who surround her, as observed in the *real* abuse of Anna Fallarino. Examples such as Anna's reveal how fiction can seep into and distort scenarios which once appeared natural – a theme explored at length, albeit with far greater levity, via the metaleptic/metatheatrical techniques utilised throughout *Doctors of Philosophy*.

Whereas *Doctors of Philosophy*'s stifling scenes from a marriage ought to be read, as I have argued, as the absurdist, experimental extension of concerns expressed throughout Spark's early fiction (in novels and short stories including 'Bang-Bang You're Dead', *The Ballad of Peckham Rye* and the unpublished 'A Dangerous Situation on the Stairs'), *Not to*

Disturb can be seen to take its author's later interest in the hyperreal celebrity culture that beamed back at her from the pages of 'the glossies and the newspapers and film mags' to a similarly delirious extreme. In '"modern society"', Lister remarks astutely, '"the popular glossy magazines have replaced the servants' hall. Our position of privilege is unparalleled in history. The career of domestic service is the thing of the future"' (83). Lister's comment, which doubles as a neat summation of Spark's gradual shift in focus from private lives to heavily mediatised public images during the period spanning the late 1950s and the early 1970s, speaks of a new, affectless postmodern age dominated by simulacra, in which 'privileged witnesses' like himself might enjoy a uniquely powerful position (Bakhtin 1981: 124). This is a superficial revolution in more than one sense; as Patricia Waugh observes, 'the upper-class engines of lust and landed inheritance [are] run down to be replaced by the new engines of publicity, fame, and acquired wealth', so that, while the Klopstocks' 'black carnival world is turned upside down', its 'order and its models of human functioning [. . .] remain fundamentally undisturbed' (2010: 77). Indeed, as demonstrated by the servants' rabid commodification of the Klopstocks' already besmirched reputations, the new order that prevails in Spark's 'break-down and build-up book' only replicates the hideous abuses and excesses of the last.

That Spark chose to populate her grotesque modern fable of fame, fortune and media exploitation with a cast of near non-entities is not evidence, then, of what Gregson describes as the author's 'Catholic antihumanism', which is 'profoundly at odds with the humanist assumptions of the classic realist novel' (2006: 6; 102). For Spark, who claimed to take issue with the 'dogmatic and absolute truth' encountered in so-called 'realistic novels' (Hosmer 2005: 147), the resolutely anti-realist aspects of *Not to Disturb* – eerily 'flat' and mechanical characters; an apparently artificial, stage-like setting; dialogue overloaded with a glut of valueless literary allusions – articulate a palpably *real* sense of Jamesonian 'depthlessness' by conjuring a cold and degraded reality in which only the surfaces of objects, texts and bodies remain. Spark had, of course, been developing such techniques over the preceding decade or so; the overtly 'staged' and 'scripted' elements of the novel hark back to *Doctors of Philosophy*, while the notion of an individual's entrapment within his or her public (and highly *publicised*) 'mould' was first explored in detail in *The Public Image*'s spectacularised contemporary Rome.

Far from supporting what I earlier named as 'the myth of Spark', the three texts that have formed the focus of the present chapter tell a different story. Despite their detached perspectives and often disturbing choices of subject matter, none exhibits the kind of performative, didactic cruelty with which Spark's fiction is so frequently associated. Cruelty is certainly prevalent, however, and each text offers a sustained exploration of an insidious, enervating masculine influence which dictates the parameters and practices of women's lives. In their worst moments, each of Spark's women – the listless, somnambulant Leonora; the impassive, shell-like Annabel; the unnervingly insubstantial Baroness Klopstock – comes to embody the uncompromising demands placed upon the female subject within the particular culture and society she inhabits. Instead of demonstrating the relative inconsequentiality of human actions when viewed from a divine perspective, Spark is shown in these texts to be concerned with abuses enacted *by* and *upon* human subjects, which render the individual self-alienated and insignificant – be this from within the constrictive space of the Delfonts' living room, the toxic marriage and manipulative media circus within which Annabel endures a waking fever dream of idealised femininity, or the crazed unreality cooked up by Baroness Klopstock's abusive husband and her exploitative, media-minded employees. Spark's restless formal and thematic experimentation undoubtedly aids her expression of such concerns, while offering occasional instances of gleeful resistance; in *Doctors of Philosophy* and the final paragraph of *The Public Image* respectively, wobbling stage sets and similarly abrupt, 'frame-breaking' shifts in narrative tone and perspective reveal possibilities (and, specifically, possibilities for women) that stretch far beyond 'the cul-de-sac of caricature' (Gregson 2006: 107).

Chapter Three

'Drama[s] of exact observation':
Spark and the *Nouveau Roman*

But now suppose the eyes of man rest on things without indulgence, insistently [. . .]. [H]is sense of sight is content to take their measurements; and his passion, similarly, rests on their surface, without attempting to penetrate them since there is nothing inside, without feigning the least appeal since they would not answer.

(Robbe-Grillet 1996b: 52–3)

Who knows her thoughts? Who can tell?

The Driver's Seat (50)

Focusing on the development of her fiction during the period spanning 1960 and 1970, this chapter examines the evolving relationship between Spark's novels and the ethos and aesthetics of the *nouveau roman*, a mode of writing associated most closely with the fiction and literary criticism of one of its leading theorists and practitioners, Alain Robbe-Grillet. As Spark recalled in a 1971 interview, exposure to the *nouveau roman* (otherwise known as the new novel or anti-novel) had proven revelatory at an early stage in her literary career: 'in the early 1950s, there was no Robbe-Grillet [. . .]. Hardly anyone was trying to write novels with all the compression and obliqueness I was aiming at' (Toynbee 1971: 73). Although Spark had initially found that the characteristic 'compression and obliqueness' of Robbe-Grillet's prose happened to match a writing style to which she herself aspired, her work would later make direct reference to, and even function as an implicit critique of, the style and philosophy of the *nouveau roman*. The diverse ways in which Spark adopts (and adapts) the anti-novel's associated theories and techniques in three distinctly different novels composed during the beginning, middle and end of the decade – *The Ballad of Peckham Rye* (1960), *The Mandelbaum Gate* (1965) and *The Driver's Seat* (1970) – form the focus of my analysis.

Having emerged in France during the 1940s and 1950s, the works of the *nouveaux romanciers* – among them, Nathalie Sarraute, Marguerite

Duras, Robert Pinget, Claude Simon, Michel Butor and Robbe-Grillet – first reached British readers in 1957, when translations of short stories by Robbe-Grillet and Butor were printed in literary magazines and periodicals including *Encounter* and *The London Magazine*. By the turn of the decade, translations of a number of novels by Robbe-Grillet, Butor and Sarraute had received notable attention and acclaim from British critics, having been printed by Calder Publications.[1] While these writers did not share a set ideology or belong to any particular school (indeed, their very association with one another is somewhat arbitrary, resulting largely from a shared publisher, Jérôme Lindon's Les Éditions de Minuit, and the coinage of '*nouveau roman*' in a 1957 *Le Monde* article by Émile Henriot, in which they were grouped together [12]), they were united in a common rejection of what they perceived to be the hackneyed conventions of Balzacian realism in favour of innovative and self-reflexive approaches to plot, character and narration. In his 1956 essay, 'A Future for the Novel' – one of a series of influential essays written by the author between 1953 and 1963, which were presented together in *For a New Novel* (1963) – Robbe-Grillet identifies the *nouveau roman's* characteristic 'destitution of the old myths of "depth"' as the feature which distinguishes it most from the 'traditional role' of authors including Balzac, Gide and Madame de La Fayette:

> The writer's traditional role consisted in excavating Nature, in burrowing deeper and deeper to reach some ever more intimate strata, in finally unearthing some fragment of a disconcerting secret. Having descended into the abyss of human passions, he would send to the seemingly tranquil world (the world on the surface) triumphant messages describing the mysteries he had actually touched with his own hands. (1996a: 23–4)

If 'traditional' fiction could be likened to an excavation project, geared towards unearthing 'the entire hidden soul of things', the *nouveau roman*, according to Robbe-Grillet, was committed purely to the surface. 'The surface of things', he wrote, 'has ceased to be for us a mask of their heart, a sentiment that led to every kind of metaphysical transcendence' (Ibid.: 24). Eliminating projections of depth thus meant that 'man and things would be cleansed of their systematic romanticism' (1996d: 39), allowing for a depiction of the world that 'is neither significant nor absurd. It *is*, quite simply [. . .]. Around us, defying the noisy pack of our animistic or projective adjectives, things *are there*. Their surfaces are distinct and smooth, *intact*' (1996a: 19, emphases in original). Numerous examples of this approach can be traced throughout the author's fiction, be it in the narrator's panoramic surveillance of a colonial banana plantation at the beginning of the 1957 novel, *Jealousy* (described by one critic as 'the novelistic equivalent of a tracking shot' [Lane 2002: 198]), or the Euclidean descriptions of household objects which permeate *The Voyeur* (1955). In the 1959 novel, *In the Labyrinth*, the narrator's precise, externalised description of the proximities and positionings of snowfall on a city street does not strive to convey the poetic significance of the scene, but resembles instead the meticulous field notes of a meteorologist:

> It lies in a thinnish layer – two inches or so – but perfectly even, covering all horizontal surfaces with the same dull, neutral whiteness. The only marks that can be seen are the rectilinear paths, parallel to the rows of houses and to the gutters which are still quite visible (made even more distinct by the vertical edge of the pavement, which remains black), and dividing the pavement into two unequal bands above their entire length. (Robbe-Grillet 2000: 19)

In the fictions of Nathalie Sarraute, on the other hand, Balzacian excess is invoked only to be subverted by the disquieting revelation that meaning lies altogether, and inaccessibly, elsewhere. As Jennifer Hodgson observes, novels including *Portrait of a Man Unknown* (1948), *The Golden Fruits* (1963) and *Between Life and Death* (1968) are sumptuously furnished, their settings becoming 'domestic fortresses of Chesterfield sofas, silver-plate cocktail shakers, Italian leather shoes' and the innumerable other 'fetish-objects of bourgeois life' (2013: 150). There is no 'hidden soul of things' (Robbe-Grillet 1996a: 23) to be unearthed by poring over these intricately drawn items; as the narrator of *Portrait of a Man Unknown* remarks, the vividly rendered paraphernalia of its protagonists' lives merely constitutes a protective 'screen' that barricades them from 'a formless, strange, threatening universe' (1959: 150). This universe, notes Hodgson, remains pointedly unknowable, yet presents itself fleetingly and terrifyingly throughout Sarraute's œuvre as something 'tentacular, molluscan, positively oozing' (2013: 150): an ancient, unfathomable, violently living depth glimpsed beneath a thin surface cluttered with dull objects.

Robbe-Grillet and Sarraute were hardly alone in conceptualising the *nouveau roman* in terms of a surface-versus-depth dialectic. In his 1952 essay, 'Objective Literature', Roland Barthes had already described the form and function of the *nouveau roman* in similar terms, as a rejection of 'the novel long established as the experience of a depth: a social depth with Balzac and Zola, a "psychological depth" with Flaubert, a memorial depth with Proust' in favour of an attempt to 'establish the novel on the surface' (1972: 23). In contrast to the novel's traditional 'endoscopic function', Barthes argued, the *nouveau roman* was a mode of writing committed solely to recording 'a direct experience of man's surroundings, without this man's being able to fall back on a psychology, a metaphysic, or a psychoanalysis in order to approach the objective milieu he discovers' (Ibid.). This mode of narration, which Barthes describes as 'not the rape of an abyss, but the rapture of a surface' (Ibid.), constitutes for Kristin Ross a 'project of redemptive *hygiene*', which 'proposes to *clean* the Augean stables of the realistic novel form of [its] fetters and archaisms'. The 'new novelist', Ross remarks, remains 'eternally vigilant, on the lookout for the tell-tale *stains* of an outmoded romanticism that lurk in the form of animistic descriptive adjectives and metaphors', so that the vision of the 'new seer' is '*cleansed* and focused to become a tool for conducting a set of technical, almost administrative operations based on criteria of efficacy' (1995: 75–6).[2] Spark's fascination with this efficacious aspect of the narration – what she identified as its 'special kind of drama – the drama of exact observation' (Toynbee 1971: 73) – would become the characteristic feature of her engagement with the *nouveau roman*.

'I was thinking the same thoughts that they were thinking, people like Robbe-Grillet,' Spark would insist in a 2002 interview, adding that she and the *nouveau romanciers* were 'breathing the same informed air' (McQuillan 2001c: 216). Despite this, critical commentary on the author's relationship to the *nouveau roman* has tended – perhaps ironically – to stop short at the surface, resting upon the aesthetic similarities that her novels of the early to mid-1970s share with the fictions of Robbe-Grillet in particular, instead of examining the ways in which her work might offer a deeper commentary, be it direct or implicit, on the theories and practices of the 'new novelists'. In an early review of *The Driver's Seat*, for example, Frank Kermode claims to detect within the novel 'a strong flavour of the *nouveau roman*', but concludes that, while 'Mrs Spark has studied Robbe-Grillet with care', she has 'decided that his methods [. . .] are useful if you want to present obsessed or manic states', such as that of the protagonist, Lise (1970: 425). Elsewhere, critics have clung faithfully to the received and revered image of the author as a Catholic novelist, taking Spark's religion as their ultimate limit of interpretation when deciphering the aims of her experimental narrative practices. For Robert Hosmer, Spark aimed only at 'creating ghastly parodies of the *nouveau roman*' by co-opting its characteristic 'commitment to distance and detachment [and] fondness for the present tense' to produce 'fictions which are deeply consistent with her long-standing, unremitting Catholic concerns'. Robbe-Grillet's well-known 'cinematic structural and narrative devices' and 'fondness for the present tense', Hosmer argues, are countered in Spark's fiction by the proleptic anticipation of the ending. In novels such as *The Driver's Seat* and *Not to Disturb*, 'it is *the End* which gives meaning and coherence, not only in aesthetic terms, but also in theological terms' (1989: 238). Adopting a near-identical reading, Ian Rankin describes *The Driver's Seat* as merely 'a homage to Robbe-Grillet's technique', in which the 'philosophy of the *nouveau roman*' is invoked only to be superseded by the future tense's revelation of God's 'divine [. . .] pattern' (1993: 43).

A more nuanced and productive reading is encountered in Aidan Day's 2007 article, 'Parodying Postmodernism', discussed in greater detail in the final section of this chapter. Focusing specifically on the various thematic and stylistic similarities between Robbe-Grillet's *Jealousy* and Spark's *The Driver's Seat*, Day examines how Spark's 'appropriation' of, and 'metacommentary' on, the various hallmarks of the *nouveau roman* 'amounts to a critical engagement with postmodern assumptions and perspectives' (Day 2007: 322). Although Day presents a thorough and incisive analysis of the ways in which Spark's prose exceeds a simple mimicry of Robbe-Grillet – an approach which supports a persuasive thesis that, by drawing upon the techniques of the *nouveau roman*, the author depicts a character 'suffering a type of despair in a world suffering from a dearth of reality' (Ibid.: 326) – his reading is limited by its near-singular focus on *The Driver's Seat*. Indeed, Day's commentary on Spark's *prior* engagement with what he terms 'postmodern assumptions and perspectives', be they derived from the *nouveau roman* or elsewhere, is notably scarce, extending only to a brief discussion of *The Mandelbaum Gate*'s digressive remarks on 'the new French writers' (Spark 1985: 177). This example aside, *The Driver's Seat*, long recognised as possessing a 'strong flavour of the *nouveau roman*', appears misleadingly as Spark's sole engagement with the art form.

The present chapter seeks to remedy this shortcoming by considering *The Driver's Seat* not as a one-off experiment, but rather as the result of Spark's sustained examination of the *nouveau roman*'s particular style and ethos, which had begun ten years earlier with the composition of her subversive social satire, *The Ballad of Peckham Rye*. In my analysis of that novel, I observe how Spark draws playfully upon the apparent depthlessness of the anti-novel's prose to depict a community in thrall to the superficial and deadened by habit and convention. The relentless exteriority of Robbe-Grillet's narration, I argue, presents Spark with an ideal means of communicating a Bergsonian form of comedy – one which involves the supposedly vital individual appearing, to humorous or even unsettling degrees, as a mindless automaton or two-dimensional stock character. This is followed by a reading of *The Mandelbaum Gate*, and in particular the novel's depiction of the trial and testimony of the Holocaust administrator, Adolf Eichmann, whose chilling lack of empathy is conveyed via direct references to 'the sensation[s] [. . .]

that the anti-novelists induce' among their readers (Spark 1985: 177). By drawing upon the studied detachment and characteristic efficacy of the anti-novel to communicate a sense of Eichmann's single-minded devotion to duty and efficient action, Spark explores the sinister implications of a mode of narrative – and, by extension, a mode of narrative *consciousness* – marked by a steadfast refusal to acknowledge psychological depths, and which thus articulates perfectly what Hannah Arendt memorably termed 'the banality of evil'. All of this leads to *The Driver's Seat*, in which Spark presents her most extensive examination of the dehumanising narrative potential of the *nouveau roman*, combining the absurd and horrific implications of its prose (as explored in the two preceding examples) with the metafictional concerns of her earliest fictions. In doing so, she depicts a nightmarish world so detached from reality that its protagonist must plot her own tragic death in order to articulate her subjectivity and engage at last with the real. I therefore treat these novels – to quote the title of Robbe-Grillet's 1962 essay collection – as valuable *snapshots* of Spark's evolving engagement with the forms, theories and functions of the *nouveau roman's* particular 'drama of exact observation'.

'Interesting finds and human remains': The Ballad of Peckham Rye

Written and published in 1960, *The Ballad of Peckham Rye* could be considered typical of Spark's early social satires, fitting neatly among a set of fictions characterised by what Alan Bold describes as a 'fascination with enclosed communities' (Bold 1986: 50). These specific, circumscribed social sets include the group of feuding septuagenarians in the morbid comedy *Memento Mori*, the desert island castaways in *Robinson*, and the Edinburgh schoolgirls and London boarding-house lodgers featured in *The Prime of Miss Jean Brodie* and *The Girls of Slender Means* respectively. In novels such as these, Spark tends to locate comic potential in patterns of thought and behaviour which have become rigid and mechanical, and codes of social conduct followed so unquestioningly that the subject becomes a target for forces of ridicule, exploitation or subversion. In *The Bachelors* (written immediately after *The Ballad of Peckham Rye*, and published in the same year), the titular characters appear – initially, at least – comical in their uncanny uniformity, as evinced by their identical morning routines: 'these men wriggled their toes when they had got back to bed and, however hard they tried, could not prevent some irritating crumbs of toast from falling on the sheets; they smoked a cigarette, slept, then rose at twelve' (Spark 1960b: 129).

What distinguishes *The Ballad of Peckham Rye* from Spark's other social satires is that its derisory effects are achieved by way of narrative techniques influenced directly by the *nouveau roman*. It was Robbe-Grillet's apparent rejection of psychological depth, Spark recalled, that inspired her own novel's externalised narrative perspective:

> I was very much impressed by Robbe-Grillet [. . .]. I was very, very interested in his methods. He got away from the novel of descriptions of people's feelings: 'he felt,' 'he thought' [. . .]. 'He said' is a fact, actually an outward fact, but 'he felt' and 'he thought' are interpolations by the author. I was very interested in this. I wrote one book without any expressed feelings and thoughts, that was *The Ballad of Peckham Rye*, although nobody has noticed that. (Hosmer 2005: 147)

This refusal of interiority in favour of 'outward fact' serves a powerful rhetorical function in *The Ballad of Peckham Rye*, enabling Spark to depict a community so beholden to prevailing economic and cultural standards that its members have come to appear curiously depthless and mechanical in their patterns of thought and physical action. From the outset, the novel's industrialised and socially stratified Peckham seems conspicuously superficial; names of residents and locations such Merle Co*verd*ale, Dixie *Morse* and *Findlater*'s Ballroom indicate both the obfuscatory character of the novel's environment, as well as the potential for the extraction and exposure of buried meanings by a revelatory force, which emerges in the form of Dougal Douglas. As his own name might imply, Dougal *Douglas* (or *Doug*las Dougal, the moniker he later adopts in order to gain secondary employment) is frequently associated with practices of excavation and exposure. A graduate of Edinburgh University, Dougal has arrived in Peckham to take up the role of Assistant to the Personnel Manager at the local textiles factory, Meadows, Meade & Grindley, a position his employers define vaguely as being geared towards 'bring[ing] vision into the lives of the workers' (Spark 1960a: 16). Declaring it his 'job to take the pulse of the people and plumb the industrial depths of Peckham' (17), Dougal sets out on a mission to uncover the repressed secrets, desires and fears of its inhabitants, his actions jolting the villagers out of the comfortingly familiar patterns of habit and convention that have rendered their behaviour as rigid and predictable as the machines they operate. Appositely, Dougal's practice of what he terms '"human research"' (18) is synchronous with the archaeological excavation of a tunnel beneath the local factories, the resulting discovery of 'interesting finds and human remains' (129) being equally applicable to his own endeavours.

Given his unnerving charisma and frequent association with the subterranean, as well as his unique physical features, including a hunched
shoulder and a forehead bearing two stumps (the remains of a pair of
surgically removed, horn-like protuberances), it is no great stretch to
claim Dougal as a diabolic or otherworldly being – not only an outsider
to Peckham, but an entity who occupies an entirely separate ontological
realm to the other characters. W. H. Auden certainly believed as much
when, in a critical overview of Spark's early novels, he described Dougal
as 'a human instrument of the devil whose name is Legion' (1962:
7). A more judicious interpretation is proffered by Avril Horner and
Sue Zlosnik, who observe that, despite Dougal's overt resemblance to
a demonic or monstrous being, 'there is nothing that [he] is or does
that cannot be explained away rationally'. Dougal, they argue, is less
a 'phantasmal figure in a spectral text' than 'a figure of hint and suggestion, intimating the power of the figurative in a world that appears
to have become determinedly literal' (2004: 112). Like Horner and
Zlosnik, I interpret Dougal as a being rooted firmly within the novel's
mortal realm, yet who stands in direct opposition to what Cairns Craig
describes as 'a world of characters so banalised by the standardised
requirements of a modern industrial environment that they are nothing
more than repetitions of each other' (1999: 173). Unlike *Not to Disturb*'s
Lister, who capitalises on a 'habit pattern' heading towards an inevitable
conclusion, Dougal exists solely *to* disturb the stagnant waters of his
new home. Indeed, within the novel's ideologically conservative and
habit-bound society, Dougal's disruptive machinations have notable,
and sometimes severe, consequences. Claiming the '"powers of exor-
cism"' and '"the ability to drive devils out of people"' (102), Dougal
assumes the role of catalyst and excavator, his interactions teasing out
the latent fears and passions of those he meets: he evokes a powerful
nonconformist streak in the browbeaten Humphrey Place, leading him
to jilt his shallow and demanding fiancée, Dixie, at the altar; he forces
his landlady, Miss Frierne, to acknowledge the brother she rejected, the
stress of which causes her to suffer a stroke; and in his interactions with
his manager, Mr Druce, who 'could not keep his eyes off Dougal' (14),
he unearths possible signs of a repressed homosexual desire.

Away from Dougal's enlivening effects, however, an aura of stultifying
mechanicity pervades *The Ballad of Peckham Rye*'s industrial Peckham,
whose residents are known to themselves and one another by their specific
workplace functions, as though they lack distinct personalities, interior
lives or individual agency: 'Dawn Waghorn, cone-winder, Annette Wren,
trainee-seamer, Elaine Kent, process-controller, Odette Hill, uptwister'
(13). These specific designations even determine the limits of characters'

social interactions; outside of work, for example, Dixie only 'addressed the men, ignoring Elaine as she had done all evening, because Elaine was factory' (43). Stranger, more extreme examples of this rigid, mechanistic behaviour can be traced throughout the wider community. It is there, for example, in the peculiar sexual proclivities of Mr Druce, who seeks erotic thrills from the shuddering motion of a department store lift, and is even detectable in the jive danced by couples in Findlater's Ballroom, which resembles the automatic movement of 'an unwound toy roundabout' (59). It is in the ballroom, a space supposedly removed from the routinised efficiency demanded in the workplace, that the mechanistic actions of the residents are at their most pronounced. Here the interactions between young men and women resemble the intricate component processes of an elaborate mechanical sequence, like those operating in the local factories:

> Most of the men looked as if they had not properly woken from deep sleep, but glided as if drugged, and with half-closed lids, towards their chosen partner. This approach found favour with the girls. The actual invitation to dance was mostly delivered by gesture; a scarcely noticeable flick of the man's head towards the dance floor. Whereupon the girl, with an outstretched movement of surrender, would swim into the hands of the summoning partner. (58)

In his analysis of this and other scenes from *The Ballad of Peckham Rye*, Peter Kemp observes that the actions of the villagers are captured in a narrative which resembles in tone 'some anthropologist's dispatch', comprised of an 'alert notation' of various 'tribal rituals' (1974: 57). This is only partly the case, however; as indicated by the 'drugged' drift of the men and the automatic 'surrender' of the women, these 'rituals' have since degraded to a kind of social autopilot, played out without evidence of natural impulse or self-awareness. What Kemp describes as the narrator's 'alert' and anthropological attention to such actions is produced, nevertheless, by way of narrative techniques associated with the *nouveau roman* – namely, the narrator's scrupulous, almost forensic, focus on surface appearances, and vigilant attention towards patterns of repeated behaviour. In the narration of the ballroom scene, form and content operate in close accord, with the blankly functional prose mimicking the robotic efficiency with which the couples pair off. Whereas a perspective limited to recording surface details articulates for Robbe-Grillet a rejection of 'the old myths of "depth"' (1996a: 23), its use here is purely rhetorical; psychological depth can be rejected, Spark demonstrates, where none is evident to begin with. Readers, rather like Dougal, thus examine the community with a mixture of fascination and suspicion, perceiving its members less like vital, adaptable beings than thoughtless drones, devoid of interiority and locked into repeating patterns of automatic behaviour.

It is here, I wish to suggest, that Spark's satirically motivated mimicry of the *nouveau roman* converges with a Bergsonian approach to comedy. In *Laughter: An Essay on the Meaning of the Comic* (1900), Henri Bergson identifies comedy as a 'kind of *absentmindedness* on the part of life', detected in circumstances wherein human vitality has been replaced by 'a certain *mechanical inelasticity*' which precludes the individual from responding spontaneously or flexibly to changing situations (1911: 10, emphases throughout in original). The philosopher's nineteenth-century axiom of the comic, developed during a period of rapid technological advancement, appears especially relevant to *The Ballad of Peckham Rye*'s absurdist depictions of mechanistic social interactions and sexual practices. The sheer *incongruity* of encountering such examples of absentmindedness and inelasticity 'just where one would expect to find the wide awake adaptability and the living pliableness of a human being' (Ibid.) is, to Bergson, inherently funny; '*the attitudes, gestures and movements of the human body*', he argues, '*are laughable in exact proportion as that body reminds us of a mere machine*' (29). Laughter, Bergson contends, is therefore a natural, necessary response to this recognition of '*something mechanical encrusted on the living*', which has caused the individual to fall back upon the 'easy automatism of acquired habits' (37; 19). All individuals, he suggests, have the propensity to slip into comedic roles:

> In one sense it might be said that all *character* is comic, provided we mean by character the *ready-made* element in our personality, that mechanical element which resembles a piece of clockwork wound up once and for all and capable of working automatically. [. . .] It is comic to wander out of one's own self. It is comic to fall into a ready-made category. And what is most comic of all is to become a category oneself into which others will fall, as into a ready-made frame; it is to crystallise into a stock character. (149)

In *The Ballad of Peckham Rye*, the danger of allowing oneself 'to fall into a ready-made category' and thus to come to resemble 'a stock character' is nowhere more apparent than in the figure of Trevor Lomas. A hollow caricature of a surly Teddy Boy, Trevor appears as the most extreme example of what Michael Gardiner identifies as the various 'spurious and over-practiced social roles' (2006: 57) exhibited throughout the text. From the curiously lifeless nature of his strut, described as a 'somnambulistic sway' (57), to the hackneyed quality of his speech (the delivery of lines such as '"Come and wriggle, snake"' [58] being his preferred means of commanding women to dance), Trevor's behaviour is that of a man going through the motions, akin to the 'piece of clockwork [. . .] working automatically' which, for Bergson, propels the figure of comedy forward. In his analysis of *The Ballad of Peckham Rye*'s representation of 1950s youth subcultures, Nick Bentley observes how, despite appearing to embody a rebellious cultural faction, Trevor is 'representative of the prevailing dominant culture rather than a potentially subversive threat to it' (2010: 28). Bentley's reading may well account for the immediate hostility that Trevor displays toward the *truly* subversive Dougal, given the threat Dougal poses to the society's unchallenged codes of conduct. It is in the ballroom that Dougal demonstrates this subversiveness in the form of an elaborate, improvised dance with a dustbin lid – an act of protest against the codified behaviour of men like Trevor, and a revelation of his own boundless imagination:

> [Dougal] pressed into the midst of the dancers, bearing before him the lid of a dust-bin [. . .]. Then he placed the lid upside down on the floor, sat cross-legged inside it, and was a man in a rocking boat rowing for his life.
>
> [. . .]
>
> Next, Dougal sat on his haunches and banged a message out on a tom-tom. [. . .] He was an ardent cyclist, crouched over the handlebars and pedalling uphill with the lid between his knees. He was an old woman with an umbrella; he stood on the upturned edges of the lid and speared fish from his rocking canoe; he was the man at the wheel of a racing car; he did many things with the lid until he finally propped the dust-bin lid up on his high shoulder, beating the cymbal rhythmically with his hand while with the other hand he limply conducted an invisible band, being, with long blank face, the band-leader. (59–60)

The description of the dance amounts to an extraordinary narrative sequence, in which form and content cohere to express Dougal's defiance of a deeply conformist ethos. Not only do his shape-shifting movements fly in the face of the community's closely regulated uniformity, but Spark's newly buoyant narration, which leaps frenetically to capture each of his imaginative impersonations, also flouts the conventions of the clinical and steadfastly literal prose applied elsewhere. In contrast to the 'mechanical inelasticity' that surrounds him, Dougal embodies and expresses Bergson's description of 'comic fancy': 'a living energy, a strange plant that has flourished on the stony portions of the social soil', which can remedy lapses into lassitude and rigidity (65). Crucially, Dougal's shape-shifting does not evince signs of supernatural powers, but is achieved by way of a physical and imaginative dexterity available to, yet feared by, the other men and women. The restorative effects of 'comic fancy' relate to what Bergson theorises more generally as *élan vital*, or 'life impulse'; a being, Bergson believes, can be alive *by degrees* – that is, he or she can be rendered more or less inert (and thus more or less comical) through habit and absentmindedness. But while the laughter provoked by Dougal might be intended to have the redemptive effect described by Bergson, its restoration of deadened sensitivities leads more often to painful confrontations with long-ignored truths; Miss Frierne, for example, 'screamed with hysterical mirth' (123) after Dougal impersonates a corpse following the news of her estranged brother's death, while Merle Coverdale 'laugh[s] from her chest' in Dougal's entertaining company, before confessing to him: '"I've had a rotten life"' (98). Dougal's playfully anarchic presence in the community, which is motivated by his desire to delve beneath the surface and elicit uncharacteristic responses from its residents, can thus be seen as an attempt to reintroduce this 'living energy' into an emotionally barren wasteland.

'Wherever there is repetition or complete similarity', argues Bergson of the source of the comic, 'we always suspect some mechanism at work behind the living' (34). In Spark's novel, however, the humour derived from the aforementioned examples of the *'mechanical encrusted on the living'* has a limit, which, if exceeded, spills over into something altogether more unsettling. This is most evident in the stagnant affair between Merle Coverdale, a typist at Meadows, Meade & Grindley, and her manager, Mr Druce. The monotony of the affair is, initially, rich in ironic humour. Despite her insistence on maintaining a distinction between her work and leisure time ('"Remind me in the morning on business premises, Vincent", she said. "I don't bring the office into my home, as you know"' [52]), the drudgery of Merle's evenings with Druce mimics the regimented processes of the factory:

> Merle switched on the television and found a play far advanced. [. . .] Then they went into the bedroom and took off their clothes in a steady rhythm. Merle took off her cardigan and Mr. Druce took off his coat. [. . .] Merle took off her blouse and Mr. Druce his waistcoat. [. . .]
>
> They stayed in bed for an hour, in the course of which Merle twice screamed because Mr. Druce had once pinched and once bit her. 'I'm covered with marks as it is', she said. [. . .]
>
> She went into the scullery and put on the kettle while he put on his trousers and went home to his wife. (53–4)

Much like the stagnated social choreography exhibited in the ballroom, the interactions between Merle and Druce are so deeply entrenched as to appear thoughtless and mechanical, their familiar 'steady rhythm' causing the pair to resemble performers in a 'play far advanced', akin to that being broadcast on the living-room television. Even Druce's bites and pinches, and the screams they elicit from Merle, appear to conform to a set formula. Left alone at the end of the evening, Merle's final resemblance to another literary typist, depicted in 'The Fire Sermon' from T. S. Eliot's *The Waste Land* (1922), appears all too obvious to be unintentional. Akin to the affair between Merle and Druce, the dull sexual encounter in Eliot's poem is framed as a mechanical act, from the description of the 'human engine' that precedes it, to the 'automatic hand' with which the woman operates the gramophone and smooths her hair afterwards (Eliot 1969: 67, l. 217; 69, l. 255). Like Eliot's typist, who endures a passionless tryst with the 'young man carbuncular' (68, l. 232), Merle ends her night in a similar state of anhedonic indifference:

> She turns and looks a moment in the glass,
> Hardly aware of her departed lover;
> Her brain allows one half-formed thought to pass:
> 'Well now that's done: and I'm glad it's over'. (69, ll. 249–52)

As a means of articulating the affair's aura of deadening rigidity, the characteristic narrative traits of the *nouveau roman* – namely, the intricate attention to exterior details, the listless narration of sequential actions, and the refusal of psychological depth – have been co-opted by Spark to disquieting effect. This was a mode of writing, she asserted, where the notable absence of expressed 'thoughts or feelings' places the reader in the more active, interpretive role of 'sighter': 'You're just observing, that's all. A sighter. You're only seeing what people do. You read between the lines what they think [. . .]. It really gives you another dimension because people fill it in' (qtd in Stannard 2009: xviii). Perhaps paradoxically, the lack of affect characteristic of Robbe-Grillet's prose is adopted to *generate* affect in Spark's novel; rather than announcing Merle's despair explicitly, Spark allows it to be inferred 'between the lines' of her pointedly depthless prose. As a 'sighter', the reader thus occupies a position similar to that of Dougal, the only character attuned to the nature of Merle's suffering. '"Are you a free woman or a slave?"', he asks Merle of her relationship with Druce. '"After six years going on seven"', she responds, '"I'm tied in a sort of way"' (99). Seemingly unable to extricate herself from the 'far advanced' routine of the affair, and having grown dependent upon Druce's payments for her flat, Merle has been drained steadily of her vitality and independence. As with the playfully didactic, yet never domineering, approach he takes with the other residents, Dougal tacitly alerts Merle to the danger that awaits her, should she remain tethered to Druce. From engaging her in discussions about the affair during strolls through the local graveyard to leaving her standing alone in the narrow hallway, 'lined with wood like a coffin' (126), of his boarding-house lodgings, Dougal frequently frames Merle as a woman in grave danger. Even his dictation of notes for Merle's transcription is an act loaded with portent; the verbal articulation of punctuation marks ('"ahead full stop"' [128]) comes to foreshadow her life's imminent end.

This sense of steadily increasing danger and dread is only heightened by a laconic, conspicuously 'neutral' narrative perspective, which dwells repeatedly upon the sinisterly banal circumstances of Merle and Druce's arrangement. In his analysis of Robbe-Grillet's *Jealousy*, Adam Shatz notes how the 'sterile, descriptive rigour' and 'eerie rhythms and hypnotic repetitions' of the novel's prose work to 'create a sense of mounting disquiet' (Shatz 2014: 24). In *Jealousy*, this 'mounting disquiet' culminates in brief, perhaps hallucinatory, instances of ambiguously expressed violence, often concerning the repeated crushing of a centipede. In an article which would be republished as the introduction to the 2008 Oneworld edition of *Jealousy*, Tom McCarthy treats such instances as abstract 'escape route[s]' from the 'vicious circle of meals, cocktails, hair-combing, [and] spying' that comprises the novel's 'stultifying, oppressive and persistent present tense' – an infernal pattern of 'loops and repetitions' punctuated only by brief sparks of violence. The violence inflicted repeatedly upon the 'venomous *Scutigera*', McCarthy asserts, thus 'serves as a meeting point for associations so overloaded that if it were a plug socket it would be smoking' (2008: 394). Merle and Druce inhabit their own version of this 'stultifying, oppressive and persistent present tense'. The pair endure a dull routine that festers with Druce's jealousy and sadism, into which the fatal violence alluded to by Dougal insidiously creeps:

> He handed over her glass of wine. [. . .] He sat down and took his shoes off. [. . .] He looked down at his watch. Merle switched on the television. Neither looked at it. [. . .] He leaned forward and tickled her neck. She drew away. He pinched the skin of her long neck, and she screamed. [. . .]
> He came towards her with the corkscrew and stabbed it into her long neck nine times, and killed her. Then he took his hat and went home to his wife. (135–6)

The brutal murder of Merle appears as merely a minor deviation from her and Druce's typical nights in. Perversely, their evening still adheres to its drearily regular formula, with the 'far advanced' routine of drinking, undressing and television leading on to pinches, screams and Druce's eventual return to his wife. Narrated with the same tonal flatness and syntactic repetitiveness of any of Druce's other actions, or any of the routinised deeds depicted in the earlier scene between the pair, the murder not only is deprived of its appropriate emotional resonance, but is presented as an unnerving extension of the affair's oppressive and deadening aura. The description of Merle's death thus constitutes a tentative exploration of the *nouveau roman*'s sinisterly dehumanising narrative effects, which Spark would draw upon to even more disturbing effect in *The Driver's Seat* a decade later.

In keeping with its broadly comical tone, however, the novel's conclusion goes some way towards remedying the disquieting effect of Merle's murder. It achieves this by staging Dougal's entertaining defeat of his main adversary, Trevor, and departure from Peckham. The pair finally come to blows within the tunnel which runs beneath the village, where Trevor stabs Dougal in the eye with one of the human bones which litter the ground, before Dougal uses the same weapon to beat his opponent unconscious and complete his exit. On one level, the scene serves as a satisfying literalisation of Dougal's earlier expressed intention to '"plumb the depths"' of the community; that he manages to access the bone-strewn tunnel above which the factories sit seems a perfect illustration of his ability, evinced throughout the novel, to venture beneath the *'mechanical encrusted on the living'*, as Bergson puts it, and unearth signs of an authentic human presence. That Trevor targets his opponent's eye articulates his continued rejection of the aforementioned 'vision' with which Dougal is associated. Of all the novel's characters, the two-dimensional Trevor is changed the least by Dougal's subversive presence, making his final, unconscious state entirely apposite; now armed with a torch, Dougal navigates a passage to daylight, leaving his opponent languishing in the dark. On another – fittingly deeper – level, the subterranean scene communicates the novel's ultimate defiance of what Spark took to be the sterile and dehumanised realm of the *nouveau roman*: a mode of writing she felt to be committed solely to 'outward fact[s]' and impenetrable surfaces (Hosmer 2005: 147). In disrupting familiar patterns of behaviour, teasing out uncharacteristic responses and emotions, and behaving in ways which flout the rigid dimensions of the narrative itself, Dougal has repeatedly demonstrated the opposite. In direct opposition to Robbe-Grillet, whose 'A Future for the Novel' rejected literature devoted to 'burrowing deeper and deeper' in order to unearth 'the entire hidden soul of things' (1996a: 23), Dougal's gradual excavation of a series of 'interesting finds and human remains' affirms the possibility, as the last words of the text affirm, of encountering 'another world than this' (143).

'The lips in the glass-bound dock': The *Nouveau Roman* and the Eichmann Trial

Unlike *The Ballad of Peckham Rye*, *The Mandelbaum Gate* never seeks to mimic or co-opt the narrative conventions of the *nouveau roman* in order to generate a particular rhetorical effect. Instead, the novel's representation of the Eichmann trial, and its disturbing impact upon Spark's protagonist, Barbara Vaughan, includes brief but direct references to 'the anti-novelists' and 'the new French writers', thoughts of whom enter Barbara's mind as she witnesses Eichmann delivering his testimony in the Jerusalem District Court:

> Minute by minute throughout the hours the prisoner discoursed on the massacre without mentioning the word, covering all aspects of every question addressed to him with the meticulous undiscriminating reflex of a computing machine. [. . .] [Barbara] thought, it all feels like a familiar dream, and presently located the sensation as one that the anti-novelists induce. [. . .] At school she usually took the novels and plays of the new French writers with the sixth form. She thought, repetition, boredom, despair, going nowhere for nothing, all of which conditions are enclosed in a tight, unbreakable statement of the times at hand. (177)

Spark's decision to refer directly to the *nouveau roman* and its practitioners (the first and only time she would do so in any of her fictions) establishes an explicit connection between the effects produced in the narratives of 'the anti-novelists' and the horror of the trial itself. Bryan Cheyette elucidates this connection when he writes that 'Eichmann, like the authors of the anti-novel, turns people into objects and drains them of their humanity by using a deadening bureaucratic language' (2000: 71).

Spark had first-hand experience of this 'deadening bureaucratic language', having attended Eichmann's trial in June of 1961 with the intention of reporting on the event for both *The Observer* and BBC Radio's Third Programme. As she later remarked in an interview with Benjamin Ivry, it was not a monster that she recalled seeing in the District Court, but rather a dull, white-collar worker, who spoke of atrocities in the sanitising language of a bureaucratic report:

> I found it absolutely horrifying to see, as Hannah Arendt said, 'the banality of evil.' This little man being tried, Eichmann, was always perfectly horrible to his own lawyer, but he clicked to attention whenever the judge spoke to him. He was accused of transporting some children to their fate in the camps, and he claimed that he wasn't responsible, because there had been a delay; if he had done it, it would have been done on time. Eichmann wasn't a huge man with horns on his head. He was a sort of weasel, but you meet his sort every day on the street, like a grocer or banker. Eichmann could only come out with these banal phrases, he never grasped the evil he had perpetrated. That's what was so shocking, that he was a little bad man, not a big bad man. (Ivry 1991: 102)

Spark's appalled reaction towards Eichmann – this 'little bad man', for whom the reality of Nazi terror was obscured beneath the 'banal' bureaucracy of transport timetables – never found its way on to the pages of *The Observer* or into any radio feature. Instead, the author wove her experience of the trial into *The Mandelbaum Gate* as an event witnessed by Barbara during her pilgrimage across Jerusalem. A Catholic convert of Jewish descent (like Spark herself), Barbara crosses the Holy Land in a determined attempt to feel at last 'all of a piece, a Gentile Jewess, a private-judging Catholic, a shy adventuress' (194). In a novel preoccupied with the themes of free will and the fluidity of identity, however, Eichmann's presence is a disturbing reminder of a mindset far removed from her own. His is a detached, mechanistic way of thinking – one Spark represents as devoid of original, independent thought and shackled instead to the conditions of Nazi law.

As her comments to Ivry reveal, Spark's response to Eichmann bears the influence of Hannah Arendt's contentious take on the criminal and his trial, *Eichmann in Jerusalem: A Report on the Banality of Evil* (1963). Eichmann, Arendt controversially argued, was neither fiendish nor monstrous; for him, the systematic annihilation of six million Jews was an impersonal, abstract exercise – merely a matter of following rules and obeying orders, of arranging schedules and timetables with the utmost dedication and efficiency. Eichmann, the former chief of the Jewish Office of the Gestapo, struck Arendt as being entirely honest when he presented himself in court as a thoughtless bureaucrat, a small and far-removed part of a vast system of oppression and genocide, who could easily have been replaced by someone else. 'The trouble with Eichmann', she claimed, 'was precisely that so many were like him, and that the many were neither perverted nor sadistic, that they were, and still are, terribly and terrifyingly normal'. This 'new type of criminal', as the prosecution had described him, was driven by neither blood lust nor sadistic cruelty, but rather a simple sense of duty to a state-sanctioned extermination scheme (2006: 276). The present section of this chapter examines Spark's translation of historical fact and first-hand experience into a fictional encounter in *The Mandelbaum Gate*, in a scene which marks a crucial turning point, not only in Barbara's quest for self-determination, but in the course and *form* of the novel itself. Throughout, however, I return to Spark's developing, and often difficult, relationship with the *nouveau roman*. The urge for extreme objectification and the absence of intersubjectivity associated with this mode of writing, Spark discovered in the course of composing her novel, possessed the unsettling power to obfuscate and annul the reality of death and suffering, and could thus articulate Eichmann's terrifying detachment from the human dimension of his crimes.

By far the longest of her characteristically spare and economical novels, *The Mandelbaum Gate* constitutes something of an anomaly within Spark's distinctive œuvre. An adventure story-cum-romantic comedy divided into two parts and centred around a set of English, Israeli and Palestinian characters scattered across a bisected Jerusalem in June of 1961, it lacks either the conceptual simplicity of the works that preceded it or the 'brief, brittle, nasty' (Nye 1971: 9) qualities of the novella-length fictions that followed in the years immediately afterwards. Spark had expressed her eagerness to visit and write about contemporary, conflicted Jerusalem in a letter to her editor. By ensuring that she saw 'different versions of the Holy Land', she believed, she might write her 'best' novel yet:

> I want to set the action of the novel in the Holy Land where I think the symbols of my grandmother's origins reside. [. . .]
> [. . .]
> The different versions of the Holy Land that I have heard are themselves significant, and part of my theme. Obviously the place is full of tensions, and I really feel I can make a good novel, probably my best.
> I could write something for the *Observer* [. . .]. The Third Programme want me to do something about the Eichmann trial when it is finished. I want to go to the Trial while I am there and I think this should be easy enough. (NLS 1961)

Racial and religious divisions; social and political unrest; familial origins; the significance of Eichmann's ongoing trial: the contents of Spark's letter read like a checklist of *The Mandelbaum Gate*'s principal themes. The title of the novel's second chapter, 'Barbara Vaughan's Identity', reveals another. Barbara's self-confessed 'state of conflict' (23) – her hyphenated identity as a Gentile Jew, combined with the antagonistic demands of her Catholic faith and her sexual relationship with her newly divorced lover, Harry Clegg (whom, she feels, she can marry only if his marriage can be annulled by the Vatican) – extends into the turbulent history of the Middle East, and is emblematised in the divided city she attempts to cross. Barbara's conviction that 'the essential thing about herself remained unspoken, uncategorized, unlocated' (28) is frequently tested, however, by the categorising impulses and competing identity claims of those around her. The Foreign Office official and spy, Freddy Hamilton, immediately reduces her to a crude list of class- and gender-based expectations: 'His first impression had been of a pleasant English spinster; she was a teacher of English at a girls' school; she was on a tour of the Holy Land' (16). As Peter Kemp notes, a kind of 'social myopia' pervades these interactions, where characters, 'unwilling to tackle the difficulty and complexity of the individual', are 'lazily prone to stop short at the type with its comfortingly familiar features'

(1974: 100). Unlike Spark, whose letter reveals a reluctance to be 'tied to one set' when it came to the religious background of her travelling companions (NLS 1961), characters such as Freddy are far happier with 'comfortingly familiar' appearances. The moment that Barbara diverges from the template of an English spinster abroad, having mentioned her Jewish heritage, fills Freddy with a 'sense of her dangerousness' (17) – a sense, that is, of her inherent otherness and unclassifiability.

So far, so familiar, it might seem. Spark has, on the surface at least, set a comedy of manners in a 'state of conflict', and loaded it with cultural misunderstandings, romantic complications and social blunders. But as evinced by the fear that grips Freddy on learning that Barbara is not quite what she appears ('he now noticed the Jewishness of her appearance, something dark and intense' [17]), even mundane encounters come to betray deep-rooted prejudices and anxieties. Later, when an Israeli tour guide insists that Barbara is, in fact, a 'whole Jew' due to her matrilineal heritage, the protagonist comes to feel like a 'victim deprived of fresh air and civil rights', sensing 'her personal identity beginning to escape like smoke from among her bones' (27). The implications here are impossible to ignore; the sustained scrutiny of Barbara's identity extends, of course, to modern Jewish history and the events of the Holocaust. The smoking bones viscerally evoke the crematoria ovens of Auschwitz, while the guide's mock outrage at the upset he has caused – '"I ask her a question, she makes a big thing of it that I am Gestapo"' (26) – refers explicitly to Nazi Germany and the Nuremberg Laws. As writes Arendt in *The Origins of Totalitarianism* (1951),

> In Nazi Germany the Nuremberg Laws with their distinction between Reich citizens (full citizens) and nationals (second-class citizens without political rights) had paved the way for a development in which eventually all nationals of 'alien blood' could lose their nationality by official decree. (288)

Whatever Barbara may make of her identity, therefore, under these laws she would, due to her Jewish mother, have been classified as a national and thus 'deprived of fresh air and civil rights' within a system representing extreme and uncompromising order.

Given Eichmann's presence in Jerusalem at the time of these identity disputes, the implications of the Nuremberg Laws loom large over the contemporary scene. Indeed, for all her insistence that the trial, by virtue of its being 'political and temporary', represents 'something apart from her purpose' (175) in the Holy Land, Barbara is confronted in the Jerusalem District Court with a logic that directly opposes and rejects her 'unique and unrepeatable' self (25). Eichmann, as Cheyette argues, represents 'the ultimate determinist and false categorizer' (2001:

108), whose chillingly measured responses to cross-examination parallel the Nazis' systematic extermination campaign. Spark constructs these responses from verbatim samples of Eichmann's real testimony, as though a purely fictional dialogue would fail to do justice to the hollow, dehumanising verbosity she had heard first-hand. Rather like Charles Reznikoff's objectivist prose-poem, *Holocaust* (1975), which draws directly from courtroom accounts (including those from the Eichmann trial) of life and death in the concentration camps, these fragments of speech transform the narrative into a sinister echo chamber, reverberating with the real 'ritualistic lines' (178) that saved Eichmann from having to speak or think for himself:

> *Bureau IV-B-4. Four-B-four*
> I was not in charge of the operation itself, only with transportation . . .
> Müller needed Himmler's consent.
> I was not in a position to make any suggestions, only to obey orders.
> And technical transport problems.
> Strictly with time-tables and technical transport problems.
> I was concerned strictly with time-tables and technical transport problems.
> *Bureau IV-B-4. Four-B-four-IV-B-4.* (178)

Even the textual arrangement of the testimony mirrors Eichmann's profound detachment from the crimes he perpetrated. Bracketed off between the twin headings, '*Bureau IV-B-4*' (a subsection of the Head Office for Reich Security, of which he was in charge), the echoes of Nazi commands are severed from their original context, becoming a dull list of routinised deeds without human significance. This is less a way of speaking than an act of burial – a relentless heaping of words on top of words, obfuscating and annulling the repercussions of Nazi terror. Both tortuous and torturous, this slow drip of information – 'technical transport problems. / Strictly with time-tables and technical transport problems' – convinces Barbara that she is losing her mind, having found herself 'caught in a conspiracy to prevent her brain from functioning' (179). Like Eichmann, she is unable to think.

Thinking, or rather the failure to do so, lies at the centre of Arendt's concept of banal evil. 'The longer one listened to him', she wrote of Eichmann, 'the more obvious it became that his inability to speak was closely connected with an inability to *think*, namely, to think from the standpoint of somebody else'. For Arendt, Eichmann's imperviousness to critical thought – his reliance on the abundance of 'stock phrases and self-invented clichés' with which he communicated – provided him with 'the most reliable of safeguards against the words and the presence of others, and hence against reality as such' (2006: 49). Eichmann, she believed, existed in a world in which language was cut off from thought and judgement, where 'matter was subject to rigid "language rules"'. 'It is rare', Arendt remarks, 'to find [Nazi] documents in which such bald words as "extermination", "liquidation", or "killing" occur. The prescribed code names for killing were "final solution", "evacuation" (*Aussiedlung*), and "special treatment" (*Sonderbehandlung*)' (Ibid.: 85). Such 'rules' betray a refusal to engage with human reality, and by extension human mortality.

It was Spark's own exposure to this surfeit of weightless language that left her, like Barbara, lost for words. The experience, she told her editor at *The New Yorker* in 1963, had proven so disturbing that it had left her unable to talk about it ever since. In the same letter, she wrote admiringly of Arendt's reportage on the trial, which had appeared in *The New Yorker* as a series of articles before its publication as a book-length report (NLS 1963). For Spark, this failure to speak for herself – her failure to make sense of Eichmann's terrifying shallowness – coincided with a paradoxical *excess* of empty words. Writing to her literary agent, John Smith, shortly after returning from Jerusalem, she noted how convoluted her recent correspondence had become, attributing this to the five long days she had spent listening to Eichmann's testimony (WUL 1961). What emerged for Spark in the aftermath of the trial, then, was a curious sensation of absence and excess – a dearth of meaning against a superfluity of meaningless language. Eichmann, and by extension the trial itself, had come to seem absurd.

The same sense of absurdity pervades the trial scene in *The Mandelbaum Gate*, where Barbara listens while '[t]he counsel for the defence consulted his document and drew [Eichmann's] attention to specific names, Misters this and that and their sons, locked in reality' (179). Changing the translation settings on her earphones between English, French and Italian fails to elucidate matters, as she wonders: 'What was he talking about? The effect was the same in any language, and the terrible paradox remained, and the actual discourse was a dead mechanical tick, while its subject, the massacre, was living' (Ibid.). Here, the 'living' memory of the massacre sits uncomfortably alongside Eichmann's meaningless regurgitations. Barbara now inhabits a glass box of her own. In a position terrifyingly similar to that of the accused, she finds herself screened off from the awful fates of 'Misters this and that', anaesthetised by a way of speaking that leaves no room for the victim to emerge. As her mind wanders, she begins to perceive Eichmann – and, by extension, herself – as 'a character from the pages of a long *anti-roman*' (179), for whom the human reality of the Holocaust has been lost in translation.

Thoughtlessness; desensitised, mechanistic behaviour; a profound disengagement from reality: what is especially striking about the way in which Spark depicts the banality of evil as embodied in the figure of Eichmann (a depiction enhanced by the author's references to the detached and dehumanised aura of the *nouveau roman*) is how closely these factors resemble the components of the comic as defined by Bergson, and explored earlier in relation to *The Ballad of Peckham Rye*. In his 2013 essay, 'Bergson and the Comedy of Horrors', John Mullarkey argues that Bergson's conceptualisation of the 'origin of the comical' – that is, of one 'having lost some of one's vitality, of becoming a living machine, a ridiculous and monstrous hybrid' – is merely 'the flip-side of the origin of horror':

> [W]here the comic concerns what is alive and of value *making itself* inert and worthless, horror relates to a subject *being made* worthless and inert *by another*. What would be truly horrific in Bergsonian terms is not the monster *as* monster (being evil and loving it), but the banality, the sheer contingency of his or her being monstrous *to us* [. . .]. Indeed, the process whereby our vitality is *disregarded* [. . .] would lead, *in extremis*, to the collapse of even sadism (and sadistic laughter), which would still be an acknowledgement of a *minimal* intersubjectivity. Eventually, we would be regarded as pure objects. The horror of Auschwitz, then, is the historical corroboration of procedural death. (248–9)

With its discussion of the banal and contingent dimensions of monstrosity, and direct references to Auschwitz and 'procedural death', Mullarkey's analysis of the horrific 'flip-side' of the Bergsonian comic bears an obvious relevance to Spark's depiction of Eichmann, whose language is terrifying because of the ease with which it renders subjects – like those 'Misters this and that' – 'worthless and inert' to murderous effect. The trial scene also maintains Eichmann's *own* inertness, the 'dead mechanical tick' of his voice, which relays verbatim streams of bureaucratic language, being certain evidence of what Bergson would identify as '*something mechanical encrusted on the living*'. As her interview with Ivry reveals, Spark had watched in horror as Eichmann '*clicked* to attention whenever the judge spoke to him' (Ivry 1991: 102), before responding with words which seem, to quote from Robbe-Grillet's manifesto for the *nouveau roman*, eerily 'without signification, without soul, without values' (Robbe-Grillet 1996b: 71) in their failure either to express the subjectivity of the speaker or to acknowledge that of the victims. That the perpetrator and victims are rendered equally inhuman accounts for the scene's pervading sense of unreality, as well as Barbara's sense that she is losing her mind.

On trial in *The Mandelbaum Gate*, then, is the purpose and human significance of the Eichmann trial itself. Before she enters the courtroom, Barbara is reminded by Saul Ephraim, an Israeli professor, that the trial is '"part of the history of the Jews"' (175). Saul has good reason to think so, too. Unlike the Nuremberg trial in 1945, in which the prosecution relied heavily on documentary evidence in their case against Nazi leaders, the Eichmann trial foregrounded the testimonies of Holocaust survivors. Whereas Nuremberg was 'a monumental documentary case', Shoshana Felman argues, 'the Eichmann trial was a monumental testimonial case' (2001: 242), designed to leave an indelible mark on the collective memory of mankind. As David Cesarani details in his meticulous accounts of the trial, the Israeli prosecution team (led by Gideon Hausner) arranged for over a hundred witnesses to testify to the impact of Nazi measures in almost every country that had been affected, while aiming at the same time to represent as many aspects of anti-Semitism in prewar Jewish life as possible (2004: 237–323). Hausner, as Arendt details in *Eichmann in Jerusalem*, even opened his address to the court on behalf not of the state he represented, but of 'six million prosecutors':

> When I stand before you, judges of Israel, in this court, to accuse Adolf Eichmann, I do not stand alone. Here with me at this moment stand six million prosecutors. But alas, they cannot rise to level the finger of accusation in the direction of the glass dock and cry out *J'accuse* against the man who sits there. [. . .] Their blood cries to Heaven, but their voice cannot be heard. Thus it falls to me to be their mouthpiece and to deliver the heinous accusation in their name. (qtd in Arendt 2006: 260)

The trial, as evinced by Hausner's emotive opening address, represented for Felman something 'jurisprudentially revolutionary' – a 'legal process of translation of thousands of private, secret traumas into one collective, public and communally acknowledged one' (2000: 492). The testimonies of the victims, televised and broadcast around the world, served not only to portray a long and brutal history of anti-Semitism, but to present the Holocaust as the latest, and most extreme, manifestation of evil within this timeline.

For Arendt, though, the efforts of the Israeli prosecution to weave a human narrative of past suffering amounted only to 'bad history and cheap rhetoric', manifesting an enormous discrepancy between the extraordinary shallowness of the perpetrator and what the prosecution could make of him on ideological grounds. 'It was clearly at cross purposes with putting Eichmann on trial', she wrote, 'suggesting that perhaps he was only an innocent executor of some mysteriously foreordained destiny' (2006: 19). What Eichmann's crimes represented instead, she believed, was a fundamental rupture in the continuity of moral and legal thought – not the endpoint of any pre-existing narrative, but a signal of the collapse of existing frames of meaning, and of the need to redefine these frames in the wake of a new kind of criminal.

'Not only are all our political concepts and definitions insufficient for an understanding of totalitarian phenomena', Arendt contends in her 1953 essay, 'Mankind and Terror', 'but also all our categories of thought and standards of judgement seem to explode in our hands the instant we try to apply them' (2005: 302). Eichmann, she felt, was not to be understood as the embodied culmination of millennia of anti-Semitism, but as a thoughtless bureaucrat whose motivations were strictly career-ist. 'Except for an extraordinary diligence in looking out for his personal advancement', she insists, 'he had no motives at all' (2006: 287).

The banality of evil thus does not serve as a comprehensive explanation for Eichmann's crimes, but points instead to a phenomenological blind spot – a space of *unknowing* – that existing categories of thought and judgement fail to elucidate. This failure, however, holds for Arendt a crucial 'lesson' of its own, distinct from the extended history lesson being taught in the District Court: 'That such remoteness from reality and such thoughtlessness can wreak more havoc than all the evil instincts taken together' (2006: 288). The sociologist Zygmunt Bauman expresses something similar when he writes that the mass destruction of the Jews 'was accompanied not by the uproar of emotions, but the dead silence of unconcern' (1991: 74). Despite his verbosity, Eichmann personifies this 'dead silence' completely – something brought into sharp focus through the transcribed extracts of his pretrial interrogation by the Israeli police officer, Captain Avner W. Less. As Eichmann describes in exhaustive detail the Byzantine structures of the Third Reich, it is his resistance to independent thought and emotional identification that emerges most prominently:

> [Bureau] IV-B-4 never decided anything on the strength of its own judgement and authority. It never would have entered my head to mess myself up with a decision of my own. And neither, as I've said before, did any of my staff ever make a decision of his own. All decisions were based on a) the relevant Reich laws and accompanying implementation orders; b) the police regulations, the decrees, orders, and instructions of Himmler and the Head of the Security Police – those were our legislative bases [. . .]. The loyalty oath in itself called for unquestioning obedience. So naturally we had to comply with the laws and regulations. (von Lang and Sibyll 1983: 124)

Notable here, against the intricate yet clearly defined operations of Nazi law, is the threat of 'mess' – the chaos heralded by emotion and personal judgement. Eichmann, it seems, would have felt guilt only if he had not acted with 'unquestioning obedience' and thus disrupted the perfect order in which he served. The criminal thus stood for something unprecedented and uniquely dangerous; his thoughtless, emotionless complicity could cause greater suffering than actions founded upon malign intent precisely because it allowed him to follow commands without contesting them, to devote himself wholly and unquestioningly (and, as he states, 'naturally') to a pre-existing order. In this sense, Eichmann might be read not only as 'a character from the pages of a long *anti-roman*', but as a deeply disturbing version of its author; he demonstrates a perspective which, committed purely to the surface, functions as a 'tool', as Kristin Ross described earlier, 'for conducting a set of technical, almost administrative operations based on criteria of efficacy' (1995: 76).

It is this shallow and single-minded devotion to duty, as opposed to a deep-rooted anti-Semitism, that Barbara registers in the courtroom. Crucially, Spark has her protagonist arrive at the trial during its 'boring phase', after 'the impassioned evidence from survivors of the death-camps was over'. Having missed the survivors' testimonies, Barbara is left with only the absent presence that remains: 'the lips in the glass-bound dock [which] continued to move' (178). Like Arendt before her, Spark chooses here to make Eichmann her prime focus, confronting Barbara directly with the methodical, detached, dehumanising and senselessly sensible language of the desk murderer, until she is 'taken in by the certainty, immediately irresistible, that this dull phase was in reality the desperate heart of the trial' (179). (Re)positioning Eichmann's cold-blooded determinism as the trial's 'desperate heart' thus constitutes a radical revisioning of the historical moment – a decentring of the witness testimonies and the ideological implications that comprised the Israeli prosecution's performance of justice. It was by taking such an approach, Spark believed, that she felt she had come to disappoint some Israeli readers of the novel: 'With the Israeli readers having suffered greatly', she later reflected, 'they obviously looked for a great deal of that suffering to be – as with the Holocaust – to be emphasised. However I didn't emphasise [this aspect of] the Eichmann trial' (Hosmer 2005: 144). The foregrounding techniques that Spark applies – her selective sampling and repetition of Eichmann's speech, her sustained focus on his moving lips, and her refusal to depict the testimonies of his victims – thus do not strive for objective realism, but announce themselves instead as aesthetic articulations of the chilling thoughtlessness and deification of duty that, she believed, lay at the core of the trial.

'It was a highly religious trial', Barbara notes sardonically – and she is right. Not religious, of course, in the sense described by Saul, as a confirmation of the survival of the Jewish faith, but in relation instead to the fascist doctrine worshipped by the man in the glass box: 'the complex theology in which not [Eichmann's] own actions, not even Hitler's, were the theme of his defence, but the honour of the Supreme Being, the system, and its least tributary, Bureau IV-B-4' (179–80).

Emotionally screened off from the barbarism of Nazi rule, Eichmann can do no more than automatically relay, *ad nauseam*, directives from the Bureau. It seems appropriate, then, for Spark to invoke the clinical factuality of the *nouveau roman* to render 'the theme of the defence' – the unnatural order followed, as Eichmann attested in his pretrial interrogation, 'naturally' and with 'unquestioning obedience'. Eichmann, as Allan Massie asserts, is a 'ghastly parody of the believer' (1984: 99). Set up against Barbara's quest for spiritual growth, his 'highly religious' submission to 'an imperative deity named Bureau IV-B-4, of whom he was the High Priest', is a vocation perversely parodied (179). In this sense, Spark's representation of Eichmann as a depthless figure from a *nouveau roman* corresponds perfectly with the suggestion, proposed by Robert Eaglestone, that 'literature or testimony about perpetrators should, if Arendt is right, [. . .] be very bad – terrible, actually – at the representation and so the understanding of this "banal" evil' (2017: 39). Eaglestone argues that 'texts about perpetrators should be about *nobodies* in this sense, failed selves (like Eichmann) rejecting an active, thoughtful subjectivity for thoughtlessness and forgetfulness', because 'the large, complex systems which make up the "banal" evil are precisely aimed at negating subjectivity, personal agency, and choice, the representation of which are [*sic*] core to literature' (Ibid.: 40).

A certain irony hangs, however, over Spark's contemptuous treatment of the '*anti-roman*' and 'the new French writers' as a form of shorthand to signify the rigidity of thought and deification of order that she registered in Eichmann. As Robbe-Grillet would attest in various works of autobiography and criticism, his approach to the *nouveau roman* (and the disorienting ordering strategies depicted therein) was predicated, in fact, upon an outright *rejection* of the extreme order represented by totalitarian systems, including Nazi Germany. In his 1977 essay, 'Order and Disorder in Film and Fiction', the author identifies the exposure and undermining of unnatural orders as the central preoccupation of novels including *Jealousy*, *The Erasers* (1953) and *The Voyeur*, along with films such as *The Immortal* (1963) and 1961's *Last Year at Marienbad* (the former directed by Robbe-Grillet and the latter by Alain Resnais, with Robbe-Grillet writing the screenplay). This preoccupation, he writes, is often expressed self-reflexively through his texts' inclusion of 'characters who organise order', or 'a narrator, who wishes to organise the world at a glance'; the inevitable undoing of such attempts only highlights the orders' various contrivances (1977: 8–9).[3] Robbe-Grillet relates this recurrent theme to political, and specifically postwar, realities:

Established order always claims to be natural. And it is rather striking that in every society, even the maddest, established order is presented to the public by its leaders as something quite natural – that is, just and definitive and so forth. [. . .] In Nazi Germany, which was a really mad society, there were theoreticians who presented as quite natural the 'fact' that the so-called Aryan race should dominate the other races. This was 'natural.' This is what Marx called ideology. In sum, ideology is established order which is masked as natural order, which pretends to be not a creation of the society but, on the contrary, a sort of divine law dictated, so to speak, by God. (Ibid.: 3–4)

Masquerading as 'natural' and God-given, the fascist desire for perfect order – the use of race, in particular, as a means of categorising, isolating and annihilating beings – comes to render the world alien and inorganic. For Robbe-Grillet, these were deeply personal concerns. In his autobiographical novel, *Ghosts in the Mirror* (1986), he recalls his childhood fear of being 'sucked reluctantly into the heart of an unknown, unstable, irrational liquid universe ready to engulf [him]' (1988: 33). This was a universe that the author associated closely with Nazi power; his parents, anti-Semites and Nazi collaborators, had themselves been 'sucked' into this very system (Miller 1993: 123–66). This formative experience, he acknowledged, had drawn him to 'problematic experimentation[s] with fiction and its contradictions [. . .] as the most promising arena in which to act out [. . .] the fight to the death between order and freedom, the insoluble conflict between rational classification and subversion, otherwise known as disorder' (1988: 133).

While Spark would wait until *The Driver's Seat* before staging her own 'fight to the death between order and freedom', *The Mandelbaum Gate* pursues its own peculiar resolution of Eichmann's unsettling presence within Barbara's plot. Recoiling from Eichmann's perverse submission to the will of an operation now in ruins, Barbara realises, as if 'without awareness' (177), that she will not only complete her pilgrimage, but will wed her lover, regardless of whether or not his marriage can be annulled by the Vatican. This curious moment of *anagnorisis*, seemingly prompted by the 'repetition, boredom, [and] despair' experienced at the trial, extends to the form of the novel itself. The languorous, protracted pace of its first half gives way to a frenzied final section, completed in a fifty-seven-hour stretch of writing that led to its author's hospitalisation (Holland 1965: 10). Awash with plot contrivances including unlikely love affairs, espionage, murder and kidnap, these final hundred or so pages culminate with the heroine (having crossed the border back into the Israeli sector of Jerusalem, while masquerading as a nun and carrying falsified identification papers) 'run[ning] along the pavements of the sweet, rational streets' (300). Having referenced the apparent stagnancy of the '*anti-roman*', Spark appears to overcompensate for its perceived plotlessness with a heightened, delirious fictionality. A generous reading of this extravagant ending might consider how, just as fractured Jerusalem once signified Barbara's conflicted sense of self, these 'sweet, rational streets' reflect the gleeful shedding of roles and rules, of resisting myopic visions and taking in a rich, expansive view of her life and surroundings (never to be 'tied to one set', as Spark wrote in her letter to her editor).

Even for Spark, though, this interpretation would ultimately prove unconvincing. Despite her initial belief, expressed to her editor, that *The Mandelbaum Gate* might become her best novel, she eventually distanced herself from it, citing its hurried and uneven ending as a particular weakness. 'I don't like that book awfully much,' she admitted five years after its publication, 'it's out of proportion. In the beginning it's slow, and in the end it's very rapid, it races [. . .]. I decided never again to write a long book, [but to] keep them short' (Gillham 1970: 412). And she did. From *The Public Image* in 1968 through to *The Hothouse by the East River* in 1973, Spark composed a series of slight, elliptical novels, all scrupulously mean in their economy, with narratives that privileged surface details over emotional depth. 'I objectified everything much more after that', she told Martin McQuillan. 'I wrote books more like *Not to Disturb* and *The Driver's Seat* and was very much more influenced by the French writers of the *nouveau roman*' (McQuillan 2001c: 215).

'Drastic reductions' and 'tell-tale stains': Writing Under/Against the Influence

Arriving late sometimes and never
Quite expected, still they come,
Bringing a folded meaning home
Between the lines, inside the letter.

'The Messengers' (ll. 11–14)

Spark's comment to McQuillan, concerning her decision to begin writing fiction that was 'influenced by the French writers of the *nouveau roman*', might seem strange, and perhaps even disconcerting, for two distinct reasons. For one, the *nouveau roman* was certainly not a new influence on the author's writing at the end of the 1960s, as evinced by her account of the composition of *The Ballad of Peckham Rye* a decade earlier. Secondly, given the unnerving likeness drawn in *The Mandelbaum Gate* between the works of 'the new French novelists' and Eichmann's deathly bureaucratic language, Spark's claim that she had begun to write under the influence of such authors might seem, at worst, a betrayal of the crimes that she had heard about at length at the Jerusalem District Court. In her 2011 study, *The Second World War in Contemporary British Fiction*, Victoria Stewart neatly encapsulates the nature of the latter 'problem': the uncomfortable notion that 'Spark somehow learns from, or even imitates, Eichmann's delivery, as much as she learns from the new novelists that their project is a shared one' (48). What I wish to suggest, however, is that what Spark describes to McQuillan is a more committed mode of engagement with the *nouveau roman* than had been seen in her previous work. Indeed, in both *The Ballad of Peckham Rye* and *The Mandelbaum Gate*, the *nouveau roman* is invoked, only to be rejected, as if in disgust, by both the narrator and the central character; *The Ballad of Peckham Rye* ends by contrasting the dispassionate murder of Merle Coverdale with a slapstick brawl and the hopeful affirmation of 'another world than this', while *The Mandelbaum Gate*'s frenetic final third is initiated by Barbara's impulsive decision to turn away from 'the character from the pages of a long *anti-roman*' and complete her pilgrimage. Rather than simply attacking the *nouveaux romanciers* for participating in a form of fascism of representation, Spark's decision to write under their influence in *The Driver's Seat* constitutes an attempt to engage with, and ultimately confront, the anti-novel's aura of objectification and dehumanisation from the inside out.

It is, of course, significant that, in discussing with McQuillan the *nouveau roman*'s influence on her fiction after *The Mandelbaum Gate*, Spark should mention her will to 'objectif[y] everything much more'. The slippery distinction between the objectivist and objectifying intentions of the *nouveaux romanciers* would form one of the key debates surrounding the 'new novel'. For early critics, including Barthes in 'Objective Literature', the work of writers such as Robbe-Grillet could be characterised by their seemingly *chosiste*, or 'thing-oriented', aesthetic, whereby individuals and their environments are represented with apparently unmediated objectivity. As one of the chief practitioners of the supposed *l'école du regard*, Robbe-Grillet was thought to 'impos[e] a unique order of apprehension: the sense of sight' in his narratives, so that 'the [narrated] object is no longer the centre of correspondences, a welter of sensations and symbols: it is merely an optical resistance' (Barthes 1972: 14). For Robbe-Grillet, however, this assessment was not entirely accurate. In 'A Future for the Novel', the author claims that '[o]bjectivity in the ordinary sense of the word – total impersonality of observation – is all too obviously an illusion' (1996a: 23). His novels are 'objective', he insists, only in so far as they relate the orientation of a *subjective* consciousness, from the specific, limited perceptual position that Barthes identifies. In 'New Novel, New Man' (1961), he attempts to clarify this earlier misreading of his fiction:

> Since there were many objects in [the *nouveau roman*], and since there was something unaccustomed about them, a special meaning was quickly attached to the word 'objectivity,' uttered in their regard by certain critics, though in a very special sense: oriented toward the object. Taken in its habitual sense – neutral, cold, impartial, the word became an absurdity. Not only is it *a man* who, in my novels for instance, describes everything, but it is the least neutral, the least impartial of men: always engaged, on the contrary, *in an emotional adventure of the most obsessive kind*, to the point of often *distorting his vision* and of producing imaginings *close to delirium*. (1996c: 138, emphasis mine)

Combining tonal flatness and forensic detail with an extreme and unmediated subjectivity, Robbe-Grillet's narratives speak not of objectivity but of *objectification*. Novels including *The Voyeur*, *Jealousy* and *In the Labyrinth* are each narrated by an unidentified objectifying consciousness – what Bruce Morrissette has termed the '*je-néant*', or 'absent-I', narrator (1975: 113) – which reduces everything in its view to a set of meticulous measurements and positionings. This reduction is achieved, as Hanna Meretoja asserts, via a narrative gaze which causes characters to 'merge into the thing-world' (2014: 94). Take, for instance, the narrator's conspicuous view of a woman, referred to simply as A..., brushing her hair in *Jealousy*:

> The brush descends the length of the loose hair with a faint noise somewhere between the sound of a breath and a crackle. No sooner has it reached the bottom than it quietly rises again toward the head, where the whole surface of its bristles sinks in before gliding over the black mass again. [. . .] The head leans to the right, offering the hair more readily to the brush. Each time the latter lands at the top of its cycle behind the nape of the neck, the head leans farther to the right and then rises again with an effort, while the right hand, holding the brush, moves away in the opposite direction. The left hand, which loosely confines the hair between the wrist, the palm and the fingers, releases it for a second and then closes on it again, gathering the strands together with a firm, mechanical gesture, while the brush continues its course to the extreme tips of hair. (Robbe-Grillet 1959: 66)

The female subject at the centre of this scene is barely identifiable, monitored with such meticulous precision that she is reduced to little more than an abstract play of shapes, lines and measurements, with her movements likened to the preprogrammed functions and 'mechanical gestures' of an automaton. A certain fear and violence is implicit in the narrator's attempts to control a perceived threat of (specifically *feminine*) disorder – evident in the 'extreme tips' of her 'black mass' of hair, for example – by reconfiguring and subsuming it within a rigid geometric order. That the woman's name is only partially revealed as A... is similarly suggestive. Is the narrator demonstrating a sense of mastery by eliding it purposefully, in a way that mirrors the fragmented representation of her body in the text, or does its incompleteness suggest that the woman has managed to elude complete narration – to remain, at least partly, private and unknowable? This ambiguity, to which I shall return in the following chapter, is only heightened by the novel's title. The French *jalousie* signifies both 'jealousy' and the *jalousie* window (the slanted glass slats of which provide the observer with only a partial outlook), and thereby underscores the text's preoccupation with the relationship between the restricted nature of its narrative viewpoint and the obsessive, emotionally distorted perception of its narrator. In this novel, notes Stephen Heath, the 'Robbe-Grillet *chosiste* is really Robbe-Grillet [the] novelist of the subjective world of the pathologically disturbed' (1972: 116).

Participating in what their author describes as 'a double movement of creation and destruction' (Robbe-Grillet 1996e: 148), the obsessively rendered scenes in Robbe-Grillet's fiction thus bear traces of a narrative *violence*, whereby the living subject is rendered increasingly obscure and inhuman with each successive description. This did not go unnoticed by Spark; Robbe-Grillet, she remarked, 'is doing something new in his precision. I believe that he was a sighter – a gunsighter – during the war, where every little millimetre counted. And one does see this in his obsession with exactitude' (Shenker 1968: 2).[4] Spark's sly conflation of voyeurism and violent intent ('a sighter – a gunsighter') is especially telling here, suggesting her recognition that a novel such as *Jealousy* does not aim at total objectivity, but carries instead a foreboding sense of its narrator's dangerous and desubjectifying presence. The same crazed compulsion to order and objectify beings and their surroundings is evident throughout *The Driver's Seat*. Described by Spark as 'a study, in a way, of self-destruction' (Gillham 1970: 412), the novel narrates, in meticulous, clinically precise detail, the final few days in the life of a woman named Lise, who plots her own murder in what Aidan Day calls 'an attempt to break out of her felt sense of distance from reality' by 'occupy[ing] – as an autonomous, willing agent – the driver's seat of her own life', and thus escaping the suffocating and unnatural order that she has come to inhabit (2007: 328–9). More than this, *The Driver's Seat* sees Spark engage more critically, and self-reflexively, with the form and function of the *nouveau roman* than anywhere else in her œuvre.

From the outset, *The Driver's Seat* appears saturated with a stifling sense of geometry redolent of the anti-novel. Lise's life, the reader learns, has long been marked by a deadening rigidity, from the curiously symmetrical distribution of her work colleagues ('she has five girls under her and two men. Over her are two women and five men'), to the fixed shape of her mouth, with its lips permanently 'pressed together like the ruled line of a balance sheet' (9). Indeed, Robbe-Grillet could himself qualify as the famously 'studious and strict-principled' architect of Lise's 'austere' designer apartment – a strictly minimalist, 'clean-lined and clear' space, the furnishings of which are built from once 'swaying tall pines', which are now 'subdued into silence and into obedient bulks' (15). Lise has come to resemble one of these lifeless bulks; she is subdued and dutifully silent, her body dissolving seamlessly 'into the dignity of unvarnished pinewood', so that her home, even when she is present, seems unnervingly 'uninhabited' (14). As she lies motionless but for her 'eye-slits open[ing] from time to time', with her body framed by 'the bed-supports, the door, the window frame, the hanging cupboard, the storage space, the shelves, the desk that extends, the tables that stack' (15), she resembles the two-dimensional subject of a Cubist painting, her form eerily indistinguishable from 'the thing-world' that encloses it (Meretoja 2014: 94) – one dull surface among many.

Examining scenes such as this one, Day notes how 'Spark's invocation [. . .] of Robbe-Grillet's descriptive exactitude' functions to serve the 'satiric point [. . .] that authentic, organic human presence is absent in a space that signifies only the repression of natural energy'. Echoing the style of the *nouveau roman*, he argues, has enabled Spark to satirise 'an entire Western world that has committed itself to an effacement of living reality, to a preoccupation with exteriors rather than interiors, surfaces rather than depths' (Day 2007: 326–7). Such a reading might envisage *The Driver's Seat*, set as it is within a myriad of anonymous and seemingly interchangeable interiors, including department stores, airports, designer apartments and chain hotels, and featuring numerous, prosaic scenes of tourism and consumption, as emblematic of what Fredric Jameson describes as 'the inner truth of that newly emergent social order of late capitalism' (1998: 3), which is distinguishable, as the previous chapter explored, by a waning of affect associated with schizophrenia. In this light, a convincing case can be made for Lise – a tourist and consumer whose exact age, surname, personal life and familial relations remain unspecified, unknown or simply inconsequential – as an avatar for the blankness of postmodernity, whose lack of history communicates the Jamesonian schizophrenia of a perpetual present (Jameson 1992: 1–54). If Spark had a target in mind, however, it is not merely a hopelessly detached and consumerist Western world, but the *nouveau roman* itself. As the details of Lise's home, appearance and work indicate, Spark does not appear to invoke the *nouveau roman* for any satirical purpose so much as to *recreate* an exaggerated version of it as a textual prison – or, perhaps more fittingly (given the preceding discussion of *The Mandelbaum Gate*), a glass box within which her protagonist finds herself trapped. In this sense, descriptions of Lise's 'detail warden of a mouth' (9) and the supposed 'dignity' inherent in her seemingly 'uninhabited' living space are particularly revealing; Lise, having internalised the objectifying and dehumanising gaze of her own *nouveau romancier*, has monitored and minimised her body and behaviour fastidiously, becoming a living embodiment of the 'distinct and smooth' surface advocated by Robbe-Grillet himself (Robbe-Grillet 1996a: 19).

That *The Driver's Seat* should begin with a reference to 'drastic reductions' (1) – relating here to the set of discounted dresses encountered by Lise in a department store – is thus far from incidental. As if obeying the philosophy of the *nouveau roman* in which they are contained, characters in the novel restrict their interactions with people and things accordingly. A customer in an airport bookshop purchases titles based purely on the colours of their covers, for example, while the attempted seduction of Lise by her lecherous admirer, Bill, is limited to Bill's demand of a daily, regimented orgasm as he 'stares ahead with glazed and quite unbalanced eyes' which are 'too wide open to signify anything but some mental distance from reality' (35). In instances such as these, the familiar components of the Bergsonian comic are evoked to absurd and unnerving effect, as characters regard themselves and one another as beings devoid of inner lives and emotional depths. In this novel, tears are stimulated by neither sadness nor hilarity, but by the lachrymatory agent released by the policemen patrolling the streets (99). Even the arrival of laughter, welcomed by Bergson as 'an immediate [social] *corrective*', which 'singles out and represses a special kind of absent-mindedness in men and events' (1911: 17), only emphasises the insensibility of the storyworld and its inhabitants. In *The Driver's Seat*, a laughing person merely comes to resemble a newly detonated 'container of laughing-gas' (17), a component part of a vast network of similarly mindless, automatic processes.

It is this agonising 'distance from reality' that Lise feels compelled to bridge. She does so by evoking what Robbe-Grillet considered anathema to the 'singular style of studied apathy' (Miller 1993: 128) encountered in his novels: human tragedy. Indeed, Robbe-Grillet would argue that tragedy serves as an unconvincing 'attempt to "recover" the distance which exists between man and things' by positing a world from which meaning can be salvaged in the form of the purgative, enlightening or morally purifying effects of catharsis (1996b: 59). The archival research undertaken for this book confirms Spark's intense interest in the nature of tragic emplotment. Her notebooks reveal that the composition of *The Driver's Seat* entailed extensive research into Aristotelian tragedy, drawing upon studies including Werner Jaeger's *Aristotle: Fundamentals of the History of His Development* (1923) and Lascelles Abercrombie's *Principles of Literary Criticism* (1932). From the latter text, Spark copied the following two passages and included them alongside a set of notes on Lise:

> The (^Aristotle's) definition of Tragedy is this: Tragedy is the imitation of an action that is serious, complete in itself, and possessing a certain magnitude; in language that gives delight appropriate to each portion of the work; in the form of drama, not of narrative its *Katharsis** of emotions.
> *Purgation[5]

> In contrast with history, in which nothing begins and nothing ends, and in which the mere sequence of events must satisfy as best it may our desire to know the secret connection of events, in poetry we see an event complete in itself, definitively beginning and definitively ending and proceeding with perfect coherence from antecedents we understand to consequences we accept as inevitable. (MFL 1969a)

That Spark had these passages in mind while conceptualising Lise's journey towards self-destruction – a journey which functions implicitly as an escape route from the 'repetition, boredom, [and] despair' encountered in the *nouveau roman* – is illuminating. If an analogy were to be drawn between Abercrombie's account of history, where 'nothing begins and nothing ends', and the looping scenes and exhaustive, often inconsequential descriptions encountered in the *nouveau roman* ('going nowhere for nothing', as Barbara puts it, dismissively), then Lise's quest acquires a new-found, almost heroic significance. Here we might observe Lise as a less explicitly metafictional version of Caroline Rose in *The Comforters*. Just as Caroline strives to disrupt what she described as '"the convenient slick plot"' (104) of the hackneyed detective novel into which she senses she has been written, Lise's construction of a tragic arc that is 'complete in itself', and carries with it a definitive and 'inevitable' *dénouement*, constitutes an attempt to counter the stalled and self-alienating quality of life beneath the gaze of her *nouveau romancier*. Seeking to arrive at such an ending, Lise assumes the grandeur of a tragic heroine, her every action geared towards leaving a trace of her subjectivity within a world that has denied it.[6] A compelling performance artist attired in garish clothes selected for how prominently they will display her eventual bloodstains, she erupts into public displays of shrieks and tears so as to 'successfully regist[er] the fact of her presence' (20) among potential eyewitnesses, before finding a man willing to stab her to death in the manner she desires and with the knife she has supplied (rather tellingly, given her desire to construct a plot of her own, the weapon is specified as a '*paper*-knife' [67]). As with the uncharacteristically buoyant description of Dougal's dancing in *The Ballad of Peckham Rye*, Lise's death drive effects a suspension of the externalised perspective of her narrator; as she seeks out her murderer and 'lays the trail' (51) of clues to be followed by investigators, journalists and her own narrator, she is described in unusually poetic terms as 'a stag scenting the breeze' (73), her purposeful search for death's thrill and finality casting ripples through the still waters of the novel's prose.

As her notes show, Spark quotes from Abercrombie's definition of Aristotelian tragedy as an imitative act which effects the '*Katharsis* of emotions', and annotates '*Katharsis*' so that it stands to mean 'Purgation'. This annotation is likely to result from the discussion that follows a few pages later in *Principles of Literary Criticism*, where Abercrombie emphatically discounts interpretations of catharsis as a mode of either moral purification or intellectual clarification in favour of a reading rooted in ancient Greek medicine:

> [I]t seems certain that 'purification' is not what [Aristotle] himself meant by *Katharsis*. Whenever he alludes to the tragic *Katharsis*, this is evidently identical with the mere fact of rousing pity and fear. [. . .] In Greek medicine, an organism could be purged of any undesirable product by the administration, in judicious doses, of something similar: as in modern homeopathy, 'like cures like.' Excess of any kind was unwholesome; health could be secured by purgation of anything which tended to be present in excess. This seems to be what Aristotle meant by *Katharsis*. Tragedy effected the purgation of pity and fear, by its administration of these very emotions. [. . .] Aristotle regarded the function of tragedy as something medical: the pity and fear of tragedy were the doses by which the tragic poet homeopathically purged his audience into emotional health. (Abercrombie 1932: 107–8)

While the physiological interpretation of Aristotelian catharsis as a homeopathic regulation of fearful and pitiful emotions (as formulated in an influential 1857 essay by the philologist Jacob Bernays) has attracted varying degrees of scepticism from contemporary scholars,[7] it evidently captured the interest of Spark, who filled an additional folder of research notes with related details from Abercrombie's study (MFL 1969b). Spark's engagement with this reading has notable implications for our understanding of her protagonist's self-directed death. Lise's intention, we might infer, is to attempt to remedy a life suffused with an 'unwholesome' excess of what she terms an '"inconceivable sorrow"' (96) by bringing about its purgation through her own tragic performance. Her elaborately stage-managed death can thus be seen to re-enact and communicate a sense of the alienated and anonymous death-in-life she has already endured; the neckties that render her body immobile are connotative of the stifling patriarchal order that has robbed her of agency, for instance, whereas the knife which pierces her throat replicates the forceful silencing of her voice that occurred long before her murder took place.

Like one of the titular tragic 'Messengers' in Spark's 1967 poem, who bring 'a folded meaning home / Between the lines, inside the letter' (ll. 13–14), Lise ('they read') presents her bound and brutalised corpse – displayed ceremonially in the grounds of a pavilion – as a monument to her misery, intended to articulate and thus exorcise that which has defined her existence. Having decided upon a suitable killer in Richard, a man whose discernible 'madhouse tremble' (102) comes to signify his propensity to murder, Lise directs him to the grounds of the pavilion and orders him, in the dead of night, to kill her in precisely the manner she specifies:

> 'I don't want any sex', she shouts. 'You can have it afterwards. Tie my feet and kill, that's all. They will come and sweep it up in the morning'.
>   All the same, he plunges into her, with the knife poised high.
>   'Kill me', she says, and repeats it in four languages. As the knife descends to her throat she screams, evidently perceiving how final is finality. [. . .]
>   He runs to the car, taking his chance and knowing that he will at last be taken, and seeing already [. . .] the sad little office where the police clank in and out and the type-writer ticks out his unnerving statement: 'She told me to kill her and I killed her' [. . .]. He sees already the gleaming buttons of the policemen's uniforms [. . .], the holsters and epaulets and all those trappings devised to protect them from the indecent exposure of fear and pity, pity and fear. (106–7)

Just as Lise appears to recognise that her tragic tableau will amount, in the object-oriented realm of the *nouveau roman*, to little more than an 'it' to be disposed of unceremoniously the following morning ('waiting for tomorrow's garbage-men' [97], her bloodied body-as-text is merely an undesirable blemish upon the clean and uncluttered surfaces of the anti-novel), her killer 'sees already' that his interrogation will be conducted by figures clinically protected 'from the indecent exposure of fear and pity, pity and fear'. These chiastic closing lines suggest the simple deflection of tragedy's intended effects against the protective surfaces of the 'sad little office', and by extension the sad little world within which *The Driver's Seat* takes place. The novel's concluding scene thus acts as an unlikely counterpart to its seemingly unremarkable *in media res* opening, where Lise listens to a saleswoman expound the virtues of stain-resistant fabrics. What first appeared as inconsequential sales patter – '"Specially treated. Won't mark. [. . .] Won't hold the stain"' (1) – can be read, in light of the ending, as indicative of an entire object world militantly resistant to the traces of individual subjectivity, figurative meaning or poetic expression. Such a world appears to have been built in accordance with Robbe-Grillet's conceptualisation of the *nouveau roman* as a literary 'mopping-up operation' (1996b: 57), which is committed, as Kristin Ross asserts, to eradicating the 'tell-tale stains' left by 'any analogical or emphatic trope that renders the world of objects tragic or conductive of any human significance whatsoever' (1995: 75). In an alternative draft of the final scene, Spark concluded her novel not with a proleptic glimpse of the police interrogation, but rather a present-tense description of Richard, who, having murdered Lise, 'stands and looks at what he has done' while 'the headlights of the cars light up their spot as the stain spreads' (MFL 1969a). In deciding against an ending that highlights – quite literally – Lise's 'tell-tale stains' in favour of one which focuses on a world '"[s]pecially treated"' against them, Spark underscores the oppressive 'neutrality' of her own version of the anti-novel, which remains pointedly and unnervingly stain-free.

We might surmise from the novel's disquietingly muted ending that Lise's death-bound journey has had little effect: Richard 'plunges into her' despite her protestations; the policemen are seemingly impervious to the effects of tragedy; 'tomorrow's garbage-men' will soon arrive to remove the stain. 'While there is a certain amount of pity, I think, to be read through the lines', Spark commented in the 1996 BBC *Bookmark* documentary, 'The Elusive Spark', 'the novel is, in the end, very cold, yes' (Yule 1996: n.p.). However, it is the very *coldness* of *The Driver's Seat* – its narrator's failure, for example, to comprehend Lise and her tragic plot, to 'read through the lines' and recognise her interiority – that affords the protagonist a unique power to unsettle, even after her death. By breaking from an existence that has long been characterised by its rigid, unnatural order, where every aspect of her appearance and actions could be measured and assessed by an exacting and objectifying narrative gaze, Lise has come to make herself strange and inscrutable, transforming her legible life into a mystery without an apparent solution (or what she herself describes as a '"whydunnit"' [101]). The narrator's relentless focus on exteriors now becomes a weak spot, as Lise's intent is made maddeningly inaccessible. The following chapter further explores Lise's role as an agent of textual disorder, who purposefully disrupts the 'clean-lined and clear' world she inhabits by unsettling the narrative gaze and provoking within her narrator a debilitating sense of interpretive anxiety. In so doing, Lise destabilises her narrator and secures the driver's seat at last for herself.

'A certain detachment'?

In an interview published in September 1968, shortly before she would begin initial work on *The Driver's Seat*, Spark spoke of Robbe-Grillet with a mixture of admiration and disdain. 'I'll always read Robbe-Grillet', she remarked, before insisting that she 'wouldn't like to write like that [her]self'. Moreover, *For a New Novel* had proven 'a pain in the neck' to read; its essays, she complained, were 'terribly insular and arrogant', their focus restricted to a 'quite obscure' set of contemporary French authors at the expense of 'Moravia, Hemingway [. . .] [or] anyone in that generation, [or] anyone outside of France'. 'But', she reasoned, 'he *is* doing something new' (Shenker 1968: 2). Unlike contemporaries such as B. S. Johnson, for example, who claimed to have taken 'the English path for the *nouveau roman*' in his own novel-writing (qtd in Guy 2014: 35), or Christine Brooke-Rose, who analysed the *nouveau roman* reverently and at length in various works of literary criticism, Spark responds to Robbe-Grillet with a measure of caution (if not outright cynicism), never subscribing wholeheartedly to his ethos or aesthetic despite her evident familiarity with both.[8] 'All I have from him', she maintained in one of her final interviews, 'is a certain detachment' (Hosmer 2005: 135).

The present chapter has sought to examine manifestations of this 'certain detachment' across three novels which, grouped together, make unlikely bedfellows. Each is attributable to a distinct phase in Spark's literary career: *The Ballad of Peckham Rye* to an early era of short, sharply observed and thematically contained social satires; the expansive, multi-plotted *The Mandelbaum Gate* to what Spark described, at the time of its composition, as her ongoing 'Mrs Tolstoy' phase (Kermode 1963: 71); *The Driver's Seat*, which Spark named in 2002 as her 'best novel to date and the creepiest' (McQuillan 2001c: 229) to a series of taut and enigmatic fictions influenced most directly by the anti-novel. Despite obvious differences in style, form and subject matter, these works can nevertheless be read alongside one another as evolving stages in Spark's conceptualisation and appropriation of Robbe-Grillet's 'special [. . .] drama of exact observation' (Toynbee 1971: 73). In *The Ballad of Peckham Rye*, the invocation of the detached and seemingly depthless aura of the *nouveau roman* allows Spark to cultivate an ironic distance from which narrator, reader and central protagonist can survey the novel's characters and depicted scenarios with wry suspicion. In *The Mandelbaum Gate*, on the other hand, direct references to the anti-novel serve to evoke a profound psychological disengagement from human suffering, which Barbara registers not only in the banal evil of Eichmann and others like him, but also in herself, having been subjected (like Spark) to his oblique and obfuscatory testimony. In both texts, the *nouveau roman* is either mimicked or mentioned for the purpose of producing a rhetorical sense of depthlessness, be it in the Bergsonian comedy of Trevor Lomas's 'somnambulistic sway' (Spark 1960a: 57), or in Eichmann's disturbing (and equally Bergsonian) status as a failed self, entirely devoid of emotional capacity.

A similarly unsettling imperviousness is conveyed throughout *The Driver's Seat*, which teems, as Cheyette observes, with 'characters who treat people, as did Eichmann, as if they were objects drained of their humanity' (2001: 109). Combining an externalised narrative perspective similar to that adopted throughout *The Ballad of Peckham Rye* with a thematic focus on extreme and dehumanising order, *The Driver's Seat* bears the influence of its author's prior novelistic engagements with the *nouveau roman*, while its self-reflexive approach to matters of plot-making and self-destruction reveals a further development in Spark's relationship with the anti-novel. Despite her insistence that she 'wouldn't like to write like [Robbe-Grillet] [her]self', *The Driver's Seat*'s tragic study of a character desperate to assert her subjectivity and evade narrative control happens to align Spark more closely with Robbe-Grillet than she perhaps anticipated; his fiction-writing, as I have discussed, is marked by a deep distrust of artificial orders, informed at least in part by his own traumatic exposure to fascist ideology. Although she might have believed otherwise, the 'certain detachment' that Spark claimed to have gained from Robbe-Grillet comes to reveal a deeper affinity between both authors.

'A study, in a way, of self-destruction': *The Driver's Seat* and the Impotent Gaze

[T]he art of the popular detective novel derives from the rhythm of desire. That is, it begins by stimulating desire, proceeds to tease it through a technique of progressive revelation interrupted by systematic digression, and finally satisfies it [. . .] in an end that reveals all.

[The anti-detective novel] ends not with a solution but with mystery enhanced, not with a *dénouement* that functions as a closure [. . .]. The end offers not the assertion of mastery and a return to order but *the surprise of impotence*. [. . .] [T]he recognition scene is also the scene of suffering.

Dennis Porter, The Pursuit of Crime (1981: 245–6; 256, emphasis mine)

Where the previous chapter discussed Lise's self-directed murder as an implicitly metafictional gesture, designed to counter the dehumanising gaze of her narrator and invoke the purgative effects of tragic catharsis, the present one shifts focus away from what is told in *The Driver's Seat* to the manner of its *telling*. That is, it examines the destabilising effects of Lise's actions upon the narrative itself. Lise's transformation of her meticulously ordered and eminently legible existence into an enthralling yet opaque drive to death effects something of a crisis of storytelling; her actions, that is, come to disorientate the objectifying gaze that has long been trained upon her, causing her narrator to spiral into impotent obsession. My analysis thus entails a thorough re-evaluation of *The Driver's Seat*'s critical reception, its approach to the inextricable relationship between gender, narrative perspective and power, its subversive treatment of the conventions of the traditional detective story, and the significance of its peculiar temporal structure.

Although numerous readings of *The Driver's Seat* have interpreted Lise's plot-making as a provocative and self-reflexive bid for narrative control, many have judged her actions to be the arrogant and misguided efforts of a fictional character to overthrow her author and thus assume an unwarranted level of authorial power. This, such readings have argued, constitutes a sin for which Lise is duly punished with sexual assault at the novel's conclusion, when her murderer, having 'stab[bed] with a turn of the wrist exactly as [Lise] instructed', proceeds to 'plung[e] into her with the knife poised high' (107). Across two separate discussions of the novel, for example, Bryan Cheyette likens Lise to one of Spark's 'one-eyed writer's [*sic*] *manqués* [. . .] who mistakenly think[s] that [her] myth-fictions can determine reality' (2001: 96), and whose killer consequently 'rapes her so as to reveal with brutal precision her ultimate inability' to do so (2000: 78). Echoing Cheyette's analyses, Maria Fackler aligns Lise with 'the artist *manqué*' for her 'presumptuous attempt to appropriate godlike authority and direct the narrative', and cites *The Driver's Seat* as an example of a text in which 'Spark's characters [. . .] are punished for their artistic pretensions, for their appropriation of the authority and power that constitute the special provenance of the novelist' (2014: 372; 375). Fackler thus identifies Lise's rape as an act designed to undermine her apparent hubris, in that it 'simultaneously ends Lise's direction of the narrative and reinstates Spark as director', while demonstrating in the process that 'the ultimate arbiter of [Lise's] fate [. . .] is *Spark*, who masquerades as a detached and limited narrator throughout' (375; 378). For Gerard Carruthers, Lise's sexual violation similarly 'represents a particularly bleak puncturing of the non-omnipotence of the individual human' (2010b: 83), which, argues Norman Page, holds a valuable didactic purpose: 'ultimately, Lise has been unable, as we all are, to control her own destiny, to write the script of her own life and death' (1990: 79).

Of added value to each of the above readings is Spark's Catholicism, and specifically the related notion that her fiction makes characteristic use of what Lorna Sage terms 'Almighty irony' (1992: 142) – the sense, outlined earlier, that the machinations of Spark's characters, however covert or confounding, are anticipated, contained and ultimately undermined within a divine 'plot' of their creator's devising. Spark's fiction-writing might thus be understood as a 'Catholic practice', in that its purpose, as Carruthers contends, is to 'acknowledge an omnipotent God, sometimes mimicked in the fabric of her novels by the narratorial or authorial character, whose implied perspective is supposed to overarch all human perspective' (2010b: 83). In *The Driver's Seat*, this perceived 'Catholic practice' is associated chiefly with the novel's well-documented use of prolepsis, whereby the narrator breaks habitually from the perspectively limited narrative present to impart details concerning the near future. One of the novel's first instances of prolepsis occurs at the beginning of its third chapter. As Lise prepares to board a plane, the intended outcome of her journey still unknown to the reader, the present tense is interrupted by the following admission:

> She will be found tomorrow morning dead from multiple stab-wounds, her wrists bound with a silk scarf and her ankles bound with a man's necktie, in the grounds of an empty villa, in a park of the foreign country to which she is travelling on the flight now boarding at Gate 14. (25)

Similar examples abound throughout the text, each related either explicitly or tangentially to the future police investigation, and media reportage, of Lise's murder. A seemingly unremarkable description of the size of the protagonist's nose, for instance, adjoins with the startling revelation that it is 'wider than it will look in the likeness constructed partly by the method of identikit, partly by actual photography, soon to be published in the newspapers of four languages' (18). What such digressions might imply, as David Lodge remarks of prolepsis more generally in *The Art of Fiction* (1992), is 'the existence of a narrator who knows the whole story' (75), and who is thus rather like the 'omnipotent God' described by Carruthers.[1]

Theological interpretations of *The Driver's Seat*'s prolepses have proven remarkably popular among critics, including even those more attentive to the more experimental facets of Spark's fiction. Despite her keen focus on Spark's various literary innovations in *Metafiction*, for example, Patricia Waugh finds the novel's repeated contrasts between present tense and proleptic narration to be analogous and thus reducible to the difference between limited human knowledge and divine omniscience. Here Waugh asserts that, while 'the present-tense narrative describing Lise in search of a man to murder her suggests that Lise is in control, is creating her own history', it is nevertheless 'counterpointed' by 'the future tense which reveals her "end" to the reader (and the "end" of Spark's plot)'. These future-tense passages can thus be seen to function 'ironically' by revealing that, despite her apparent agency in the narrative present, 'Lise's "script" exists within a larger "script" (Spark's) which exists within a final script (God's)' (1988: 121–2). Offering a near-identical reading to Waugh, Aidan Day perceives the protagonist as a minor authorial figure who finds herself enveloped within a *matryoshka*-like nesting pattern of plots both authorial and divine, so that 'behind Lise's plot stands the author's and the author's perspective is subsumed by God's' (2007: 333). Long before her sexual assault, both readings suggest, Lise's control of the 'script' of her life is placed firmly in doubt by proleptic indications of her ultimate powerlessness.

In light of such interpretations, it is perhaps unsurprising that *The Driver's Seat*'s conclusion, read as an unnerving extension of the proleptic undermining of Lise's carefully organised plot, has attracted notable criticism. For Aileen Christianson, the apparently didactic sexual violence that attends Lise's final moments as divine and authorial retribution for her 'temerity to attempt control of [her] life' only 'excuses and underplays the ferocity of male violence against women' in society at large (2000: 100). In her study of contemporary, women-authored Gothic novels, *Femicidal Fears* (2001), Helene Meyers levels similar criticisms rather more abruptly; 'the story of Lise', she asserts, 'suggests that women who choose this strategy [to attempt to assume autonomy over their lives] are fucked by both God and men' (84). Such condemnations are understandable. If we are to read the ending as others have, its apparently offhand allusion to rape seems an extravagantly cruel way of destabilising the protagonist's appropriation of authorial power, which trivialises sexual assault by reducing it to the brutal punchline of what Paddy Lyons terms the novel's 'theological twist' (2010: 94). As a consequence, *The Driver's Seat* has come to be viewed as Spark's most bitter and starkly drawn parable of human fallibility versus divine omniscience, as dictated by a pitiless author whose fingernails are not pared, but rather sharpened and poised to attack.

My own analysis differs markedly from those referenced above, in that it does not involve attributing to Spark's narrator the properties of God-like omniscience, nor does it read the sexual violence inflicted upon Lise as a mode of punishment meted out by a vengeful authorial surrogate in service of 'Almighty irony' or a particular didactic purpose. Most importantly, my reading rejects the idea – expressed most prominently in the work of Day, Carruthers and Waugh – that Lise's self-directed plot is neatly contained and controlled within the extradiegetic and existential 'scripts' of her narrator and God. My interpretation of the narrator is therefore closer to the model proposed by Bran Nicol, who notes how, throughout the novel, 'Lise's actions come across as being observed by someone following her', so that the narration 'resembles a less supernatural, more sinister, voyeuristic practice, like stalking' (2010: 123). Nicol's description of the narrative as emanating from 'a small-scale, prurient, menacing entity' (113) has significant implications not only for our understanding of the narrator's character and capabilities – it accounts, for example, for the narrative's obsessive and unwavering focus on the minutiae of Lise's appearance and movements, as well as its failure to provide psychological insight – but also for its diegetic position. A narrator who is 'more like a stalker than a deity' (Ibid.), that is, is necessarily situated *within* the diegesis, *loitering with intent* within the same storyworld inhabited by Lise, rather than surveying her actions from a lofty diegetic remove.

How might these limited capabilities be reconciled, however, with the narrative's frequent flashforwards, which pepper the ambiguous present with certainties from the near future, and thus appear to confirm the existence of extradiegetic knowledge? One explanation, offered earlier by Fackler, and related to Sage's notion of 'Almighty irony' or the 'theological twist' outlined by Lyons, is that Spark's supposedly God-like narrator is merely feigning the non-omniscience exhibited for much of the text, only to emphasise the opposite via proleptic digressions designed to demonstrate that Lise's sense of authorial control was always, in fact, hopelessly misguided. This would mean that the majority of *The Driver's Seat* is narrated from what Judith Roof describes as 'the vantage point of a disingenuous present marked by a certain dissimulation' before the author's hand is revealed (Roof 2001: 55). This reasoning is plausible, yet somewhat unsatisfactory. For one, the novel's glimpses of the future are not expansive or particularly detailed, but are limited instead to the discovery of Lise's corpse the following morning and the initial stages of the ensuing police investigation and media coverage; the reader never discovers, for instance, how Lise's murderer fares in court, or how her family or work colleagues react to the news of her death. Similarly, the narrator's professed uncertainties regarding Lise's thoughts and motivations (or even mundanely tangible details concerning her exact age or natural hair colour) are never elucidated in the prolepses. If Spark's intention had been to illustrate the containment of Lise's self-spun plot within various existentially and epistemologically superior 'scripts', then this is hardly an effective means of doing so. To the end, Lise remains unknown and unknowable.

An alternative, and arguably more convincing, interpretation would consider the narrator to be situated firmly within the diegesis (as implied in Nicol's reading), and aware of the investigation into Lise's murder not through powers of omniscience, but because it is *this* moment which, in fact constitutes the narrative present. The seemingly concurrent narration of Lise's behaviour can thus be reread as a retrospective retracing of the hours preceding her death, so that the prolepses come to return the narrator to the present moment, during which time the police investigation is under way. This (re)conceptualisation of *The Driver's Seat*'s narrative and temporal design has notable implications for our understanding of the narrator's relationship to the protagonist. No longer are Lise's present plans thought to be anticipated and undermined by her narrator's proleptic digressions; instead, the narrator can be seen to be preoccupied with the ambiguous and unsettling nature of Lise's *prior* actions and thus compelled to return continually to the recent past, replaying previously witnessed scenes and dialogue in the vain hope of elucidation. This sense of an investigative consciousness caught spiralling between present and past is even alluded to in one of the future-tense passages, wherein 'the interrogators' in the 'sad little office' go 'round and round again [. . .], always bearing the same questions like the whorling shell of a snail' (107). The same 'whorling' pattern is replicated in Spark's narrative; we might observe, following the proleptic leap to Lise being 'found tomorrow morning dead' in the passage quoted earlier, the occurrence of a backward spatial and temporal *rewinding* from 'the 'grounds of an empty villa' to the 'foreign country to which she is travelling', and to 'the flight now boarding at Gate 14', only to be followed by another future-tense projection (and subsequent rewinding) some pages later.

The 'whorling', shell-like structure of Spark's narrative demonstrates an immediate continuity between its present tense and proleptic dimensions, so that the narrative resembles something akin to a Möbius strip, whereby past and present (configured in the novel as present and future, respectively) are shown to intertwine inexorably and obsessively. This is the very opposite of omniscience: the narrator can claim no authority over, nor cleavage from, the subject of narration, and is condemned instead to spiral fascinatedly around Lise, in thrall to her mystery. As such, the obsessive, fraught and ultimately inconclusive circularity of *The Driver's Seat* only reaffirms the influence of Robbe-Grillet, who insisted that, in each of his novels, 'it is a *man* who sees, who feels, who imagines, a man situated in space and time, conditioned by his passions', so that 'the book reports nothing but his experience, limited and uncertain as it is' (Robbe-Grillet 1996c: 139). It was this aspect of the author's prose that Spark most admired; she claimed to have been fascinated by Robbe-Grillet's novelistic expressions of 'a train of consciousness that doesn't necessarily wind up to a pretty end' (Shenker 1968: 2).

Perceived in this way, the balance of power between character and narrator shifts dramatically, so that the future-tense digressions are not, as A. S. Byatt remarked in one of the novel's earliest reviews, 'cool prophetic forecasts' emanating authoritatively 'from outside, [from] the film-director's view-point, or God's' (Byatt 1970: 14) but reflective instead of a narrating consciousness that is located *inside* the storyworld, and anxiously preoccupied with the recent past. This chapter explores this drastic shift by moving away from previous readings of Lise as the hopeless object of a God-like narrative perspective, and considering her instead as a captivating figure who, even after death, commands the epistemologically limited gaze of her hopelessly fascinated narrator–voyeur. What Spark presents in *The Driver's Seat* is not simply the story of a woman determined to assert control over her life by plotting its end, as so many critics have argued, but also one of narrative mediation, epistemological impotence and, as I shall demonstrate with reference to the author's manuscripts, a specifically *masculine* anxiety to penetrate the mystery of the female Other. Spark's description of the novel as 'a study, in a way, of self-destruction' can thus be seen to relate not only to Lise's drive to death, but to the unravelling of the narrating 'self', which finds itself tormented and undone by its perennially unknowable subject.

'A whydunnit in q-sharp major'

In his biography of Spark, Martin Stannard identifies as the 'germ' of *The Driver's Seat* a newspaper article encountered by the author during a period of 'obsessive reading' in June of 1969 (2009: 363–4). The article, which Stannard describes in detail but does not cite directly, reportedly concerned the rape and murder of a German woman who had been travelling alone in Rome, and whose garishly attired body was later discovered in a park in the city. While the influence of the story ought not to be overlooked – garish clothing, sexual violence and a foreign location (and, specifically, a park as the site of a murder) all feature prominently in Spark's novel – its status as *The Driver's Seat*'s 'germ' should be discounted. A folder of the author's research material, consulted in the present study, reveals that a slightly earlier news report had first captured Spark's attention as she began to conceptualise the novel. This was a *Times* article from the previous March, which detailed an alleged 'invitation to murder' offered by a British woman to her male murderer. The woman, Brenda Gibson, had been strangled to death with a necktie after her murderer, Frank Hatton, had reportedly refused her initial request to be killed with an axe. As well as a necktie, Gibson had supplied Hatton (and, presumably, the authorities who would later investigate her death) with a handwritten note, reading simply: '"I want Frank Hatton to kill me – Brenda."' Spark had underlined this, along with the article's concluding sentences:

> Counsel said that the accused told police that he declined the invitation to axe Mrs Gibson to death, and had tried to strangle her. 'But I couldn't do it, because she was looking at me', he added.
>
> The alleged statement added: 'She then gave me a black and yellow tie. I put it around her neck and pulled it until it snapped.
>
> I was only doing it as a favour. I only did it because she asked me to.' (Anon. 1969: 2, in MFL 1969a)

The circumstances surrounding Gibson's death, discussed in the *Times* as 'a most extraordinary case' (Ibid.), share a number of immediate similarities with Spark's depiction of Lise and the nature of her murder. The women are not only of a similar age (Lise is described imprecisely as being 'as young as twenty-nine or as old as thirty-six, but hardly younger, hardly older' [18], while the *Times* article lists Gibson's age as thirty-three), but both supply their chosen male murderers with neckties as weapons, and offer explicit instructions that they wish to be killed. More significant is the manner in which both the novel and article end; each concludes with the 'unnerving statement' (107) of each woman's killer, as well as an enduring sense of mystery. Despite a number of established details concerning the identities of murderer and victim, the exact methods of killing and the items used as weapons (the knowledge of which would probably comprise the satisfying solution of a traditional detective story), the motivations behind each woman's prearranged death remain unanswered. What the newspaper report appeared to offer Spark was an example of a mystery without a clear solution, wherein the accumulation of knowledge fails to amount to a sense of either clarity or closure.

The Driver's Seat, which David Lodge describes in a dust-jacket blurb as 'a crime story turned inside out' (1974 edition, n.p.), is by no means a straightforward fictionalisation of the *Times* article, however, but rather a self-reflexive play on its ambiguous subject matter. Lise exists in the novel as a metafictional version of Gibson herself; her actions, that is, are geared not only towards bringing about a violent murder that is notably similar to the one inflicted upon her real-life counterpart, but are designed purposefully to captivate and confound her narrator's investigative and objectifying gaze. Throughout the novel, Lise demonstrates an acutely self-reflexive awareness that her death will come to be looked upon, much like Gibson's, as 'a most extraordinary case' which defies easy comprehension, and thus undermines any sense of objectifying power or epistemological mastery her narrator might have been thought to possess. Before boarding her flight at the beginning of the novel, for example, she purchases a paperback from the airport bookshop, which she clutches to her chest for the remainder of her journey, even appearing 'to display it deliberately' at various intervals (39). The book, which remains unopened and unread, and which sports a brightly coloured dust-jacket that matches Lise's own gaudy exterior, functions as a *mise en abyme* of its enigmatic owner, and, by extension, her captivating yet ultimately impenetrable self-directed plot. When Lise hands the book to a hotel porter before heading, finally, to the site of her murder, her description of the text as '"a whydunnit in q-sharp major"' (101) underscores her own status as a mystery without a tangible resolution, the key to which lies remotely outside the diatonic scale.

The Driver's Seat is itself, of course, a text for which the label 'why-dunnit' takes precedence over the conventional *who*dunnit. Indeed, that Lise's eventual murderer turns out to be Richard (instead of any other man from the novel's roll-call of undesirables, including the lecherous garage owner, Carlo, and the equally unsavoury businessman, Bill) seems almost incidental against the greater, unresolved mystery of Lise's origins and intent. This shift in emphasis – from unmasked murderer to still-elusive motive – aligns the novel with what has been termed the metaphysical detective (or 'anti-detective') story. Such a story, Patricia Merivale and Susan Elizabeth Sweeney explain in the introduction to their edited collection, *Detecting Texts: The Metaphysical Detective Story from Poe to Postmodernism* (1999), 'parodies or subverts traditional detective-story conventions – such as narrative closure and the detective's role as surrogate reader' in order to generate 'questions about mysteries of being and knowing which transcend the mere machinations of the mystery plot' (2).[2] While Merivale and Sweeney acknowledge that examples of metaphysical detective fiction can be traced back to Poe's 'self-reflexive, philosophical, consciously literary detective stories of the 1840s' (4), they attribute a groundswell of critical discourse on the genre during the late 1960s and early 1970s to literary theorists' efforts to conceptualise broad differences between modernist and postmodernist literature. If the traditional detective novel, defined by Brian McHale as 'the epistemological genre *par excellence*' (1987: 9), appeared to encapsulate modernism's broadly epistemological concerns (its faith, for instance, on positivism, teleology and totalisation), its metaphysical successor signals a shift to an ontological dominant, so that mystery spins out into mystification. Such were the claims of Michael Holquist's influential 1971 essay, 'Whodunit and Other Questions', which discussed the parodic, self-reflexive and inconclusive detective text as a reaction against 'the narcotising effect of its progenitor; instead of familiarity, it gives strangeness [. . .], instead of reassuring, they disturb. They are not an escape, but an attack' (67). The metaphysical detective story, argues Holquist, 'is non-teleological', and 'is not concerned to have a neat ending in which all the questions are answered, and which can therefore be forgotten'; by 'jumbling the well-known patterns of classical detective stories', such texts '*dramatise the void*', so that 'if, in the detective story, death must be solved, in the metaphysical detective story it is *life* which must be solved' (68).

A discussion of detective novels that are jumbled and inconclusive, and which narrativise the collapse of logic and linearity, sends us 'whorling' back once more to Robbe-Grillet. In a *prière d'insérer* for the first edition of his first published novel, *The Erasers*, the author describes the text that follows as 'a detective story event – that is, there is a murder, a detective, a victim. In one sense their roles are conventional: the murderer shoots the victim, the detective solves the problem, the victim dies' (qtd in Ewert 1999: 186). In the novel's tale of the doomed quest of Special Agent Wallas to solve the mystery surrounding a political assassination, however, these components are radically rearranged. Wallas's search proves not only fruitless (much of it is spent walking in circles around an unspecified Flemish city, while straining to interpret a series of tenuous signs as vital clues) but also self-destructive; ultimately, and with Oedipal circularity, it is *he* who commits the murder that he has been sent to investigate, after shooting Professor Dupont, who he had presumed already dead. The reported death, apparent resurrection and subsequent killing of Dupont, whose name pointedly evokes that of Poe's detective hero, C. Auguste Dupin, can be read as an acknowledgement of Poe's influence on the novel's tricksy, disorienting application of the detective plot. 'In a very Poesque way', writes Stefano Tani in his aptly titled study, *The Doomed Detective* (1984),

> the confrontation [in metaphysical detective fiction] is no longer between a detective and a murderer, but between the detective and reality, or between the detective's mind and his sense of identity, which is falling apart, between the detective and the 'murderer' in his own self. (76)

The implosive 'confrontation [. . .] between the detective and reality' is nowhere more apparent in Robbe-Grillet's œuvre than in *Jealousy*, where, as the previous chapter began to discuss, an investigative point of view surveys with mounting delirium the dimensions and positionings of the crops of a banana plantation, the architecture and furnishings of a plantation house, the changing physical dimensions of a venomous centipede, and the body and behaviour of A..., as she spends time alone or in the company of her neighbour, Franck. While less explicit in its appropriation of detective story elements than *The Erasers* or *The Voyeur* (in which a series of similarly forensic descriptions come to imply the concealed murder and sexual assault of a teenage girl), *Jealousy* retains the epistemological methods encountered in those texts only to frustrate them further, by training the investigative gaze not upon a crime scene, but repetitive, prosaic sequences of hair-brushing and table-setting, the significance of which remains either unfathomable or non-existent to begin with. Robbe-Grillet would himself insist that, contrary to the *chosiste* idea that his aim in *Jealousy* was to conjure a 'serene, whitewashed world in which man seems perfectly reconciled with his environment', his intention was to do 'exactly the opposite', and that the novel, in fact, constitutes '*an experiment with anxiety*' (Guppy 1986: n.p.). In the absence of any of the hallmarks of a conventional mystery, however (such as a crime, corpse or vital clue), *Jealousy* prompts its readers to query why the narrator's suspicion and anxiety should be aroused to begin with. A popular interpretation, first elaborated upon at length by Bruce Morrissette, posits that 'the story with its three characters – the husband, the wife, the presumed lover [Franck] – is "narrated" by the husband [. . .] who, from the vantage points in his banana plantation house [. . .] suspiciously keeps watch over his wife' (1975: 112–3). If such a reading is to be accepted – and more recent analyses of the novel have made convincing cases in its favour[3] – then it is through the obsessive, anxious quality of the novel's prose that 'the helpless figure of the cuckolded voyeur emerges' (Mäkelä 2012: 147).

By exposing its readers to the troubled cogitations of a 'cuckolded voyeur' (as opposed to the assurances of a perceptive sleuth, for instance) *Jealousy*'s 'experiment with anxiety' constitutes its author's most drastic subversion of the detective story and, in particular, the genre's archetypal protagonist. In the introduction to her study of feminism and crime fiction, *Murder by the Book?* (1994), Sally Munt characterises both the form and content of the traditional detective story as 'iconically masculine', describing the typical (and typically male) 'detective hero' as the 'focus of morality', and 'the controlled centre surrounded by chaos'. An 'effective reading' of such a text, she argues, 'must involve identification with this mediator of action, truth, and finally pleasure and relief through closure' (1). To read *Jealousy* is, by contrast, to read *jealously*. It is to read in uneasy identification with a narrative consciousness whose covetous desire for knowledge and mastery will remain frustrated and unfulfilled. Whereas Munt's 'detective hero' guides his reader authoritatively away from chaos and uncertainty and towards closure and epistemological plenitude, *Jealousy*'s impotent investigator remains caught in a feedback loop of obsessive paranoia, replaying scenes until they acquire an undue significance. In *Reading Unruly* (2014), Zahi Zalloua articulates the effect that this comes to have on the reader:

> The circular structure of [*Jealousy*] ultimately short-circuits any definitive sense of closure, halting any progression from textual obscurity to interpretive clarity. Moreover, in the absence of a linear unfolding of the narrator's jealousy, we could say that the reader enters the state of jealousy, itself a state of anxiety and irresolution, *in media res*. (122)

Jealousy's inconclusive circularity and '*in media res*' anxiety are mirrored in *The Driver's Seat* by the restless 'whorling' of its narrator's attention between present and past. What distinguishes Spark's novel from Robbe-Grillet's is its narrator's knowledge of the end; whereas

Jealousy's narrator–voyeur scrutinises the actions of A… for possible evidence of a past transgression, or to determine her propensity to commit one, Spark's narrator is in no doubt that the journey undertaken by Lise will conclude with the crime of her murder, and thus necessitates investigation. Rather than affording the narrator any sense of epistemological mastery, however, the novel's overdetermined ending functions – to return to Holquist's earlier definition of the metaphysical detective story – to 'dramatise the void' further by foregrounding crucial gaps in its narrator's knowledge. The narrative's 'acknowledgement of having knowledge', notes Judith Roof, establishes within it a 'doubled consciousness – a consciousness of telling a story and a consciousness of the story's shape', which 'makes telling itself the subject of the novel' (2001: 53). As this process of telling never comes to align the reader with any definite comprehension of Lise's thoughts or desires, however, the clearly demarcated 'shape' of her story remains curiously hollow, so that a series of effects are presented without their attendant causes. *The Driver's Seat* is thus less a novel about telling, as Roof would insist, than the failure to do so with any accuracy or authority. The novel's concern, that is, is with that which eludes and undermines the grasp and gaze of the teller. 'I admire good detective stories, their lack of frills and nonsense', Spark remarked in 2005, before describing her long-held 'fascinat[ion] [with] suspense, on which many detective stories lean. I think suspense is often heightened if the author "gives away" the plot from the beginning.' By learning of what is to come, she explained, 'the reader is then all the more anxious to find out how the conclusion came about' (Hosmer 2005: 146). It is to the novel's generation of suspense, which in turn foregrounds the interpretative anxiety experienced by its narrator (an anxiety shared by the extratextual reader), that this chapter will turn.

Doomed Deduction in the Tense Present

In a 1993 profile piece for *The New Yorker*, Spark was asked about what her interviewer, Stephen Schiff, described as her 'utterly unconventional' tendency to 'create suspense not by hiding a secret and building toward its discovery but by giving all her secrets away, again and again' (1993: 42). Of the untimely revelations Schiff had in mind – the future betrayal of Jean Brodie; the eventual martyrdom of Nicholas Farringdon in *The Girls of Slender Means* – it was Lise's heavily forecasted murder that he would cite most reverently. Perhaps to Schiff's surprise, however, Spark admitted that she had adopted the technique not from the experimental temporalities encountered in the works of postmodern contemporaries such as Brooke-Rose or Robbe-Grillet, but rather the gentle authorial assurances interspersed throughout the narratives of Anthony Trollope:

> I'll tell you what gave me that idea of giving things away. [. . .] I read that Trollope used to write some of his books in serial form for magazines. [. . .] And people wrote to him – young ladies wrote to him and said, 'Oh, please don't let the hero die or be banished or let her marry the man she doesn't love.' So he began one serial saying, 'Fair reader, do not be dismayed. She will marry the hero in the end, but just be patient while I tell you about it.' And it didn't at all take away from the suspense. They still went on reading it. It was a very interesting thing to me. I thought, well, suspense isn't just holding it back from the reader. Suspense is created even more by telling people what's going to happen. (Ibid.)

For an example of one of Trollope's amiable authorial intrusions, designed to placate readers by revealing the ending far in advance, we might look to the benevolent address which concludes Chapter Fifteen of the first volume of *Barchester Towers* (1857). Here the author assures his 'gentle-hearted' audience of the heroine's happy fate, while insisting on the importance of transparency in 'the art of telling tales':

> [L]et the gentle-hearted readers be under no apprehension whatsoever. It is not destined that Eleanor shall marry Mr. Slope or Bertie Stanhope. And here, perhaps, it may be allowed to the novelist to explain his views on a very important point in the art of telling tales. He ventures to reprobate that system which goes so far to violate all proper confidence between the author and his readers, by maintaining nearly to the end of the third volume a mystery as to the fate of their favourite personage.
> [. . .]
> Our doctrine is that the author and the reader should move along together in full confidence with each other. Let the personages of the drama undergo ever so complete a comedy of errors among themselves, but let the spectator never mistake the Syracusan for the Ephesian; otherwise he is one of the dupes, and the part of a dupe is never dignified. (1996: 155)

Keen to spare his readers the indignity of playing 'the part of a dupe', Trollope's narrator, as Meir Sternberg observes, 'elevat[es] [them] to his own level of awareness from the beginning' by sharing with his audience 'his overwhelming advantage over the characters'. It is by way of a 'rigorous abstention from withholding information through chronological displacements', notes Sternberg, that 'the narrator ensures that we shall be at every point in possession of all the material that is necessary for such a full comprehension of the present state of affairs as none of the agents [characters] can ever dream of attaining to' (1978: 271). In Spark's novel, however, any similar sense of superiority proves illusory. Having determined that 'telling people what's going to happen' might heighten suspense just as easily as relieve it, Spark locates subversive potential in Trollope's magnanimous 'doctrine'; the epistemological 'advantage' that the reader may sense that s/he possesses over a character, she recognises, can be threatened and undermined by a narrative which fails to make good on its promise.

In *The Driver's Seat*, Spark's own 'chronological displacements' – her rendering of the past as an uncertain present which unfurls before a future that is already known and set in place – come to highlight her narrator's failure of comprehension by undermining the sense of clarity and coherence that is often implicit in the retrospective mode. Barthes, in *Writing Degree Zero* (1953), identifies the French preterite (the tense otherwise known as the simple past or past historic) as the 'cornerstone of narration' and 'the ideal instrument for every construction of a world', behind which 'there always lurks a demiurge, a God or a reciter'. When using the preterite, argues Barthes, 'the narrator reduces exploded reality to a slim and pure logos, without density, without volume, without spread, and whose sole function is to unite as rapidly as possible a cause and an end' (1968: 30–1). Reconfigured in Spark's novel as a sprawling present, the preterite lacks the sense of certainty, causality and narrative mastery at the hands of 'a demiurge, a God or a reciter' that Barthes describes. Instead, the narrated past resembles most closely the 'exploded reality' of the unprocessed moment at hand. For large portions of its prose, in fact, the novel assumes the qualities that the narratologist Uri Margolin would attribute to concurrent narration, where 'the narrator does not possess [. . .] any temporal distance from the actions and events, no external later point of vantage from which s/he could survey and define the structuredness of the reported sequence as one integrated whole' (1999: 152). In the concurrent mode, Margolin explains, 'the narrated domain is a world in the process of becoming, progressively taking shape as it is being narrated, not a bounded whole', so that 'it is not yet possible [. . .] to elicit a pattern from the succession', or to 'describe it in terms of macro-coherence, plot or narrative theme' (Ibid.). This is nowhere more evident than when, while retracing Lise's movements across the foreign city to which she has travelled, the narrator fixates on a procession of figures emerging from the entrance of a hotel:

> There emerge down the steps of the hotel two women who seem to be identical twins, [. . .] followed by an important-looking Arabian figure, sheikh-like in his head dress and robes [. . .]. Two black-robed women with the lower parts of their faces veiled and their heads shrouded in drapery then make their descent, and behind them another pair appear, men-servants with arms raised, bearing aloft numerous plastic-enveloped garments on coat-hangers. (83–4)

This prolonged, bewildering narrative detour runs on exhaustively until each of the pairs, and several more besides, have completed the short journey down the steps. Instead of identifying with an authoritative investigative gaze, which might facilitate narrative progression and an increasing sense of clarity, the reader shares the narrator's passive abandonment to the moment at hand. Everything is described successively, without the assurance that might be appended to retrospective narration (the two women only 'seem' to be identical twins, for example, while the 'Arabian figure' is described as vaguely 'important-looking'). As a draft version of the same scene shows, Spark had originally presented the sequence in more concise, and considerably less ambiguous, terms:

> The newly-dethroned potentate leaves the Hilton accompanied by three men, ten suits on hangers, a wife, two daughters, two baskets containing two jumbo-sized vacuum flasks, and twenty-five other people, one a black-yashmaked woman. There is a man wearing a fez, and six crates of oranges. (MFL 1969a)

Less 'a world in the process of becoming' (in Margolin's words) than one 'reduced to significant lines' (in Barthes's), Spark's original rendering of the scene does much of the interpretive work on the reader's behalf. Here, the 'important-looking Arabian figure' is presented as a *'newly-dethroned* potentate', who '*leaves* the Hilton' accompanied by, among other people, his wife and daughters. These small details provide the scene with a motivation and *telos* that is entirely absent from the blankly successive procession of figures and objects narrated in the final version of the text; having been stripped of his title and power, one might infer, the now deposed leader, along with his family and aides, appears to be fleeing his residence to seek exile elsewhere. Similarly, the narrator's precise description of the veiled woman as 'black-yashmaked' reveals a level of narrative specificity that is unparalleled in the published novel, where the more ambiguous 'black-robed' and 'drapery' appear instead. In removing these specificities, Spark is effectively covering her authorial tracks, and confining knowledge and attention purely to the moment at hand.

Such revisions are consistent with Spark's conception of her narrator as an entity who speaks purely 'from the point of view of someone who doesn't know what anyone is thinking, but who can see, who can observe' (Frankel 1987: 454). Rather like the enfeebled figure of the 'newly-dethroned potentate', her narrator is reduced bathetically from an apparent source of wisdom and mastery (as suggested by the novel's first proleptic leap, evocative as it is of a Trollopean assurance) to a hopeless gazer, unable to offer more than a running commentary on each unfolding scene. This, as I have discussed, is a recognisable feature of the fiction of Robbe-Grillet, to whom Spark referred admiringly as a 'sighter'. As several critics have observed, the perceptual and epistemological limitations placed upon the Robbe-Grilletian narrator (particularly as encountered in *Jealousy*) come to enhance readerly identification with the disturbed source of the gaze. The author, argues Wayne C. Booth of *Jealousy*, 'wants us to receive the very touch and feel' of the novel's titular mental state 'with an intensity that is almost unbearable':

> [B]y never describing the person, actions, or thoughts of the husband, but simply leaving us to infer his reality through what is left out, [Robbe-Grillet] locks us inside the camera box, as it were, more completely than in any previous fiction. [. . .] The effect of such a novel is of an extended dramatic monologue, an intense expression of one quality of mind and soul, deliberately not judged, deliberately left unplaced, isolated from the rest of human experience. (1961: 62–3)

Over forty years after Booth's analysis, Tom McCarthy would return to the 'camera box' analogy as a means of articulating the disquieting effect produced by *Jealousy*'s intensely insular narrative. Through the novel's domestic setting, he asserts, travels 'a camera and mic-like "node" of seeing and hearing', which produces 'the effect of stating the hero's subjectivity negatively, by implication rather than affirmation' (McCarthy 2008: 392). McCarthy locates a number of cinematic parallels for this 'eerie and troubling' subjective presence, including the sinister perspective of 'The Shape' in John Carpenter's 1978 horror, *Halloween*, which the audience are forced to adopt during the film's first few minutes, as well as the viewpoint of the unidentified, crepuscular voyeur in David Lynch's *Lost Highway* (1997), who prowls the hallway and bedroom of a maritally troubled home 'armed with a camera' (the apparatus through which Lynch's viewers watch the scene; Ibid.). Such a sensation is only heightened by the paratext provided in English editions of *Jealousy* – a highly detailed floor plan of the novel's plantation house setting, not unlike those drawn up by architects, or perhaps used to scrutinise crime scenes. As Dorrit Cohn observes, this visual aid, which allows the more assiduous reader to determine with queasy accuracy the exact position of the narrator's 'node' in relation to A..., 'prompt[s] the reader to postulate a human eye (and "I") behind the [narrative] voice – not just a camera eye' (1978: 207). Such an approach may well have informed Spark's own writing practice. Her meticulous depictions of *The Driver's Seat*'s various interiors were often modelled on the layouts and dimensions of real examples. Spark used a floor-by-floor guide of Rome's La Rinascente department store, for instance, to map with perfect precision Lise's movements during her shopping trip with

her temporary travelling companion, Mrs Fiedke.⁴ Her narrator, these
aids suggest, is constructed as an investigator-cum-voyeur – a strictly
surveillant entity able to capture Lise's every action and movement with
painstaking exactitude from a set of specific vantage points, and yet
incapable, like *Jealousy*'s frustrated observer, of accessing and assessing
her state of mind.

At occasional intervals throughout *The Driver's Seat*, the narrator
pauses to acknowledge the limits of looking. A description of Lise
'lifting the corners of her carefully packed things' after arriving at her
hotel room, for instance, adjoins the speculation that she does so 'as if
in absent-minded accompaniment to some thought, who knows what?'
(49). While such questions pass without further reflection in the published text (indeed, their use might appear purely rhetorical, designed to
express an air of cool indifference towards Lise's inner life), this is not
the case in some of the draft passages written in the author's notebooks.
In one such passage, intended to appear during the narration of Lise's
flight abroad, Spark has her narrator digress from a seemingly detached
description of the interaction between Lise and Bill, who are seated
beside one another on the plane, to expound self-consciously and at
length on the impossibility of reading her mind:

> (Her thoughts) – Who knows? Largely, all that we have to go on, we of
> the ethos of human individuality, when summing up a passing stranger, are
> sound-effects and visual appearances. At this present moment, when Lise sits
> by Bill in the plane, it is not permissible to approach another member of our
> species as do cats, who not only prick their ears for sound and watchfully
> fix their eyes, but also cautiously smell, who perhaps rub against each other
> and lick each other, all by way of conquering the unknown by all five senses.
> With us, after the formal handshake, which generally tells us nothing except
> whether the hitherto unknown person shakes too roughly, has clammy hands,
> or is nice enough to take our hand and respond in a simple, unremarkable
> way. In love-affairs and in marriage, there all our five senses sooner or later
> begin to penetrate the other's mystery. But even then, who in our civilisation
> has not been left wondering still? (MFL 1969a)

What is encountered here is neither the objective, dispassionate mode
of narration outlined in a *chosiste* interpretation of the *nouveau roman*,
for example, nor the assured proclamation of an omniscient observer.
Instead, Spark's narrator is cast as an anxious and eminently fallible
entity, who, being 'of the ethos of human individuality', is capable only
of producing limited, subjective recordings of various 'sound-effects
and visual appearances'. There is something clumsy and convoluted
about these phrases, which betray their speaker's discomfort at being
faced with the mystery of 'another member of our species'. It is perhaps

understandable, then, that the narrator should entertain the idea of 'conquering the unknown' with the heightened sensory perceptivity of a cat. In the published text, as I discussed in the last chapter, similar animal sensitivities are assigned to Lise herself: 'she is a stag scenting the breeze', notes her observer (with a degree of envy, we might now infer), 'moving step by step [. . .], search[ing] for a certain air-current, a glimpse and an intimation' (72–3). This rare, and ultimately expunged, instance of narratorial self-reflection, in which the 'absent-I' of the *nouveau romancier* gazes fretfully inward, articulates most clearly what I have claimed to be the novel's central concern: the investigator–narrator's anxious and unsatisfied desire to gain epistemological purchase by 'penetrat[ing] the other's mystery'.

The Driver's Seat is thus a text which functions, as both Spark's debt to Trollope and the content of the above passage indicate so persuasively, as a fictional account of thwarted reading and doomed detection. To an extent, the novel is self-reflexive in the sense that Garrett Stewart, in his 1996 study, *Dear Reader: The Conscripted Audience in Nineteenth-Century British Fiction*, claims novels by authors including Trollope, Austen and Dickens to be. Through their production of 'narrative parables of which reading is itself the subject', argues Stewart, such authors position their readers 'to extrapolate some adjusted orientation towards the continuing event of reading' (1996: 343–4). Readers of *The Driver's Seat* – finding themselves positioned indeterminately between the nineteenth century and the *nouveau roman* – are oriented instead towards the continued *failure* of the 'event of reading'. By revealing its ending up front, before confining its audience to a dilated narrative present which fails to offer more than a surface-level account of the various sights and sounds registered by a narrator 'of human individuality', Spark's novel (an 'experiment with anxiety' just as unnervingly resistant to comprehension as *Jealousy*) can be seen first to invite, then drastically and deliberately to frustrate, its own investigatory premise. What this uncomfortable imbrication of certainty and doubt comes to foreground, of course, is the essential illegibility of Lise herself. The narrator can but look on in bemusement as Lise forges determinedly ahead – a closed and unreadable book: a detective in her own right, her senses attuned to a frequency to which her narrator lacks access – to a certain yet perplexing *dénouement*. Spark's foregrounding of the ending, from which the investigation ensues, thus induces an estrangement in Brechtian terms (another 'certain detachment') that makes readers recognise their own voyeuristic positioning.

Taking the Reins: The Gaze and its Return

Who sees in *The Driver's Seat*? Who strives and strains to scrutinise Lise's image and actions in the hope of 'penetrat[ing] [her] mystery'? To compose the novel, Spark told one interviewer, had entailed 'finding the tone, deciding who the unseen, invisible narrator *is*, and what role he's going to play' (Frankel 1987: 454). Although it remains unclear as to whether Spark's use of 'he' points to a specifically *male* narrator, there are reasonable grounds for suspecting this to be the case. Indeed, the diegetic world of *The Driver's Seat* – within which, argues Bran Nicol, the novel's narrator lurks 'like a stalker' (Nicol 2010: 113) – is positively *defined* by male perspectives, teeming as it does with men who view Lise with varying degrees of fear, desire, opprobrium, bewilderment and revulsion. The novel begins, for example, with a description of the 'frightened eyeglasses' of Lise's 'quivering [male] superior', who looks on in horror as his obstreperous employee erupts into fits of laughter and tears, 'all in a flood' (9). Lise later becomes a source of untrammelled lust for men including Bill, whose expressions of rabid licentiousness remind her of '"Red Riding-Hood's grandmother"' ('"Do you want to eat me up?"' she responds, returning his gaze – *all the better to see him with* – with a raised eyebrow and a mocking laugh [27]). She is to Carlo the hideous yet covetable product of generations of prostitution and infidelity – appearing simultaneously as an 'exotic [. . .], clearly available treasure', and a whore 'conceived in some ditch and born in another', her grandfather having been 'ten times cuckolded' long before (75) – who not only escapes his predatory sexual advances, but vanishes from view, having stolen his car. To Richard, she is a tempting yet terrifying reminder of his own murderous capabilities, a living Medusa who 'cause[s] a kind of paralysis' (27) when her eyes look back at his (we might here recall Frank Hatton's remark, underlined in the *Times* article kept by Spark, that he had initially struggled to murder Brenda Gibson '"because she was looking at me"').

Perhaps most prominent among the novel's numerous anxious and anguished male gazes, however, are those belonging to 'the policemen', whose 'hot and [. . .] barking voices' resound throughout their 'sad little office' as they struggle to retrace Lise's movements and uncover her motives (107). As I earlier suggested, the office is a space in which the novel's proleptic digressions (concerned as they are with the discovery and investigation of Lise's murder) might find their diegetic locus, making the viewpoints of such men fundamental to the production and progression of the narrative itself. While critical analyses have largely neglected such an interpretation, preferring instead to consider how Lise's death might look from the lofty perspectives of her God and/or author, cinematic and theatrical adaptations of the novel have brought it to the fore. In Giuseppe Patroni Griffi's ambitious yet critically maligned 1974 film, *The Driver's Seat* (released in some countries as *Identikit*, a title which underscores the centrality of the police investigation to the progression of its plot), the on-screen action is regularly halted by freeze-frames, so that the once moving colour image, now presented as a monochrome still, is recontextualised as an item of evidence on the male detectives' office wall. A similar approach is taken in Laurie Sansom's 2015 theatrical adaptation, which utilises a series of staging techniques, including live video projections, transparent partition walls and revolving stage sets, to foreground the ongoing nature of the men's discussions, from which the on-stage performance appears to germinate as both collaborative, piecemeal recollection and dramatic reconstruction. To borrow a term applied by Thomas Elsaesser in his analysis of the disorienting framing and reframing devices encountered in Michael Haneke's psychological thriller, *Hidden* (2005), the recontextualisation of on-screen events as police evidence in Patroni Griffi's film and Sansom's play constitutes a major 'ontological switch'. This effect, achieved by way of 'editing, camera movement, [and] framing' in Haneke's film, induces 'a particular kind of vertigo' within the viewer, who must suddenly adjust his or her orientation towards what has been viewed (Elsaesser 2010: 64). A similar effect can be seen to be produced in the final scene of Spark's novel, which suggests that the preceding narrative emanates from a space *within* the story, rather than an omniscient, authoritative external position.

To (re)conceptualise *The Driver's Seat* as a text which emerges metaleptically from the 'sad little office' – spilling, perhaps, from the 'typewriter' that 'ticks out' details of the inconclusive investigation (107) – is to align the fictive gaze that orders novelistic narration with the investigative (and emphatically masculine) one depicted within the story. Lise is thus presented to readers as the elusive, and therefore unnerving, object of male perception, whose behaviour confounds and unsettles her narrator in much the same way as it does the various men she encounters over the course of her journey. Consequently, the novel's subversive power emerges through its presentation of an act of apparent masculine dominance – the subjection of a woman to an intense and exacting narrative gaze – as one which exists, in fact, in an uneasy dialectic with the feminine, indecipherable sight/site of visual fascination. In this respect, the novel invites further comparison with *Jealousy*, whose 'husband–narrator', as Jeremy Lane argues, is transformed into an 'anxious subject of desire' when confronted with A...'s enduring mystery (2002: 199). The narrator's exhaustive efforts to locate conclusive evidence of A...'s 'brazen sexuality', Lane continues, should thus be read as a series of 'displacements of a more general anxiety about the potential for bound- ary loss and loss of male control', which bear particular relevance to the novel's 'colonial context' (201). Zahi Zalloua, noting that 'jealousy' is 'etymologically derived from the ancient Greek *zelos*', similarly argues that Robbe-Grillet's narrative is driven by 'a fervent desire or *zeal* [. . .] for an object that lies beyond [the narrator's] mastery', which 'robs the narrator's gaze of its habitual sense of power' (2014: 119–20).

A striking parallel emerges here between the staging, in each novel, of an objectifying masculine perspective that is directed towards a threaten- ingly enigmatic female figure, and the conceptualisation of the male gaze as a sadistic scopic drive in Laura Mulvey's seminal 1975 essay, 'Visual Pleasure and Narrative Cinema'. With her own gaze trained upon the workings of classical Hollywood cinema, Mulvey utilises aspects of Lacanian psychoanalysis to analyse the ways in which such films come to reproduce and reaffirm structures of patriarchal authority and male narcissism by reconstituting their viewers as omnipotent masculine sub- jects (regardless of the individual viewer's gender). The filmic spectator, argues Mulvey, identifies with the central male protagonist and 'projects his look onto that of his like, his screen surrogate, so that the power of the male protagonist as he controls events coincides with the active power of the erotic look, giving a satisfying sense of omnipotence' (1989: 20). The plot and action of traditional Hollywood narratives, therefore, are the exclusive domain of male characters, whereas women appear as the subservient spectacles of masculine desire; the viewer's gaze is thus scopophilic in the sense outlined by Freud, who 'associated scopophilia with taking other people as objects, subjecting them to a controlling and curious gaze' (16). In a sexually imbalanced world, Mulvey asserts, 'pleasure in looking has been split between active/male and passive/ female', so that 'the determining male gaze projects its fantasy on to the female figure', who finds herself 'simultaneously looked at and dis- played, with [her] appearance coded for strong visual and erotic impact so that [she] can be said to connote *to-be-looked-at-ness*' (19). This priv- ileged, 'active' and heterosexual male gaze, Mulvey argues, is dictated by Oedipal anxieties concerning loss and castration, which revolve around the threatening figure of the female Other. Such anxieties, she asserts, are resolved through the psychic mechanisms of voyeurism and fetishism. Whereas the former is related to the scopophilic desire to investigate the hitherto unknown Other from a vantage point of privilege and power, the latter seeks to avoid investigation entirely by transforming the source of anxiety into an unthreatening object of desire. Hollywood cinema is thus shown to abound with imaginary strategies and scenarios geared towards achieving either end – from voyeuristic narratives of investigation and detection, to the fetishistic fragmentation of the female body through close-up shots and nimble editing techniques. We can see a fluctuation between the two strategies in both *The Driver's Seat* and *Jealousy*. In each text, the female protagonists are figuratively and fetishistically dismembered by an objectifying narrative gaze; A...'s narrator fixates obsessively on her 'black mass' of hair (Robbe-Grillet 1959: 66), for example, while Lise's makes exhaustive references to her 'slightly parted' lips. Similarly, both A... and Lise are subjected to an investigative viewpoint which seeks to 'solve' their central mystery and establish their guilt or madness. Such techniques might work to allay, as Mulvey contends, the masculine fear of castration and disempowerment.

In the decades since its emergence, Mulvey's thesis has been criticised for its rigid representation of the woman on screen as an objectified 'Other', its deterministic application of Lacanian psychoanalysis, and its constrictive view of masculinity as only ever prevailing and possessive.[5] Indeed, given the Oedipal anxieties which underpin it, Mulvey's theory offers scant exploration of the male gaze as vulnerable, fearful or impotent; nor does it consider either the numerous cultural, social and historical factors which might differentiate masculinities, for example, or the existence of a specifically female or *feminine* gaze in place of her own model's inflexibly gendered binary of active/passive looking. It is for reasons such as these that Alice Ferrebe, in an incisive essay on scopic power and sexual politics in the fiction of John Fowles, chooses to 'quibble with the nomenclature of Mulvey's "male gaze" in Hollywood cinema' (2004: 207). Here Ferrebe cites not only 'the essentialism inherent in the adjective "male"', but also 'the fact that, striving as it does to transfer all intimations of weakness to the subaltern characters within the diegesis, it is in fact panicked, fraught with inadequacy'. What Mulvey might define as an 'omniscient, omnipotent, objectifying mode of looking' is thus, for Ferrebe, 'looking at its most lacking' (208–9).

Ferrebe's reassessment of Mulvey's 'male gaze' as ultimately 'panicked' and 'fraught with inadequacy' (208) is especially pertinent to my own examination of the anguished and epistemologically limited perspective of Spark's narrator. Rather than simply expose such limitations, however, Spark has Lise anticipate and ironise the machinations of the male, investigative gaze that will later struggle to comprehend her. As she heads defiantly towards her tragic *dénouement*, Lise assumes and discards public images and identities at will. She speaks, as she prepares to board her flight at the beginning of the novel, in a naive and docile 'little-girl tone' (19), and then in a 'foreignly accented English' while masquerading, shortly thereafter, as an effervescent holidaymaker who claims to be '"look[ing] for a gay time"' (22–3). Some hours later she will adopt the invented persona of a widowed New Jersey schoolteacher, before switching to that of 'a temptress in the old-fashioned style' (78). At other intervals she will accost a policeman with a handgun, make a public display of discarding her passport, become embroiled in a student demonstration, shriek angrily at a chambermaid, perform a rendition of a nursery rhyme, and – perhaps most incongruously of all – scrawl an obscure message in lipstick across a pair of gift-wrapped slippers. Lise's shape-shifting efforts are even aided, to some extent, by the various oppressive and essentialising cultural standards to which women in *The Driver's Seat* are subjected; if, in the Northern European city where the novel begins, her outlandish outfit marks her out as a madwoman and therefore deserving of 'the high, hacking cough-like ancestral laughter of the streets' (17), it signifies that she is 'of the street prostitute class' (51) when she arrives in Southern Europe. As she transitions effortlessly between various voices, guises and spaces, Lise (whose name reads ana-grammatically as 'lies') skilfully manipulates her *'to-be-looked-at-ness'* so that she may hide in plain sight, wearing 'a look of satisfaction at her own dominance over the situation' all the while (9). In doing so, she eludes and undermines the multiple, suspicious gazes of the men around her, while ironically offering scraps of these invented identities to the devouring gaze of her narrator (none of which will, of course, reveal anything of her essential self).

Rather like the dazzling dress that she tries on in the novel's opening scene – its disorienting pattern of 'green and purple squares on a white background, with blue spots within the green squares, cyclamen spots within the purple' proving 'too vivid for most customers' taste' (1) – Lise blinds her narrator with a kaleidoscopic procession of mesmeric, fabricated selves. As a consequence, she casts doubt upon any simple correlation between scopic apprehension and epistemological power; to see, her actions imply, is not necessarily to comprehend and control, but rather to risk succumbing to endless fascination. In her 1990 article, '"The Situation of the Looker-On": Gender, Narration and Gaze in *Wuthering Heights*', Beth Newman follows Mulvey in claiming the gaze as 'the privilege of a male subject, a means of relegating women [. . .] to the status of object (of representation, discourse, desire, etc.)' (1990: 1031). Newman qualifies this stance, however, with reference to the Medusa – described elsewhere as 'a spectacular subject of the gaze, the ultimate example of the terrible effects of looking, a prime example of male gazing with potentially fatal results' (Greven 2006: 137). What makes the Medusa so threatening to her spectator, Newman suggests, is the spectator's 'knowledge that the other sees and therefore resists being reduced to an appropriable object', thus 'disturbing the pleasure the male subject takes in gazing and the hierarchical relations by which he asserts his dominance' (1990: 1031). Here Newman engages with Stephen Heath's reading of Lacan's seminars on the gaze, in which Heath argues that woman is absent as the subject of the gaze *except* when she 'sees herself seeing herself' – when she recognises herself, that is, as the object of the gaze. 'If the woman looks', argues Heath, 'the spectacle provokes, castration is in the air, the Medusa's head is not far off; thus, she must not look, is absorbed herself on the side of the seen' (1978: 92).

As evinced by her interactions with the likes of Richard, Carlo and Bill, Lise is extraordinarily adept at unsettling these 'hierarchical relations' by anticipating and returning the gazes directed towards her. The same is true on a metafictional level; no longer a submissive spectacle 'absorbed [. . .] on the side of the seen', or flattened into the *nouveau roman*'s depthless 'thing-world' (Meretoja 2014: 94), Lise demonstrates, through her incongruous exhibitionism, an acute awareness of her status as the fascinating subject of an incomprehensible mystery. Her behaviour thus amounts to a destabilising *returned gaze*, in that it confronts the narrator (and, by extension, the extratextual reader) with her radical resistance to 'representation, discourse, desire' (Newman 1990: 1031). As Newman asserts, 'when a woman looks back she asserts her "existence" as a subject, her place outside the position of object to which the male gaze relegates her and by which it defines her as "woman"' (1032). With this in mind, we might briefly observe the ironic tendency, among male critics in particular, to attempt to *solve* Lise definitively by minimising the components of her self-spun mystery to a set of uncomplicated indicators of mental illness: 'Lise's terrible outfits are clues to her derangement', deduces John Lanchester in his introductory essay to a recent edition of the novel (2006: x); 'Throughout the novel', observes Norman Page, '[Lise] complains, quarrels, speaks more loudly than is normal [. . .] and this behaviour is [. . .] evidence of her serious mental instability' (1990: 72); '[Lise] is committing suicide', Ian Rankin surmises from a scant selection of details concerning the protagonist's private life, 'because she has been a lonely anonymous woman' (1985: 154). Each reading constitutes a vain attempt to discern and dictate the meaning of Lise's quest, and thus betrays an anxious refusal to attend to the significance of her defiant inscrutability.

Spark would make Lise's subversive resistance to the gaze rather more explicit in drafted dialogue between the protagonist and her father, who never appears in the published text. In a telephone conversation between the pair, Lise's father berates his daughter for her alleged history of waywardness and sexual promiscuity, before reminding her of the duty she owes to both her family and her faith. Immediately afterwards, Lise dismisses her father's orders as ridiculous in a call to her aunt, who is sympathetic to her grievances and mindful of her absent mother. Quoted below, these exchanges take place the evening before Lise's journey, the first beginning – like her interaction with the shop assistant at the start of the novel – *in media res*:

> Her father's voice says on the telephone, 'With Margot and with me. Your father and your sister. You should be home to join your sister after she has been away at school all these months. She looks for you and you're never here. You want to go on your own to meet men. Men all the time. You will never meet a good man going through the streets like a . . .'
>
> She laughs happily and waits for him to go on. [. . .]
>
> 'You will never prosper, Lise. A daughter. God knows your heart. The Lord is at the helm. The Lord holds the reins. You will never go against the Lord'.
>
> She says, 'What about modern travel? Is the Lord in the pilot's cabin and in the driver's seat, or did it all stop with ocean voyages?'
>
> 'What do you say? I don't understand you?'
>
> 'I've got to go now, Pa'. She laughs and hangs up. For a second. Then she dials another number and the voice answers.
>
> 'Auntie Bell?'
>
> 'Lise. You're off tomorrow'.
>
> 'Yes, early. I've just had a call from Pa. He's crazy'.
>
> 'What can you do?' says the aunt.
>
> 'You can't take him seriously', says Lise. 'Religious mania'.
>
> 'Your poor mother', says her aunt, 'is well out of it'.
>
> 'Absolutely'. (MFL 1969a)

In the published version of *The Driver's Seat*, Spark replaced these exchanges with two brief and uneventful telephone calls: one with Margot (who, the above passage reveals, is in fact Lise's sister – a detail that the novel neglects to mention), concerning the banal practicalities of the coming day's journey, and another with an unidentified well-wisher, who asks Lise to send a postcard from her travels. In contrast, the conversations with Lise's father and aunt possess far greater significance in terms of what they reveal about the life and authority that she is preparing to leave behind. What Lise refers to as her father's '"Religious mania"' concerns his belief that her intentions are known to both himself and God, neither of whom she will dare disobey. In proclaiming (incorrectly, as it will transpire) his knowledge of Lise's desire for sexual liaisons with men, the father paraphrases from the Book of Jeremiah:

The heart is deceitful above all things, and desperately wicked: who can know it? I the Lord search the heart, I try the reins, even to give every man according to his ways, and according to the fruit of his doings. (Jeremiah 17: 9–10)

'Reins' is an archaic term for the kidneys, which, in conjunction with the heart, are referred to throughout the Bible as the figurative locus of the desires, thoughts and emotions that constitute 'the central essence of a person' (Eknoyan 2005: 3468). As internal organs, the reins are 'hidden from view but accessible to the look of God' (Ibid.), who may examine them in order to judge the purity of the mortal soul. Drawing a connection between the apparent visibility of Lise's desires and her powerlessness before God, her father switches to the more conventional usage of 'reins', having reminded his daughter that '"the Lord is at the helm"'. Lise responds by co-opting the metaphor – *taking the reins*, as it were – with literal references to the modes of '"modern travel"' by which she will make her journey, and of which, she suggests, the Lord is not in command. This playful and cryptic response, which bemuses her father and cuts dead his castigation, is also notable for its mention of '"the driver's seat"' a phrase which is never uttered by Lise or any other character in the published text. Although the novel's title might seem a rather uncomplicated metaphor for personal autonomy and free will, its use here suggests, more specifically, Lise's rebellious assertion of her essential *illegibility* to man (or to *men*) and God alike. While her father associates God's scrutiny of one's 'reins' with the divine 'reins' that keep her or him under control, Lise's stated possession of '"the driver's seat"' articulates her steadfast rejection of both principles.

More intriguing still is the possibility, raised during her telephone call with Auntie Bell, that Lise is not the first in her family to seek to evade the father's scrutiny; Lise's '"poor mother"', remarks her aunt, is now '"well out of it"'. While it is conceivable that Lise's mother has chosen of her own volition to live contentedly apart from the family unit, Auntie Bell's sympathetic use of '"poor"' may indicate that she is dead or in some way ill or incapacitated, and yet still better off for being free of the father. This ambiguous fate raises further questions concerning the motivation behind Lise's journey. Is Lise, in rejecting her daughterly responsibilities and engineering her own mysterious and violent death, attempting, perhaps like her mother before her, to escape the persistent, judgemental gaze of her father by making herself strange and unknowable? If Lise is a 'spectacle [who] provokes', then her mother is one who vanishes altogether. In both cases, the father's control is lost, and the reins (in both uses of the word) are obscured and out of reach. The spectre of jealousy/*Jealousy* is evoked once more; the voyeuristic threat, as in Robbe-Grillet's novel, is installed within the family unit, and linked closely to a diminished masculine authority and to an anxiety over a steadily waning influence.

Although Spark chose to remove the father's voice and other details concerning Lise's family from the published text, a similarly anxious interplay between spectator and spectacle is discernible in the narrator's intense preoccupation with keeping Lise permanently in view, accessing her thoughts and uncovering her secrets. In this sense, the narrative can be read in its entirety as an extended attempt, on the narrator's part, to guard against the threat of the female Other by investigating and objectifying her, after which she may be put finally to rest. This endeavour, as we have seen, results only in continued failure and frustration. In anticipating and returning the male gaze with her own spectacular display, Lise effects the Medusa-like paralysis of her observer; instead of telling her story and making it – and her – his own, the narrator is frozen in fascination, and tortured by a maddening inability to 'penetrate the other's mystery'. We might thus read the novel's deeply unsettling ending, in which Richard 'plunges into' Lise against her will, in terms of this unfulfilled masculine desire to 'penetrate' and possess. Treated here as a vile assertion of phallic power, the act of rape becomes a pathetic retaliation against a threatened castration, which makes explicit the psychosexual dimensions of the male gaze. This applies not only to Richard, who seeks to overpower Lise's emasculatory ability to return his gaze and instruct him on how to murder her, but also to the narrator, whose grim fixation upon the attacker's penetrative 'plunge' betrays his own frustrated need to comprehend and control her. Far from demonstrating Lise's failure, as an artist *manqué*, to avoid having her plans scuppered by superior creative forces, the closing scene depicts the endless collapse of the fictive gaze – a scopic drive that is masculine, vulnerable and eminently self-destructive.

'Is the Lord in the pilot's cabin and in the driver's seat?'

While Lise's question to her father (along with the rest of the terse exchange shared between the pair) never found its way into *The Driver's Seat*, its implications ironically anticipate the predominant tone of the novel's critical reception. Indeed, if the majority of readings of *The Driver's Seat* are to be accepted, the answer to her question is an emphatic *yes*. The novel, such readings contend, is concerned almost exclusively with the containment of Lise's 'plot' within a divine 'script', over which she lacks any control. Lise's macabre machinations, such readings assume, occur within a still-unfolding narrative present, yet are known to – and even anticipated by – an existentially and epistemologically superior narrator, who stands rather uncomplicatedly for both her mighty author and almighty God. A thorough re-evaluation of Spark's 'spiny and treacherous masterpiece' (Schiff 1993: 42) is long overdue. Spark's narrator is neither assured nor authoritative, and the text's proleptic digressions demonstrate little in the way of omniscience. What is more, Lise remains utterly inscrutable, even as her journey reaches its end.

Contrary to the assumption that her plot-making is contained, comprehended and consequently undermined by the revelation of a wider temporal frame, Lise's practice of fashioning her life and death into an unfathomable mystery comes to hold her narrator in rapt fascination. The narrative, then, can be seen to fixate obsessively and unwaveringly on Lise's actions, rather than demonstrate their insignificance in relation to a greater 'script'. The narrator – something of a cross between *Jealousy*'s disintegrating husband and the disoriented investigator of a metaphysical detective text – is doomed to remain caught on her trail, repeating a story that moves in a shell-like spiral rather than towards a definitive, illuminating conclusion. A similar effect is transferred to the audience; seduced by Spark's textual machinations, the reader is lulled into a false sense of mastery, believing erroneously that s/he possesses an advantage over Lise by knowing the ending in advance. The seemingly climactic moment of Lise's murder arrives, however, without elucidation. We are soon back to the 'sad little office', where her steps shall be retraced once more.

Given her association with death, deviance and secrecy, Lise can be aligned quite comfortably with the *femme fatale*, described in Mary Ann Doane's influential study of feminism and classical Hollywood cinema, *Femmes Fatales* (1991), as 'the figure of a certain discursive unease, a potential epistemological trauma', whose 'most striking characteristic, perhaps, is that she never really is what she seems to be' (1). For Doane, films featuring the *femme fatale* tend to be concerned with 'transforming the threat of the woman into a secret, something which must be aggressively revealed, unmasked, discovered', thus ensuring that 'the figure is fully compatible with the epistemological drive of narrative, the hermeneutic structuration of the classical text' (Ibid.). Amending one of the central tenets of Mulvey's thesis in light of Doane's, Katherine Farrimond proposes that 'the femme fatale [. . .] is presented not merely as to-be-looked-at, but as to-be-*solved*' (2017: 16). Lise, however, inhabits no such 'classical text', and no conventional *femme fatale* role. Her self-described 'whydunnit' remains clasped tightly shut, her 'slightly parted' lips refuse to tell her secrets, and any act of 'unmask[ing]' only reveals a proliferation of other masks layered beneath. Her elusive presence thus evokes Doane's discussion of the masquerade:

> The masquerade, in flaunting femininity, holds it at a distance. [. . .] The masquerade's resistance to patriarchal positioning would therefore lie in its denial of the production of femininity as closeness, as presence-to-itself [. . .]. To masquerade is to manufacture lack in the form of a certain distance between oneself and one's image. (1991: 25–6)

In this sense, Lise is the ultimate embodiment of what Ruth Whittaker terms 'the Sparkian woman' – one who is a masterful 'creator of fictions', and who 'efficiently reorganises events in her favour' (1982: 113). Intended by Spark to appear as a 'destiny-driven creature', preoccupied with 'going direct' to the ending that she has so clearly envisaged (Frankel 1987: 452), Lise fosters the same sense of 'discursive unease' described by Doane by making herself illegible ('manufactur[ing] lack') and thus evading control. This 'unease' remains pointedly unrelieved, as Lise's mesmeric drive to death comes to subsume the 'epistemological drive' through which narrator and reader each attempt to solve her mystery. Indeed, in deciding against including details of Lise's domineering father and mysteriously absent mother, Spark further frustrates the readerly desire for origins and interpretive 'keys', so that her text becomes instead an encounter with loss – of knowledge and bearings, beginnings and conclusions. It is grimly fitting, then, that Spark's bewildering chronicle of a death foretold should close not with a restoration of logic and order, but rather a desperate stab in the dark.

Conclusion: Leaving the Hothouse

If it were only true that all's well that ends well, if only it were true.
The Hothouse by the East River (1)

This book seeks to end well by taking in the fetid, febrile air of Spark's most extravagant work of metafiction, *The Hothouse by the East River*, as a means of uniting the various strands of literary experimentation, satire, subversion and social critique discussed over the course of the preceding chapters. First, however, I wish to focus on an obscure and hitherto unexamined by-product of that novel's tortuous gestation. *The Hothouse by the East River* was written over the course of seven years, an unprecedented amount of time for Spark to spend on a novel (*The Mandelbaum Gate*, her previous longest, had taken a little over two). Within this lengthy period of writing and rumination, Spark conducted extensive research into an eccentrically diverse selection of subjects – among them, the pathophysiology of electric shocks, the specificities of hotel cuisine, the workings of telephone wires and the hatching of silkworm eggs – that bear only tangential relevance to the content of the novel she eventually wrote. Spark also composed strange fragments of poetic verse during this time, which she compiled among her ever-growing collection of notes and research for *Hothouse*. One such fragment, quoted in full below, depicts a world of desperate squalor and contagion, which the poem's speaker looks upon with apparent confusion and despair:

Who are there that contaminate the spring,
That bring lousy associations to the nightingales
And who follow not even the laws of the Congo jungles
of the world, but of the treacherous gutter
the gutter of diphtheria, the gutters of profound contagion
and polluted words? (MFL c.1968–73)

The poem fragment may seem to be little more than a scrap of marginalia, and thus inconsequential to the end result of Spark's years-long project. What this fragment reveals, in fact, is a subject that would become central to the published novel: the destruction of a seductive ideal by a force of 'profound contagion'. The nature of that ideal is represented by the nightingales, whose appearance calls to mind the theme and content of John Keats's 'Ode to a Nightingale' (1819). In Keats's poem, the titular bird appears to sing from beyond the parameters of human life, and thus entices the speaker with the prospect of 'transgress[ing] the melancholy laws of mortality' (Roe 1997: 200) and arriving in an idealised imaginative realm, far removed from human suffering and death. The speaker envisages how, following his own death, his body shall merge into the earth while the nightingale's eternal song plays on without pause:

> While thou art pouring forth thy soul abroad
> In such an ecstasy!
> Still wouldst thou sing, and I have ears in vain –
>   To thy high requiem become a sod. (Keats 1995: 214, ll. 56–8)

In Spark's verse, by contrast, something is unnervingly amiss. The nightingale, described by Keats as an 'immortal Bird' who 'wast not born for death' (Ibid. l. 61), here inhabits a putrid, 'contaminate[d]' world where it finds itself infested with 'lousy associations'. The dream of transcendence is now diseased and dying, the 'spring' of eternal life having since degraded into the dismal 'gutter of diphtheria'. Whereas 'Ode to a Nightingale' entertains the possibility of escaping into an idyllic realm far removed from mortal concerns, Spark's poem fixates instead on the foul stagnancy that follows after 'pouring forth thy soul abroad'. How did this awful state come to be? Crucially, 'Ode to a Nightingale' ends with the speaker rejecting the idealism captured in the bird's song ('Adieu!' he cries to the nightingale, 'the fancy cannot cheat so well / As she is fam'd to do, deceiving elf'), leaving the creature to depart to 'the next valley-glades' to enthral another passing poet (Ibid. ll. 73–4; l. 78). Spark's poem suggests the opposite; the 'deceiving elf' of the imagination has taken over, producing a false and 'treacherous' unreality built entirely from 'polluted words'.

Much like Spark's untitled, unpublished and likely unfinished poem, *The Hothouse by the East River* concerns itself with a fantasy of 'transgress[ing] the melancholy laws of mortality' that has since run rampant and turned toxic and grotesque. The novel narrates a posthumous fever dream emanating from the unquiet spirit of Paul Hazlett (his surname, 'has let', indicates his mind's submission to an unruly fiction), who has denied the plain fact of his death with a placatory vision of eternal life, abundant wealth, omniscient control and a subservient wife. Paul's name is therefore also, perhaps, an allusion to William Hazlitt's *Liber Amoris; or, The New Pygmalion* (1823). Hazlitt's narrative, described as 'one of the first extended treatments in a line of modern writing on men who try to make women fit their illusions', retells the Pygmalion legend as a man's attempt to force the object of his affections 'into the mold of a goddess' (Ready 1975: 46; 42). While Paul cannot be said to love or indeed idolise his wife, his entrapment of Elsa within a rigid role inside the hothouse of his spectral imagination bears a certain similarity to the themes at play in Hazlitt's text (and the Pygmalion legend). As he and the reader discover simultaneously at the end of the novel, Paul had been killed in a V-2 blitz of London in 1944, when a bomb obliterated the train in which he and Elsa were preparing to leave the city. What precedes this illusion-shattering revelation is a dream of life in 1970s New York, where Paul and Elsa (along with their two invented children, Pierre and Katerina) live affluently in a luxurious apartment 'fourteen stories above everything' (14).[1] The eye snags on those 'stories'; Paul, the word signifies, resides high above New York inside an exceedingly tall tale of his own construction. This is the novel's second clue that all is not as it seems. The first arrives in the form of Elsa's shadow, which falls toward the sun rather than against it. By defying the physics of light, the shadow's strange angle poses a nagging challenge to the validity of the (un)reality that Paul has summoned into being. Not that he is prepared to take notice of this: 'Paul cannot acknowledge it', remarks the narrator, '[a] mirage, that shadow of hers. Not a fact' (8).

Paul can only ignore Elsa for so long, however. No longer content with having her errant shadow offset her photographed image in the family portraits that decorate the apartment, she now seeks to demolish Paul's edifice of world-sustaining 'stories' with destabilising tales of her own devising. At the outset of the novel, Elsa deliberately incites her husband's jealousy with news of a recent encounter with Helmut Kiel, a German prisoner of war with whom she had an affair while she and Paul were stationed at a Political Intelligence compound during wartime. Paul denounces her claims as nonsensical (another of Elsa's non-facts), knowing Kiel to have died in the intervening years, but soon descends into a state of febrile paranoia. Attempts at interrogating Elsa only exacerbate Paul's latent fears; his wife responds to his questions by communicating in arcane metaphors and oblique literary allusions, thus contaminating Paul's self-made and eminently legible universe with a series of threateningly impenetrable mysteries. Submitting Elsa to psychoanalysis results in further failure and frustration. '"He hasn't got his material yet,"' Elsa remarks gleefully of her bemused analyst, Garven: '"He's looking for the cause, and all I'm giving him are effects. It's lovely"' (48). In instances such as these, Elsa, with her indecipherable language and her swooping, scythe-like shadow, lacerates Paul's dream of eternal life and omniscient control with fleeting reminders of the reality of his death:

> His heart thumps for help. 'Help me! Help me!' cries his heart, battering the sides of the coffin. 'The schizophrenic has imposed her will. Her delusion, her fragment, her nothing-there, has come to pass.' (15)

> His heart's panic begins to rotate: I'm on the wrong train, he silently screams, an express train going miles in the opposite direction from where I want to go, and I can't get off. (85–6)

> How long, cries Paul in his heart, will these people, this city, haunt me? (88)

In this respect, Elsa's attempts to mystify and disempower Paul furnish the themes at play in Spark's strange poem with further significance. Like the lice-ridden nightingales described in its second line, the poem is itself infested with references to the disquiet and confusion caused by human utterances ('lousy associations', 'treacherous gutter', 'polluted words'), which have caused the utopian spring to spoil. By muddying the waters of Paul's world with her cryptic comments, as well as distressing allusions to her past treachery and present deathliness, Elsa articulates her resistance to the normative family fiction in which she has been expected to assume a silent, passive role. By the end of the novel, her slim shadow has thickened into a 'faithful and lithe cloud of unknowing' (147) – a reliably impermeable barrier against interpretation and mastery.

In the figure of Elsa, whose very name signifies her radical alterity, Spark thus forges a link between errant femininity and narrative disintegration. This link finds its physical embodiment in Elsa's closest friend, the wildly eccentric Princess Poppy Xavier, who causes pandemonium after allowing the silkworm eggs that she has stored beneath the folds of her breasts to hatch in the high temperature of the Hazletts' apartment, sending worms spilling from her flesh and into the living room. This outrageous scene – inspired, perhaps, by the extraordinary habits of Spark's close friend, Patricia Highsmith, who was known to smuggle her pet snails under her breasts when travelling abroad (Wilson 2010: 267) – thwarts the progress of Paul's investigation and exacerbates his bewilderment and distress; to watch the body of Poppy, another lively socialite of vast and implausible wealth, so quickly come to resemble a decomposing corpse is to be reminded of the deathly decay that is barely kept at bay by the sleek structures and sumptuous interiors of his New York fantasy. Having co-opted Paul's phallocentric 'master' narrative of elongated existence, rigid 'facts' and epistemological control, Elsa announces mockingly that her own '"psyche is [now] like a skyscraper, stretching up and up, practically all glass and steel so that one can look out over everything, and one never bends"' (85). Elsa does not aspire to such qualities, of course, but is instead ridiculing the ideal of perfect omniscience and eternal life that she has so successfully dismantled ('"It was you with your terrible and jealous dreams"', she later tells Paul, '"who set the whole edifice soaring"' [95]). Her ridicule does not end there, however. When she and Paul attend a bizarre theatrical production of J. M. Barrie's *Peter Pan; or, the Boy Who Wouldn't Grow Up* (1904), in which a group of geriatrics are cast as the Lost Boys, Elsa chucks rotten tomatoes at the players in mockery and disgust. That the decaying fruit is retrieved from inside her 'big crocodile bag' (92–3) is far from incidental; in Barrie's play (and his 1911 novel), the crocodile contains within its stomach an audibly ticking clock, the sound of which comes to terrify Captain Hook far more than the ferocious creature who swallowed it. In her riotous tomato-hurling display, Elsa similarly calls time on the ridiculous New York Neverland within which her spirit has festered for far too long. If Peter Pan's slippery shadow marks his happy separation from (and denial of) his mortality, the wayward direction of Elsa's guides her decisively toward her own.

Associated throughout the novel with sweltering temperatures and blazing fires (she dresses in a 'flame-coloured' evening gown [85], for instance, and insists that the central heating in her and Paul's home is set at the highest possible level), Elsa exists in stark contrast to her permanently wintry surroundings, her fiery presence indicating the strain she exerts on a story that struggles to contain her. When the apartment's excessive heat causes a maid to suffer a 'brainstorm' and drop a tray of afternoon tea, for example, the narrative is forced to switch focus from a scene of controlled decorum to an account of the 'wreckage on the carpet', involving 'the silver teapot on its side oozing leafy tea, the cream crawling its way among the jagged fragments' of broken china, and 'the sugar cubes scattered over the carpet like children's discarded playing-blocks seen from a far height' (39). An assortment of luxury brands ('Coalport china, [. . .] petit-fours and scones from Schrafft's, Fifth Avenue, [. . .] pineapple preserves from Charles's, Madison Avenue' [Ibid.]) find themselves juxtaposed with language which recalls the 'laws of the Congo jungles' described in Spark's poem ('oozing', 'leafy', 'crawling'), thus evoking a sense of the wild disorder that lurks just beneath the surface of Paul's meticulously arranged and placidly narrated existence. This 'wreckage' of 'jagged fragments' and 'scattered' sugar cubes prefigures the altogether more drastic destruction of Paul's 'stories' that arrives at the novel's close, when the titular 'Hothouse' of stifling fictions is at last demolished to make way for real death:

> [Paul and Elsa] stand outside their apartment block, looking at the scaffolding. The upper stories are already gone and the lower part is a shell. A demolition truck waits for the new day's shift to begin. The morning breeze from the East River is already spreading the dust.
>
> Elsa stands in the morning light reading the billboard. It announces the new block of apartments to be built on the old.
>
> "Now we can have some peace," says Elsa. (139–40)

Just before this point, Elsa leads us on a merry dance through the haunts and hotspots of her New York afterlife. Like another skewed shadow, the reader joins Paul at her heels, struggling to keep pace as she twirls breathlessly in and out of a sequence of nightclubs bearing the names The Personality Cult, The Sensual Experience, The Throb and Roloff's. At Roloff's, her final destination, she mesmerises a crowd of admirers by dancing with Paul beneath spinning multi-coloured lights, magnifying in the process a shadow that falls the wrong way. '"This deadly body of mine can dance, too"' (134), she beams, making explicit what Paul has long attempted to deny. It is no great stretch to read the trajectory of Elsa's last night on the tiles as a final, slightly crude, dig at her husband's depleted powers. Elsa has indeed managed to evacuate the cult of Paul's personality, having purposely corrupted his self-aggrandising dreamland and staged his final humiliation before a sea of onlookers. She has done so, too, by summoning the ghost of Kiel, and with him the spectre of a jealousy that is both romantic (via intimations of the pair's shared *sensual experience*) and sexual (their quick trysts are hinted at winkingly, perhaps, in *throb* and *roll-offs*). The husband and wife had spent the final years of their lives working, like Spark herself, at a Political Intelligence compound outside London, where they devised modes of 'black propaganda and psychological warfare' (50) intended to undermine and demoralise Nazi Germany. But old habits die hard, and Elsa's flamboyant floorshow works to deal her husband's mythmaking powers a final blow.

The boiling air of Spark's *Hothouse* reverberates with echoes of her earlier fictions. Indeed, the entire narrative, manifesting as it does from Paul's fervent refusal to accept the cold fact of his own mortality, reads as a realisation of the failure to adhere to the ghostly telephone message repeated throughout *Memento Mori*: '"Remember you must die."' Like *The Girls of Slender Means* and *The Bachelors* before it, it is set within an enclosed, increasingly febrile world populated by a specific *type*:

affluent ex-pats living *far* beyond their means. Elsa's claustrophobic containment within a man's world, meanwhile, recalls the plight of January Marlow in Spark's second novel, *Robinson*, who finds herself stranded on an island that shares not only the name of its chief inhabitant, but – as evinced by a map provided on the inside cover – his physical shape. There are riotous echoes here, too, of the anarchic spectral revelry that transmits from the adjacent flat in Spark's radio play, 'The Party Through the Wall', and of the tyrannies of narrow familial roles in the unnerving 1958 short story, 'A Member of the Family'.

Perhaps the loudest of these echoes, however, is that of Spark's best-known work, *The Prime of Miss Jean Brodie*. That novel famously depicts the consequences of inhabiting a world shaped in accordance with a singular, sinister, egomaniacal vision. Just as she tailors the school curriculum to suit her private passions (in *her* classroom, art appreciation replaces science lessons, for example, while pupils are to worship at the altars of figures as diverse as Mussolini, Pavlova, Giotto and Sybil Thorndike), Jean Brodie attempts to curate and control the lives of the six schoolgirls selected specially for her 'Brodie set' (5). Elsewhere, she enraptures her pupils with a florid account of her '"felled fiancé"', a soldier named Hugh Carruthers, who '"fell like an autumn leaf"' on Flanders Field shortly before Armistice was declared (9). Carruthers, as Marina MacKay observes, is 'more textual than fleshly', appearing in the tale as an amalgamation of literary references (from John Keats and Robert Burns, to Wilfred Owen and Scottish folk ballads), and revealing Brodie to be a masterful 'textual bricoleuse and improviser' (2010: 102–3), who is uncannily adept at transfiguring the commonplace at every turn. Brodie's romantic mythmaking, as evinced by the delight taken by Sandy Stranger and Jenny Gray in imagining the 'love correspondence' between Brodie and Gordon Lowther (94), proves positively intoxicating among her 'set'; captivated by their teacher, the girls submit as if unconsciously to her grander designs. Among these machinations is a plan to steer Rose Stanley (introduced from the outset as being 'famous for sex' [5]) into bed with another of Brodie's ex-lovers, the art teacher Teddy Lloyd. The power Brodie seeks to assume is thus *authorial*; she is adept at 'making patterns with facts' (72), as Sandy notes sagely to herself, and expecting the lives and freedoms of those around her to be compromised accordingly. '"Give me a girl at an impressionable age"', Brodie famously boasts, '"and she is mine for life"' (9).

Rather like Paul Hazlett's death-denying high-rise, Brodie's classroom becomes a hothouse of compensatory fictions, within which her girls exist as surrogates for her own unrealised (or, as in the case of Teddy Lloyd, unrevisited) desires and ambitions. This is not to say, however, that the novel seeks to communicate Brodie's subjectivity; instead, the reader – like another member of the 'Brodie set' – experiences the teacher on what Paddy Lyons describes as 'an entirely theatrical basis', perceiving her as 'purely dramatic, a performance artist, [. . .] presenting herself as she invents herself' (2010: 90). We are, in other words, breathing the intoxicating hothouse air of Brodie's classroom as we hang on her every word and mannerism (it comes as little surprise that this novel is arguably Spark's best known and loved, and the source of an enduringly popular film adaptation, as well as regular theatrical productions – audiences of various kinds relish their time in Brodie's classroom). But while some members of the 'Brodie set' function to indulge their teacher's romantic or sexual flights of fancy, others serve as vessels for her political fervour. Brodie, who is recognised by Sandy as a '"born Fascist"' (134), makes her political leanings known to her class when she speaks fondly of her tours of fascist Italy and Nazi-occupied Germany and Austria in 1939 ('"Hitler *was* rather naughty"' [131], she admits in a flashforward set after the Second World War, her sole concession to the horrors of Nazi genocide). It is Sandy who first notices the awful parallel between the photograph, proudly presented by Brodie, of Mussolini's troops 'marching in the straightest of files', and the girls themselves, who appear like 'Brodie's fascisti [. . .] all knit together [. . .] marching along' (31). It is Sandy, too, who brings about Brodie's downfall, when, after a classmate dies, having been compelled to fight for Franco's fascist army in Spain, she presents incriminating evidence of Brodie's malign influence to the school. Her act of defiance – she would not call it a betrayal, believing that '"it is only possible to betray where loyalty is due"' (127) – forms a fissure in Brodie's hothouse, ending her career and allowing her 'set' to glimpse possibilities beyond their scripted selves.

It might therefore be tempting to view Sandy as Elsa's natural predecessor. Both characters have sought to effect the demise of a stifling, singular, tyrannical worldview by corrupting it from within. But whereas Elsa arrives at '"some peace"' as she watches Paul's stories tumble away into nothingness, Sandy achieves neither contentment nor independence. Having supplanted Rose Stanley as Teddy Lloyd's lover (a decision predicated less on her attraction to Lloyd or a rebellious desire to disrupt Brodie's plans, and more on an irresistible 'curios[ity] about the man that loved [Brodie]'), she quickly 'los[es] interest in the man himself' and leaves him, having 'extracted [. . .] his [Catholicism] as a pith from a husk' (136) and joined a convent. Less a free-thinking disruptor than a palimpsest of competing influences, Sandy retreats to a life of solemn, ambiguous devotion; glimpsed at in proleptic passages interspersed throughout the novel, the older Sandy – now known as Sister Helena of the Transfiguration, and famed for having written a 'strange book of psychology' entitled 'The Transfiguration of the Commonplace' (128) – remains a woman firmly under the influence. When an enquiring young reader visits the convent to ask Sandy about '"the main influences of [her] school days"', be they '"literary or political or personal [. . .] [or] Calvinism"', she responds simply that '"there was a Miss Jean Brodie in her prime"' (Ibid.). Sandy's revelation is hardly surprising – for what is the title of her famous book if not a lasting tribute to Brodie's seductive ability to envisage hidden possibilities and romanticise the everyday? Like a parodic version of the Sparkian woman, Sandy has undergone no such transfiguration, and languishes instead in a knot of tortured piety and penance: we leave her 'clutch[ing] the bars of her grille more desperately than ever' (Ibid.), still a stranger to herself and others.

By ending on a scene of enclosure, with Sandy agonised and alone within the confines of her cell, *The Prime of Miss Jean Brodie* can be seen to sit alongside Spark's subsequent 'anti-novels', *The Driver's Seat* and *Not to Disturb*, as a kind of *hothouse fiction*. Rather than offering the fresh air of transformation (or, indeed, transfiguration) in their last pages – as the endings of *The Comforters* and *The Ballad of Peckham Rye* do, for example – those 'anti-novels' restrict the reader to scenes of claustrophobic containment, with the troubling implication that the potential for understanding or change lies altogether elsewhere. What is more, the texts themselves appear to have emerged metaleptically from the stifling settings of their final scenes, be it *The Driver's Seat*'s 'sad little office' (107) or *Not to Disturb*'s squalid servants' hall, as if cultivated by the febrile chatter and 'hot and [. . .] barking' (Ibid.) panic of those dreadful spaces. *The Prime of Miss Jean Brodie* achieves a similar effect. Despite Brodie's downfall, the hot air of her classroom never entirely dissipates; like Sandy in her cell, the narrator circles fascinatedly around Brodie's elegant performance and the legend of her 'prime' without ever accessing her private life. What the narrative comes to exhibit, then, is a rapt curiosity and paucity of vision that is comparable with Sandy's. Indeed, Sandy is described throughout the novel by way of references to her poor eyesight, spectacles and 'little pig-like eyes', which are so small as to be 'almost non-existent' (66; 7). Such eyes can neither fully comprehend Brodie's 'soaring and diving spirit' (85), nor escape succumbing to endless fascination, even long after Brodie's demise. To the end, her own 'cloud of unknowing' remains as 'faithful and lithe' as Elsa's. In this sense, *The Hothouse by the East River* reads as an unlikely companion piece to *The Prime of Miss Jean Brodie*. Whereas Brodie cultivates the alluring mystery of a personal 'prime' to enrapture and influence the lives of her 'set', Elsa adopts the same twinned strategy of mythmaking and mystification precisely to *evade* control and leave the hothouse for good.

* * *

I have chosen to conclude this book with a discussion of *The Hothouse by the East River* because in this, by far the most outlandish of all of Spark's fictions, aspects of each of the experimental, defamiliarising strategies discussed in the preceding chapters can be identified. Like *The Driver's Seat* almost immediately before it, *Hothouse* stages the operation and gradual deconstruction of a masculine ideal of all-knowing omnipotence. Much in the same way that Lise evades and consequently undermines the objectifying impulse of her own narrator (whose gaze, I have argued, mirrors those of the men depicted within the diegesis) by fashioning her final days into an enduringly mystifying spectacle, Elsa's predilection toward manifesting indecipherable '"effects"' over readily comprehendible '"causes"' comes to destabilise her husband's powers of deduction, causing him to spiral into impotent obsession before his edifice of 'stories' crashes into rubble. Before this point, Paul has enjoyed exploiting the kind of manipulative authority exhibited by the likes of *The Public Image*'s Frederick Christopher, *Not to Disturb*'s Baron Klopstock, *The Ballad of Peckham Rye*'s Mr Druce and *Doctors of Philosophy*'s Charlie Delfont. Like the female characters in those texts (Annabel Christopher, Baroness Klopstock, Merle Coverdale and Leonora Chase, most notably), Elsa has come to languish within a narrow, preconstructed role, before seizing her opportunity, as Leonora and Annabel do, to abandon it entirely. The cataclysmic consequences of Elsa's refusal to participate in her husband's fantasy can thus be read as an extreme realisation of the warning issued by Charlie Delfont of recalcitrant women like Leonora: 'Once they break out, they break out' (5). Indeed, one of Paul's fearful remarks concerning Elsa's newfound resistance bears a distinct similarity to Charlie's comment: Elsa, Paul tells Garven, '"is a development of an idea, that's all. She's not my conception anymore. She took a life of her own. She's grotesque"' (129).

As well as exhibiting a recognisably subversive approach to aspects of plot, narration and characterisation, *The Hothouse by the East River* seeks to effect 'a certain detachment' between reader and text that is comparable to Spark's earlier experiments with the conventions of the ghost story. In *The Comforters*, I earlier observed, the self-reflexive spooking of Caroline Rose (and her retaliatory haunting of her Typing Ghost) initiates the metafictional unravelling of the text itself, by laying bare the various narrative contrivances that would have otherwise reduced Caroline to a bit player in what she refers to as a '"cheap mystery piece"' (93). Spark's supernaturally inflected short stories gear their hauntings toward more pointed instances of gendered social critique, from the stifling conditions of colonial life that are examined so sharply in 'Bang-Bang You're Dead', to the themes of female subservience and self-alienation explored in 'The Girl I Left Behind Me'. In this respect, *Hothouse* can be seen to combine both aspects of Spark's earlier ghost stories. Paul's spectral fantasy of omniscient control, eternal life and infinite wealth operates, for instance, rather like the suffocating script dictated by Caroline's Typing Ghost, with rigidly defined characters and a leaden, carefully controlled plot (one need only think of those extravagantly dull afternoon teas). The implications of such a fantasy, furthermore, are undoubtedly gendered; for his 'stories' to remain strong, Paul requires the participation of a servile spectre of his wife, as opposed to the feisty and libidinous flesh-and-blood woman he once knew. As in 'Bang-Bang You're Dead' and 'The Girl I Left Behind Me', Elsa's ghostliness is communicated by way of her silence and passivity – attributes she need not be physically dead to possess. Ironically, it is when she transforms into a more morbid, '"grotesque"' presence (with her uncanny shadow, burning flesh and rotting fruits, for example) that Elsa seems most riotously alive; much like Needle in 'The Portobello Road', Elsa's awareness of her own ghostliness provides her with the key to upending the 'master' narrative which once defined her, so that she may finally be free.

Spark's longstanding interest in the style and ethos of the *nouveau roman*, meanwhile, is discernible throughout *Hothouse*, set as it is within an antiseptic afterlife of geometric glass and steel structures seemingly lifted from the pages of an anti-novel (in a fittingly spooky coincidence, in fact, a sense of this spectral setting is captured in the title of Robbe-Grillet's 1976 novel, *Topology of a Phantom City*, published three years later). As with Spark's earlier explorations of the humorous and horrific potentialities of Robbe-Grillet's 'certain detachment' in *The Ballad of Peckham Rye* and *The Mandelbaum Gate* respectively, *Hothouse* examines the unsettling absurdity of a world operating in outright denial of human mortality and self-scrutiny. Rather like Lise before her, Elsa manages to evacuate such a world by articulating her subjectivity and confronting her husband with the tragedy of the pair's untimely deaths. A 'Sparkian woman' every bit as resistant to control as Caroline, Needle, Leonora, Annabel or Lise, she disrupts the eerily depthless and dispassionate narration of Paul's stultifying Neverland (described – in a guilty shriek from Paul's coffin – as a 'sedative chamber where you don't think at all [. . .] and talk your head off all day, all night' [76]) with scenes of lively chaos and wild fury. The novel thus constitutes an experiment with form in the double sense outlined in my Introduction; Elsa, a force of 'profound contagion / and polluted words', flouts the 'sterile, descriptive rigour' (Shatz 2014: 24) of the anti-novel into which she has been written, while also articulating her unwillingness to remain a subservient, spectral participant within an oppressive family fiction.

This book, as the preceding few paragraphs demonstrate, has sought to examine the various experiments with form that came to preoccupy Spark during the first two decades of her fiction-writing career. If the eccentric, genre-busting approach taken in *The Comforters* constitutes a 'joyful' and irreverent exercise in 'break[ing] the obvious rules of fiction and get[ting] away with it' (Spark 1959: 18), then subsequent works like *Doctors of Philosophy*, *The Mandelbaum Gate* and *Not to Disturb* can be seen to combine formal innovation with a decidedly more serious interrogation of contemporary concerns, from sexual politics to postwar political realities and the machinations of the modern media. In retaining a degree of the derisory wit advocated by Spark in 'The Desegregation of Art', such works can be said to be 'disorienting', to return to the content of Christine Brooke-Rose's letter, in that they elude easy classification while possessing the power to unnerve and undermine. The temporal scope of this book should certainly not be taken as an indication that Spark ceased to experiment with the form and purpose of fiction after the publication of *Hothouse*. Later texts, including 1981's playfully metafictional *Loitering with Intent*, and 1990's multi-plotted medita- tion on intersubjectivity and individual free will, *Symposium* (1990), undoubtedly continued the author's innovative streak over the decades that followed. *Reality and Dreams* (1996), meanwhile, begins with an image of capsized male megalomania redolent of *Hothouse*'s climax, when its protagonist, a film director named Tom Richards, falls from a crane while giving orders to his cast. In the earlier texts I have chosen to discuss, however, Spark's self-declared intention to 'write fiction [. . .] with all the intensity that [she is] capable of concentrating on the idea of fiction' (MFL 1961) is at its most pronounced, subversive and politically engaged.

This book does not seek to provide the last word on Spark's strange and self-reflexive body of fiction (her so-called 'author's ghosts' would surely thwart any such attempt, anyway). I have sought instead to plot an alternative route through the first two decades of Spark's fiction-writing by deviating from the enduring myth of the author as a 'Catholic comic writer' (Bradbury 1992: 187), committed to a narrowly didactic mode of writing, and instead tracing her evolving and expansive attempts at realising 'an honest creative process' born of a 'rediscovery of form' and a refinement of 'the arts of pretence and counterfeit' (MFL 1961).

There, of course, remains more to be said of Spark. More demands to be written of her literary inheritances (the influence of the Scottish border ballads, in particular), her work as a poet and playwright, her interest in writing for radio, her archived correspondence with contemporaries including Christine Brooke-Rose and Doris Lessing, the impact of her varied and mobile life on her writing, her enduring influence on contemporary authors such as Ali Smith, Deborah Levy and A. L. Kennedy, as well the numerous novels, short stories, poems, plays and screenplays that were left unfinished, unpublished, or used instead as starting points for all manner of alternative creative projects.[2] These and other potential areas of study will inevitably return, however, to Spark's endlessly inventive approach to form – her eagerness, that is, to collapse and rebuild the story being told, to depict the entrapment, manipulation and possible metamorphosis of her characters, to subvert the conventions of genre and plot, to shake the scenery and to question seemingly stable structures of narrative authority. Like Elsa, Spark was permanently seeking ways of evacuating the stale air of the hothouse, and of demolishing old stories.

Shortly before writing her first short story, the shapeshifting 'The Seraph and the Zambesi', Spark completed a poem entitled 'Chrysalis' (1951). The following few lines, which fixate on 'the scene of the small violence' wherein a new form emerges from its 'broken shell', would define the following half-century of Spark's literary career, and therefore seem a fitting place for this author – who for too long has been another of Spark's Typing Ghosts, stalking the pages of her old works in the hope of writing something new – to reach an end:

> There was the broken shell with what was once
> The head askew; and what was once the worm
> Was away out the window, out of the warm,
> Out of the scene of the small violence. (ll. 9–12)

Notes

1. For a comprehensive account of such attacks, see Gasiorek 1995: 1–22. 'The idea about experiment being the life-blood of the English novel is one that dies hard,' wrote Kingsley Amis. His own fiction, in contrast, was made up of 'believable stories about understandable characters' that were delivered 'in a reasonably straightforward style: no tricks, no experimental foolery'. William Cooper, more virulently, claimed that the experimental novel represented an attack on 'intellect in general, made by intellectuals so decadent that they no longer mind if intellect persists' (both qtd in Gasiorek 1995: 3).
2. Brooke-Rose's exasperated comments were made in regard to the imminent publication of her latest novel, *Xorandor* (1986), and the baffled critical reception that she expected it to generate.
3. Brooke-Rose wrote reverently and at length of the influence of the *nouveau roman* and postmodernism on her own fiction ('The Real as Unreal: Robbe-Grillet' [1981]; 'The Author is Dead, Long Live the Author' [2002a]), as well as on Spark's ('A Writer's Constraints' [2002b]).
4. As detailed in NLS 1956.

Chapter One: 'Author's Ghosts': Manifestations of the Supernatural in Spark's Early Fiction

1. Spark's short article included brief reviews of two collections of ghost stories: Shane Leslie's *Ghost Book* (1956) and Cynthia Asquith's *The Third Ghost Book* (1955).
2. In his biography of Spark, Martin Stannard describes Spark's unfinished *Warrender Chase* erroneously as 'a novel' (2009: 444), perhaps because it is used as the title of Fleur Talbot's novel in *Loitering with Intent*.
3. Spark copied copious notes from, among various other studies, Kenneth Walker's *Commentary on Age* (1952) and Joseph Harold Sheldon's 1948 report, 'The Social Medicine of Old Age' (see NLS c.1958). In amassing such a great deal of research on old age, Spark comes to bear an ironic resemblance to *Memento Mori*'s Alec Warner, an amateur gerontologist

who conducts increasingly intrusive research into the impacts of old age, before his enormous personal archive is destroyed in a house fire.

4. Spark includes quotations from, among other sources, Shakespeare's *Hamlet*, Plato's *The Republic* and Cicero's *Cato Maior de Senectute* (*On Old Age*).

5. Spark's interest in the ghost story might also be investigated in relation to her lifelong enjoyment of the Scottish border ballads, renowned for their tales of bloody violence and vengeful spirits. The 'steel and bite' of such stories, Spark remarked of her childhood reading habits in *Curriculum Vitae*, 'entered my literary bloodstream, never to depart' (1992a: 98). For a useful discussion of the influence of the border ballad on Spark's fiction, see Gardiner 2006: 55–61.

6. Although 'Bang-Bang You're Dead' was not published until 1961, when it appeared in Spark's collection of short fiction and radio plays, *Voices at Play*, records of the author's correspondence with *The New Yorker* reveal that the story was submitted to, and rejected by, the publication in 1958 (at the same time that Spark was working on 'The Girl I Left Behind Me' and 'The Portobello Road', which contain similar themes). 'The Portobello Road' was also turned down by the publication in 1957, despite positive reviews from its editors. For a detailed study of Spark's relationship with *The New Yorker*, in which several of her short stories *were* published and where Spark would later work, see Harrison 2010: 39–60.

7. Spark, too, had sought retreat following her own period of mental illness. As Alan Bold notes, Spark wrote *The Comforters* 'while living near Allington Castle, Kent, in a cottage owned by the Carmelite Friars of Aylesford Priory' (1986: 36). For a more detailed account of this period, see Stannard 2009: 161.

8. Even when referring to the original, 1953 version of 'Harper and Wilton', I quote from Spark's 1996 revision. This is because, as the present chapter will shortly discuss, Spark includes the original short story in its entirety in the revised version.

9. 'Created and Abandoned' is, incidentally, the title of a 1979 poem by Spark, which concerns the 'limbo'd' status of 'characters / in a story one has started to write and set aside', and the responsibility their author might owe them. The poem concludes:

> I hope you're not looking for me
> night after night, not waiting for me to come back.
> I feel a definite responsibility for your welfare.
> Are you all right?' (ll. 12–13; ll. 15–18)

10. The sudden powerlessness of the haunted men in ghost stories (and, indeed, the *reversal* of power between men and women that this might effect) is acknowledged by Jennifer Uglow, who observes that 'the experience of seeing a ghost pushes men into conventional female roles: timid, nervous and helpless' (1988: xvii).

11. Examples are numerous, ranging from Charlotte Perkins Gilman's *The Yellow Wallpaper* (1892), in which the ghost trope is used to support the short story's critique of patriarchal oppression, to the repudiation of so-called 'male rationality' in the modernist ghost stories of May Sinclair and

Edith Nesbit, which valorise the perspectives of 'female outsiders such as spinsters and mistresses, who validate their own oddity or power through their uncanny capacity to see, hear or feel what others cannot' (Liggins 2015: 44).

12. In his biography of Spark, Martin Stannard writes that Nita McEwan's murder 'seemed like an omen' for the author's fate, should she remain in her own abusive marriage to Sidney Oswald Spark (2009: 50). 'S.O.S.', notes Stannard, was Spark's 'wry name' for her violent husband – a tacit admission, perhaps, of the danger that she felt that he posed to her (61).

Chapter Two: 'The role in which you've cast me': Reassessing the Myth of Spark

1. Bradbury is referring here to the description of the artist in James Joyce's *A Portrait of the Artist as a Young Man* (1916): 'The artist, like the God of creation, remains within or behind or beyond or above his handiwork, invisible, refined out of existence, indifferent, paring his fingernails' (2000: 181).

2. When presented with Bradbury's conception of the Sparkian author by her interviewer, Martin McQuillan, Spark rejected it without hesitation: 'No! [. . .] No, no I don't think so. I don't think I like that [idea] very much. However, perhaps that's the impression I give' (McQuillan 2001c: 218).

3. 'I define *postmodern* as incredulity toward metanarratives,' announces Lyotard in *The Postmodern Condition: A Report on Knowledge* (1984: xxiii).

4. Spark took the resolutely anti-realist decision to name all three of *Doctors of Philosophy*'s male characters Charlie. 'Men', she remarked of this decision, 'are irrelevant for the purposes of the play' (it was, after all, 'a woman's play') (Frankel 1987: 451). The play's producer, Michael Codron, was so taken by this decision that he urged Spark to change the name of the play to *Charlie is My Darling* (see Stannard 2009: 282).

5. According to Spark, the premise of *The Public Image* came to her in a dream, just before she would complete a move from New York to Rome in 1966. 'I dreamt the whole thing in New York', she recalled, 'and when I arrived in Rome I wrote the book. It was the easiest book I ever wrote' (Frankel 1987: 453).

6. The 'Leopard' contained in the surname of Luigi Leopardi, the chief mastermind behind Annabel's *Tiger*-Lady persona, is surely ironic: '"What is personality but the effect one has on others?"' Luigi asks Annabel. '"Life is all the achievement of an effect. *Only the animals remain natural*"' (34, emphasis mine).

7. Spark's notes contain two of these disturbing, pornographic mock-diaries: *Il Diario della Marchesa Anna Fallarino Casati* and *The Splendours and Miseries of Marquis Casati: The Diary of an Eccentric*. The first of these is presented from the perspective of Anna Fallarino, and the second from that of her husband (see NLS 1970b, where both diaries are located).

8. For similar readings, see, *inter alia*, Hynes 1988: 155–76.

Chapter Three: 'Drama[s] of exact observation': Spark and the *Nouveau Roman*

1. See, for example: Duchene 1959: 11; Hogan 1959: 4; Toynbee 1959: 22.
2. Ross's references to 'hygiene', 'stains' and 'cleansed' vision are far from incidental; her study of modernisation and decolonisation in relation to bourgeois life in postwar, metropolitan France interprets the *nouveau roman*, associated as it is with unmediated objectivity and precise, surface-level descriptions, as part of a 'generalised postwar atmosphere of moral purification, national cleansing, and literary laundering' (Ross 1995: 76). Ross identifies the prominence of metaphors of cleanliness within French postwar culture (ranging from those found in literature, film and advertising to accounts of 'clean' modes of torture in Algeria), and attributes them to the end of empire and the consequent displacement of French colonial authority. This heightened emphasis on cleanliness in domestic, public and cultural life, Ross's study argues, served not only as the means by which the French maintained a sense of superiority over the newly decolonised, but also as a way of purging the stains of the Occupation by cultivating and propagating a belief in their nation's 'moral purification' (Ibid.).
3. We might note, for example, the doomed and ultimately self-destructive attempts of the detective in *The Erasers* to piece together the narrative of a murder, the subject of *In the Labyrinth*'s failed quest to shape the chaotic flux of his reality into something resembling a coherent order, or (perhaps most famously) the plight of the couple in *Last Year at Marienbad*, who find themselves condemned to stalk the rooms of a labyrinthine hotel in the vain hope of determining whether or not they had met the year before, and, if so, what might have taken place between them.
4. A detailed account of Robbe-Grillet's wartime experience is provided throughout Ilona Leki's *Alain Robbe-Grillet* (1983).
5. '(^Aristotle's)' and the asterisked 'Purgation' are additions that Spark made to her notes from Abercrombie's study. Here, Spark quotes Abercrombie's text partially and imperfectly. The complete passage reads as follows: 'The definition of tragedy, then, is this: Tragedy is the imitation of an action that is serious, complete in itself, and possessing a certain magnitude; in language that gives delight appropriate to each portion of the work; in the form of drama, not of narrative; through pity and fear accomplishing its *Katharsis* of such emotions' (Abercrombie 1932: 96).
6. It is perhaps significant, given her intention to weave a personal narrative dictated by the components of classical tragedy, that Lise's sole addition to her anonymous-looking and seemingly 'uninhabited' home is a 'patterned rug from Greece' (14).
7. For comprehensive overviews of critical responses towards the work of Bernays and the physiological interpretation of catharsis more generally, see, for example: Golden 1976: 21–33; Kruse 1979: 162–71; Porter 2015: 15–41.
8. See, for example: Brooke-Rose 1981: 291–310; Brooke-Rose 2002a: 130–55.

Chapter Four: 'A study, in a way, of self-destruction': *The Driver's Seat* and the Impotent Gaze

1. This mode of reading *The Driver's Seat* (and Spark's handling of plot and narration more generally) has proved enduringly popular. In her analysis of the novel, Maria Fackler asserts that 'the play with time' indicates 'a kind of omniscience'. The narrator, she argues, 'is all-knowing in terms of time and chronology [. . .] and insists on time as a whole, rather than as a series of episodic moments' (2014: 378). James Wood also draws upon Spark's distinctive use of prolepsis to argue that 'Spark always exercises ruthless control over her fictional characters'. Her 'flash-forwards' thus 'remind us that Muriel Spark has powers of ultimate control over her creations' (2008: 89).
2. Among the wide range of authors discussed in the essays included in Merivale and Sweeney's edited collection are Robbe-Grillet, Vladimir Nabokov, Paul Auster, Iris Murdoch, Graham Greene, Umberto Eco and Italo Calvino. Spark's omission is surprising, given that a great number of her novels and short stories (including *The Driver's Seat*, *Not to Disturb*, *Robinson*, *A Far Cry from Kensington*, *The Comforters*, *Memento Mori*, 'The Thing About Police Stations' [1963], 'The Girl I Left Behind Me' and 'Chimes' [1995]) allude to and subvert the conventions of the traditional detective story or murder mystery.
3. Brian Richardson argues convincingly that, in *Jealousy*, 'the inferred perceiver, the jealous husband, is certainly the sole focaliser of the text' (2006: 8), whereas Peter Toohey asserts that, by 'reporting the tiniest details of [A...'s] movements', Robbe-Grillet 'captures perfectly the obsessively studious psychology of the jealous individual', who 'constantly replays what he has seen and what he suspects' (2014: 11)
4. See MFL 1969a. This detail might offer decisive proof that *The Driver's Seat*'s unspecified setting is indeed Rome, as various readings of the novel have speculated.
5. See, *inter alia*, De Lauretis 1984; Doane 1982; Yates 2007; Greven 2013.

Conclusion: Leaving the Hothouse

1. Paul's fantasy thus constitutes an example of 'spectral incognisance', as defined earlier by Aviva Briefel. The entire novel, in fact, bears an uncanny similarity to one of the films discussed in Briefel's essay, Adrian Lyne's *Jacob's Ladder* (1990). As with *The Hothouse by the East River*, Lyne's film narrates the gradual destruction of a dream of extended life in contemporary New York, emanating from the unquiet spirit of a man killed during the war (in this case, the Vietnam War).
2. I am thinking specifically of *Watling Street*, the aborted yet extensively researched historical novel detailed in the Introduction to the present study. Alongside this more substantial work, it is likely that Spark's enormous Tulsa and Edinburgh archives contain unpublished poems, plays and short stories additional to those I encountered over the course of my research.

Another potentially fruitful area of archival research concerns Spark's active role in devising adaptations of her fiction for film, stage, television, radio and even opera. In my analysis of *Not to Disturb*, I discussed how Spark commissioned three playwrights to submit scripts for a proposed theatrical adaptation. Alongside evidence of this, her correspondence reveals her interest in working alongside the classical composer, Thomas Ades, to adapt either *Not to Disturb* or *The Abbess of Crewe* as an opera. The Edinburgh archive also contains a screenplay, written by Spark herself, for a film version of *The Takeover*; this came to nothing following the death of the film's proposed director, Joseph Losey. Closer scholarly attention to these and other aspects of Spark's diverse body of work would advance the task of 'desegregating' the author from the rigid mode of criticism that has traditionally been applied to her fiction.

Bibliography

Archives

All sources have been written by Muriel Spark, unless stated otherwise.

NLS: Muriel Spark Archive, National Library of Scotland, Edinburgh
1951: Letter from Muriel Spark to John Masefield, 26 May 1951, from 8 Sussex Mansions, 65 Old Brompton Road, London. Muriel Spark Archive, Acc.10607/89.
1952a: 'Warrender Chase' (notebook of handwritten notes), Muriel Spark Archive, Acc.11621: Miscellaneous Notes, Poems, Plays (1954–7), National Library of Scotland. It should be noted that, according to correspondence dates included among these notes, the play was developed in 1952, despite it being grouped among notes for poems and plays spanning 1954–7.
1952b: Muriel Spark, 'Act 1, Scene 1 of Warrender Chase' (unpaginated draft). Muriel Spark Archive, Acc.11621: Miscellaneous Notes, Poems, Plays (1954–7), National Library of Scotland.
1952c: Letter from Emmanuel Wax (ACTAC [Theatrical & Cinematic] Ltd) to Muriel Spark, 16 May 1952, from 33 Haymarket, London. Muriel Spark Archive, Acc.11621: Miscellaneous Notes, Poems, Plays (1954–7).
c.1955: Muriel Spark, 'Unpublished review of *Job and His Friends* (1954) by T. H. Robinson (4pp.)'. Muriel Spark Archive, Acc.11621: Miscellaneous Notes, Poems, Plays (1954–7).
1956: Letter from Evelyn Waugh to 'Mr. Fielding' [the nom de plume of Alan Barnsley, Spark's literary agent], 29 October 1956, from Piers Court, Strithcombe, Gloucestershire. Muriel Spark Archive, Acc.10607/92: Original Letters, 1956–75, National Library of Scotland.
c.1958: Muriel Spark Archive, Acc.10989: *Memento Mori* Notes and Research (unpaginated).
1961: Letter from Muriel Spark to Lovat 'Rache' Dickson, 26 May 1961, from 13 Baldwin Crescent, Camberwell, London. Muriel Spark Archive, Acc.10607/15: Correspondence 1941–92.
1963: Letter from Muriel Spark to Robert Henderson, 20 March 1963, from 13 Baldwin Crescent, Camberwell, London. Muriel Spark Archive, Acc.10607/18: General Correspondence, 1963.

1970a: Ian Gillham, Unedited transcript of 'Keeping it Short: Muriel Spark Talks about Her Books to Ian Gillham'. Muriel Spark Archive, Acc.10989/195: Biographical Notes and Interviews, 1953–70 (published in abridged form in *The Listener*, 24 September 1970, pp. 411–13).

1970b: Loose handwritten notes and *Il Diario della Marchesa Anna Fallarino Casati*. Muriel Spark Archive, Acc.11344: Papers and Correspondence 1986–95. It should be noted that Spark's notes and research for *Not to Disturb*, along with many other items from this accession, lie far outside the 1986–95 bracket.

1970c: Anon., 'Secret Diary Tells of Sex Games', *Rome Daily American*, 4 September 1970, p. 47. Muriel Spark Archive, Acc.11344: Papers and Correspondence 1986–95.

1971a: W. Gordon Smith, '*Not to Disturb* [unpublished dramatic adaptation, June 1971, 134 pages]'. Muriel Spark Archive, Acc.11344.

1971b: Brian de Breffny, '*Not to Disturb* [unpublished dramatic adaptation, July 1971, 118 pages]'. Muriel Spark Archive, Acc.11344.

1971c: Christopher Holme, '*Not to Disturb* [unpublished dramatic adaptation, June 1971, 168 pages]'. Muriel Spark Archive, Acc.11344.

1986: Letter from Christine Brooke-Rose to Muriel Spark, 15 June 1986. Muriel Spark Archive, Acc.10607/85: Correspondence and Related Papers, 1941–91.

c.1991: Loose handwritten note entitled 'My Contribution to Literary History' (grouped among notes and drafts for *Curriculum Vitae*). Muriel Spark Archive, Acc.10989/134: Research Notes.

MFL: Muriel Spark Papers, McFarlin Library, University of Tulsa

c.1955a: 'Sub-plot: diamond smuggling (2p.)', in 'Handwritten notes and draft fragments in three notebooks and one exercise book (*The Comforters*)', Muriel Spark Papers, Box 13, Folder 7.

c.1955b: Muriel Spark, 'The Loving of Mrs. Hogg (4p.)', in 'Handwritten notes and draft fragments in three notebooks and one exercise book (*The Comforters*)', Muriel Spark Papers, Box 13, Folder 7.

c.1955c: Loose draft fragment[s], 'Handwritten notes and fragments (*The Comforters*) (40 pieces, pages unnumbered)', Muriel Spark Papers, Box 13, Folder 6.

c.1960–1: 'A Dangerous Situation on the Stairs (handwritten short story, 4pp.)', in '*The Prime of Miss Jean Brodie*, handwritten notes and draft fragments, 44pp.)', Muriel Spark Papers, Box 59, Folder 1.

1961: Loose handwritten note entitled 'Author's Note', in 'Handwritten notes and draft fragments, 44pp. [*The Prime of Miss Jean Brodie*]', Muriel Spark Papers, Box 59, Folder 1.

1966: 'The Parquet Floor (1p.)', in '*The Public Image*, handwritten and typed notes and draft fragments (52pp.)', Muriel Spark Papers, Box 61, Folder 5.

c.1968–73: Untitled poem (typed, loose fragment), 'Typed and Carbon Copy Typed General Notes [*The Hothouse by the East River*, 1968–73, 89 pieces]', Muriel Spark Papers, Box 28, Folder 4.

1969a: Loose research notes and draft fragments, 'Handwritten notes and draft fragments (*The Driver's Seat*; pages unnumbered)', Muriel Spark Papers, Box 16, Folder 8. This folder includes the following newspaper article, to which I refer in Chapter Four: Anon. (1969), 'Note an invitation to murder, QC says', *The Times*, 20 March, p. 2.

1969b: 'Aristotle (unnumbered handwritten notes)', Muriel Spark Papers, Box 83, Folder 10.

1970: Loose draft fragments, '*Not to Disturb*, handwritten and typed notes and chapter outlines, character lists and draft fragments, 197 pieces (unpaginated)', Muriel Spark Papers, Box 53, Folder 5.

WUL: John Smith Archive, Washington University in St Louis Library
1961: Letter from Muriel Spark to John Smith, 3 July 1961, from 13 Baldwin Crescent, Camberwell, London. Muriel Spark Papers, Box 1, Folder 10: Correspondence with John Smith: May–September 1961.

Works by Muriel Spark

Novels by Muriel Spark
(1975), *The Abbess of Crewe* [1974], Harmondsworth: Penguin.
(1960b), *The Bachelors* [1960], Harmondsworth: Penguin.
(1960a), *The Ballad of Peckham Rye* [1960], Harmondsworth: Penguin.
(1963), *The Comforters* [1957], Harmondsworth: Penguin.
(1994), *The Driver's Seat* [1970], New York: New Directions.
(1963), *The Girls of Slender Means* [1963], New York: Knopf.
(2004), *The Finishing School*, London: Viking.
(1975), *The Hothouse by the East River* [1973], London: Penguin.
(1982), *Loitering with Intent* [1981], London: Triad/Granada.
(1985), *The Mandelbaum Gate* [1965], London: Penguin.
(1992), *Memento Mori* [1959], London: Penguin.
(1971), *Not to Disturb* [1971], London: Macmillan.
(1972), *The Prime of Miss Jean Brodie* [1961], Harmondsworth: Penguin.
(1970), *The Public Image* [1968], Harmondsworth: Penguin.
(1997), *Reality and Dreams* [1996], London: Penguin.
(1976), *The Takeover*, London: Macmillan.

Short Stories by Muriel Spark
Each of Spark's short stories is quoted from 2011's *The Complete Short Stories*, Edinburgh: Canongate. The page references are as follows:
'Bang-Bang You're Dead' [1961], pp. 83–120.
'The Girl I Left Behind Me' [1957], pp. 278–83.
'Harper and Wilton' [1953/Revised in 1996], pp. 243–51.
'The House of the Famous Poet' [1952], pp. 338–49.
'The Leaf-Sweeper' [1952], pp. 235–42.
'The Pearly Shadow' [1955], pp. 293–301.
'The Portobello Road' [1958], pp. 495–524.

Poems by Muriel Spark
The following poems are quoted from 2004's *All the Poems*, Manchester: Carcanet Press.
'Author's Ghosts' [2004], p. 13.

உ

'Chrysalis' [1951], p .63.
'Created and Abandoned' [1979], p. 74.
'The Messengers' [1967], p. 37.

Plays by Muriel Spark
(1966) *Doctors of Philosophy: A Play* [1963], New York: Knopf.
(1958), 'The Interview', in *Voices at Play*, London: Macmillan, 1961, pp. 129–49.
(1957), 'The Party Through the Wall', in *Voices at Play*, London: Macmillan, 1961, pp. 175–88.

Criticism, Biography and Autobiography by Muriel Spark
(1992a), *Curriculum Vitae: A Volume of Autobiography* [1992], Harmondsworth: Penguin.
(2014) *The Golden Fleece: Essays*, ed. by Penelope Jardine, Manchester: Carcanet Press.
(1992b), *John Masefield* [1962], London: Macmillan.

Essays, Articles and Reviews by Muriel Spark
(1959), 'Breaking the Novelist's Rules', *The Observer*, 21 June, p. 18.
(1992c) 'The Desegregation of Art' [1970], in *Critical Essays on Muriel Spark*, ed. by Joseph Hynes, New York: Hall, pp. 33–7.
(1992d) 'Edinburgh-Born', in *Critical Essays on Muriel Spark*, ed. by Joseph Hynes (New York: Hall, 1992), pp. 21–3.
(1956) 'Ghosts', *The Observer*, 1 January, p. 7.
(1960c) 'How I Became a Novelist', *John O'London's Weekly*, 1 December, p. 683.
(1961), 'My Conversion', *Twentieth Century*, Vol. 170 (Autumn), pp. 58–63.
(1955), 'The Mystery of Job's Suffering: Jung's New Interpretation Examined [Review of Carl Jung's *Answer to Job*]', *The Church of England Newspaper*, 15 April, p. 7.
(2014a), '*Pensée*: The Supernatural' [2003], in *The Golden Fleece: Essays*, p. 161.
(2014b), 'The Sitter's Tale' [1999], in *The Golden Fleece: Essays*, p. 99.

Interviews with Muriel Spark

Brooker, James, and Saá, Margarita Estévez (2004), 'Interview with Dame Muriel Spark', *Women's Studies*, 33, pp. 1035–46.
Devoize, Jeanne, and Valette, Pamela (2003), 'Muriel Spark – b.1918 [Interview]', *Journal of the Short Story in English*, Vol. 41 (Autumn), pp. 243–54.
Frankel, Sarah (1987), 'An Interview with Muriel Spark', *Partisan Review*, Vol. 54 (Summer), pp. 443–57.
Gilbert, Harriett (2001), '*Meridian*: Muriel Spark', BBC World Service, 15 November.
Gillham, Ian (1970), 'Keeping it Short – Muriel Spark Talks about Her Books to Ian Gillham', *The Listener*, 24 September, pp. 411–13.

Greig, Geordie (1996), 'The Dame's Fortunes', *The Sunday Times*, 22 September, pp. 8–9.

Holland, Mary (1965), 'The Prime of Muriel Spark', *The Observer* (Colour Supplement), 17 October, pp. 8–10.

Hosmer, Robert E. (2005), 'An Interview with Dame Muriel Spark', *Salmagundi*, Vol. 146/7 (Spring/Summer), pp. 127–59.

Hosmer, Robert E. (2014), '"Fascinated by Suspense": An Interview with Dame Muriel Spark', in *Hidden Possibilities: Essays in Honor of Muriel Spark*, ed. by Robert E. Hosmer (Notre Dame, IN: Notre Dame University Press), pp. 227–55.

Ivry, Benjamin (1991), 'A Sinister Affair: Muriel Spark in Conversation', *The Economist* (US), 23 November, p. 102.

Kermode, Frank (1963), 'The House of Fiction: Interviews with Seven English Novelists', *Partisan Review*, 30, pp. 61–82.

Lawson, Mark (2004), '*Front Row*: Muriel Spark', BBC Radio 4, 26 February.

McQuillan, Martin (2001c), '"The Same Informed Air": An Interview with Muriel Spark', in *Theorising Muriel Spark: Gender, Race, Deconstruction*, ed. by Martin McQuillan, Basingstoke and New York: Palgrave, pp. 210–229.

Schiff, Stephen (1993), 'Muriel Spark Between the Lines', *The New Yorker*, 24 May, pp. 36–43.

Shenker, Israel (1968), 'Portrait of a Woman Reading: Muriel Spark Interviewed by Israel Shenker', *Book World*, 29 September, p. 2.

Smith, Sarah (1998), 'Columbia Talks with Muriel Spark', *Columbia: A Journal of Literature and Art*, No. 30 (Autumn), pp. 199–214.

Smith, W. Gordon (1971), 'Scope: Muriel Spark', BBC Television, 3 December.

Taylor, Alan (2004), 'The Gospel According to Spark', *Sunday Herald*, 22 February, p. 27.

Toynbee, Philip (1971), 'Interview with Muriel Spark', *The Observer Colour Magazine*, 7 November, pp. 73–4.

Yule, Eleanor (1996), '*Bookmark*: The Elusive Spark', BBC Scotland, 2 March.

Critical Texts on, or Containing Analysis of, Muriel Spark

Auden, W. H. (1962), 'A Disturbing Novelist', *The Mid-Century*, Vol. 39, pp. 5–8.

Bailey, James (2015), '"Haunted, whether we like it or not": The Ghost Stories of Muriel Spark', in *British Women Short Story Writers: The New Woman to Now*, ed. by Emma Young and James Bailey, Edinburgh: Edinburgh University Press, pp. 81–95.

Bailey, James (2011), '"Repetition, boredom, despair": Muriel Spark and the Eichmann Trial', in *Holocaust Studies*, Vol. 17, No. 2–3, pp. 185–206.

Bailey, James (2015), 'Salutary Scars: The "Disorienting" Fictions of Muriel Spark', *Contemporary Women's Writing*, Vol. 9, No. 1 (March), pp. 35–52.

Bentley, Nick (2010), '"New Elizabethans": The Representation of Youth Subcultures in 1950s British Fiction', *Literature & History*, Vol. 19, No. 1 (Spring), pp. 16–33.

Bold, Alan (1986), *Muriel Spark*, London and New York: Methuen.

Bold, Alan, ed. (1984), *Muriel Spark: An Odd Capacity for Vision*, London: Vision Press.

Bold, Alan (1992), '"Poet and Dreamer"', in *Critical Essays on Muriel Spark*, ed. by Joseph Hynes, New York: G. K. Hall, pp. 85–103.

Bradbury, Malcolm (1992), 'Muriel Spark's Fingernails' [1972], in *Critical Essays on Muriel Spark*, ed. by Joseph Hynes, New York: G. K. Hall, pp. 187–93.

Brown, Peter Robert, '"There's Something about Mary": Narrative and Ethics in *The Prime of Miss Jean Brodie*', *Journal of Narrative Theory*, Vol. 36, No. 2 (Summer 2006), pp. 228–53.

Byrne, Eleanor (2001), 'Muriel Spark Shot in Africa', in *Theorising Muriel Spark: Gender, Race, Deconstruction*, ed. by Martin McQuillan, Basingstoke and New York: Palgrave, pp. 113–26.

Carruthers, Gerard (2010a), '"Fully to Savour Her Position": Muriel Spark and Scottish Identity', in *Muriel Spark: Twenty-First-Century Perspectives*, ed. by David Herman, Baltimore: Johns Hopkins University Press, pp. 21–38.

Carruthers, Gerard (2010b), 'Muriel Spark as Catholic Novelist', in *The Edinburgh Companion to Muriel Spark*, ed. by Michael Gardiner and Willy Maley, Edinburgh: Edinburgh University Press, pp. 74–84.

Cheyette, Bryan (2000), *Muriel Spark*, Tavistock: Northcote House.

Cheyette, Bryan (2001), 'Writing Against Conversion: Muriel Spark and the Gentile Jewess', in *Theorising Muriel Spark: Gender, Race, Deconstruction*, ed. by Martin McQuillan, Basingstoke and New York: Palgrave, pp. 95–112.

Christianson, Aileen (2000), 'Muriel Spark and Candia McWilliam: Continuities', in *Contemporary Scottish Women Writers*, ed. by Aileen Christianson and Alison Lumsden, Edinburgh: Edinburgh University Press, pp. 95–110.

Cixous, Hélène (2001a), 'Grimacing Catholicism: Muriel Spark's Macabre Farce' [1968; trans. by Christine Irizzary], in *Theorising Muriel Spark: Gender, Race, Deconstruction*, ed. by Martin McQuillan, Basingstoke and New York: Palgrave, pp. 204–7.

Crace, John (2008), 'Digested Classics: *The Prime of Miss Jean Brodie* by Muriel Spark', *The Guardian*, 13 December, <https://www.theguardian.com/books/2008/dec/13/prime-of-miss-jean-brodie>(last accessed 3 July 2017).

Craig, Cairns (1999), *The Modern Scottish Novel: Narrative and the National Imagination*, Edinburgh: Edinburgh University Press.

Dalsimer, Katherine (1986), *Female Adolescence: Psychoanalytic Reflections on Literature*, New Haven, CT, and London: Yale University Press.

Day, Aidan (2007), 'Parodying Postmodernism: Muriel Spark (*The Driver's Seat*) and Robbe-Grillet (*Jealousy*)', *English*, Vol. 56, No. 216 (Autumn), pp. 321–37.

Drabble, Margaret (2018), 'Snapshots of Muriel Spark', *Times Literary Supplement*, 26 June, <https://www.the-tls.co.uk/articles/public/muriel-spark-margaret-drabble>(last accessed 27 June 2018).

Edgecombe, Rodney Stenning (1990), *Vocation and Identity in the Fiction of Muriel Spark*, Columbia: University of Missouri Press.

Fackler, Maria Francesca (2014), 'Imagining Female Authorship After 1945: Lessing's and Spark's Portraits of the Artist *Manqué*', in *A Companion to British Literature, Volume IV: Victorian and Twentieth-Century Literature*

1837–2000, ed. by Robert DeMaria Jr, Heesok Chang and Samatha Zacher, Chichester: Wiley-Blackwell, pp. 367–84.

Foxwell, John (2016), 'Enacting Hallucinatory Experience in Fiction: Metalepsis, Agency, and the Phenomenology of Reading in Muriel Spark's *The Comforters*', *Style*, Vol. 50, No. 2, pp. 139–57.

Gardiner, Michael (2006), *From Trocchi to Trainspotting: Scottish Critical Theory Since 1960*, Edinburgh: Edinburgh University Press.

Gardiner, Michael, and Maley, Willy, eds (2010), *The Edinburgh Companion to Muriel Spark*, Edinburgh: Edinburgh University Press.

Glavin, John (2000), 'Muriel Spark: Beginning Again', in *British Women Writing Fiction*, ed. by Abby H. P. Werlock, Alabama: University of Alabama Press, pp. 293–313.

Gregson, Ian (2006), *Character and Satire in Postwar Fiction*, New York: Continuum.

Gutkin, Len (2017), 'Muriel Spark's Camp Metafiction', *Contemporary Literature*, Vol. 58, No. 1 (Winter 2017), pp. 53–81.

Harrison, Bernard (1976), 'Muriel Spark and Jane Austen', in *The Modern English Novel: The Reader, The Writer, and the Work*, ed. by Gabriel Josipovici, New York: Barnes & Noble, pp. 225–51.

Harrison, Lisa (2010), '"The Magazine That Is Considered the Best in the World": Muriel Spark and the *New Yorker*', in *Muriel Spark: Twenty-First-Century Perspectives*, ed. by David Herman, Baltimore: Johns Hopkins University Press, pp. 39–60.

Herman, David (2008), '"A Salutary Scar": Muriel Spark's Desegregated Art in the Twenty-First Century', *Modern Fiction Studies*, Vol. 54, No. 3, pp. 473–86.

Herman, David, ed. (2010), *Muriel Spark: Twenty-First-Century Perspectives*, Baltimore: Johns Hopkins University Press.

Horner, Avril, and Zlosnik, Sue (2004), *Gothic and the Comic Turn*, Basingstoke and New York: Palgrave.

Hosmer, Robert E. (2012), 'Muriel Spark', in *The Cambridge Companion to Scottish Literature*, ed. by Gerard Carruthers and Liam McIlvaney, Cambridge: Cambridge University Press, pp. 203–16.

Hosmer, Robert E. (1989), 'Writing with Intent: The Artistry of Muriel Spark', *Commonweal*, Vol. 118, pp. 233–41.

Hynes, Joseph (1988), *The Art of the Real: Muriel Spark's Novels*, London: Associated University Presses.

Hynes, Joseph, ed. (1992), *Critical Essays on Muriel Spark*, New York: G. K. Hall.

Hynes, Joseph (1993), 'Muriel Spark and the Oxymoronic Vision', in *Contemporary British Women Writers: Texts and Strategies*, ed. by Robert E. Hosmer, London: Macmillan, pp. 161–87.

Kemp, Jonathan (2010), '"Her Lips Are Slightly Parted": The Ineffability of Erotic Sociality in Muriel Spark's *The Driver's Seat*', in *Muriel Spark: Twenty-First-Century Perspectives*, ed. by David Herman, Baltimore: Johns Hopkins University Press, pp. 173–86.

Kemp, Peter (1974), *Muriel Spark*, London: Paul Elek.

Kolocotroni, Vassiliki (2010), 'Poetic Perception in the Fiction of Muriel Spark', in *The Edinburgh Companion to Muriel Spark*, ed. by Michael

Gardiner and Willy Maley, Edinburgh: Edinburgh University Press, pp. 16–26.

Lanchester, John (2006), 'Introduction', in Muriel Spark, *The Driver's Seat*, London: Penguin, pp. i–xv.

Lodge, David (1992), 'The Uses and Abuses of Omniscience: Method and Meaning in Muriel Spark's *The Prime of Miss Jean Brodie*', in *Critical Essays on Muriel Spark*, ed. by Joseph Hynes, New York: G. K. Hall, pp. 151–73.

Lyons, Paddy (2010), 'Muriel Spark's Break with Romanticism', in *The Edinburgh Companion to Muriel Spark*, ed. by Michael Gardiner and Willy Maley, Edinburgh: Edinburgh University Press, pp. 85–97.

MacKay, Marina (2000), 'Catholicism, Character, and the Invention of the Liberal Novel Tradition', *Twentieth Century Literature*, Vol. 48, No. 2 (Summer), pp. 215–38.

MacKay, Marina (2010), 'Muriel Spark and the Meaning of Treason', in *Muriel Spark: Twenty-First-Century Perspectives*, ed. by David Herman, Baltimore: Johns Hopkins University Press, pp. 94–111.

McQuillan, Martin (2001a), 'Introduction: "I Don't Know Anything about Freud": Muriel Spark Meets Contemporary Criticism', in *Theorising Muriel Spark: Gender, Race, Deconstruction*, ed. by Martin McQuillan, Basingstoke and New York: Palgrave, pp. 1–31.

McQuillan, Martin (2001b), 'In Bed with Muriel Spark: Mourning, Metonymy and Autobiography', in *Theorising Muriel Spark: Gender, Race, Deconstruction*, ed. by Martin McQuillan, Basingstoke and New York: Palgrave, pp. 78–91.

Maley, Willy (2001), 'Not to Deconstruct? Righting and Deference in *Not to Disturb*', in *Theorising Muriel Spark: Gender, Race, Deconstruction*, ed. by Martin McQuillan, Basingstoke and New York: Palgrave, pp. 170–88.

Malkoff, Karl (1968), *Muriel Spark*, New York: Columbia University Press.

Massie, Allan (1984), 'Calvinism and Catholicism in Muriel Spark', in *Muriel Spark: An Odd Capacity for Vision*, ed. by Alan Bold, London: Vision Press, pp. 94–107.

Massie, Allan (1979), *Muriel Spark*, Edinburgh: Ramsay Head Press.

Moseley, Merritt (1999), 'Muriel Spark', in *The Cambridge Guide to Women's Writing in English*, ed. by Lorna Sage, Cambridge: Cambridge University Press, p. 592.

Nicol, Bran (2010), 'Reading Spark in the Age of Suspicion', in *Muriel Spark: Twenty-First-Century Perspectives*, ed. by David Herman, Baltimore: Johns Hopkins University Press, pp. 112–28.

Page, Norman (1990), *Muriel Spark*, London: Macmillan.

Piette, Adam (2010), 'Muriel Spark and the Politics of the Contemporary', in *The Edinburgh Companion to Muriel Spark*, ed. by Michael Gardiner and Willy Maley, Edinburgh: Edinburgh University Press, pp. 52–62.

Rankin, Ian (1993), 'The Deliberate Cunning of Muriel Spark', in *The Scottish Novel Since the Seventies: New Visions, Old Dreams*, ed. by Gavin Wallace and Randall Stevenson, Edinburgh: Edinburgh University Press, pp. 41–53.

Rankin, Ian (1985), 'Surface and Structure: Reading Muriel Spark's *The Driver's Seat*', *The Journal of Narrative Technique*, Vol. 15, No. 2 (Spring), pp. 146–55.

Richmond, Velma Bourgeois (1984), *Muriel Spark*, New York: Frederick Ungar.

Roof, Judith (2001), 'The Future Perfect's Perfect Future: Spark's and Duras's Narrative Drive', in *Theorising Muriel Spark: Gender, Race, Deconstruction*, ed. by Martin McQuillan, Basingstoke and New York: Palgrave, pp. 49–66.

Royle, Nicholas (2001), 'Memento Mori', in *Theorising Muriel Spark: Gender, Race, Deconstruction*, ed. by Martin McQuillan, Basingstoke and New York: Palgrave, pp. 189–203.

Sage, Lorna (1992), *Women in the House of Fiction*, London: Macmillan.

Sehgal, Parul (2014), 'What Muriel Spark Saw', *The New Yorker*, 8 April, <https://www.newyorker.com/books/page-turner/what-muriel-spark-saw> (last accessed 13 October 2014).

Sellers, Susan (2001), '*Tales of Love*: Narcissism and Idealization in *The Public Image*', in *Theorising Muriel Spark: Gender, Race, Deconstruction*, ed. by Martin McQuillan, Basingstoke and New York: Palgrave, pp. 35–48.

Showalter, Elaine (1981), 'Rethinking the Seventies: Women Writers and Violence', *Antioch Review*, Vol. 39, No. 2 (Spring), pp. 156–70.

Sproxton, Judy (1992), *The Women of Muriel Spark*, London: Constable.

Stannard, Martin (2009), *Muriel Spark: The Biography*, London: Weidenfeld & Nicolson.

Stevenson, Randall (2010), 'The Postwar Contexts of Spark's Writing', in *The Edinburgh Companion to Muriel Spark*, ed. by Michael Gardiner and Willy Maley, Edinburgh: Edinburgh University Press, pp. 98–109.

Stewart, Victoria (2011), *The Second World War in Contemporary British Fiction: Secret Histories*, Edinburgh: Edinburgh University Press.

Stubbs, Patricia (1973), *Muriel Spark*, Harlow: Longman for the British Council.

Summers-Bremner, Eluned (2012), '"Another world than this": Muriel Spark's Postwar Investigations', *The Yearbook of English Studies*, Vol. 42, pp. 151–67.

Todd, Richard (1986), 'The Crystalline Novels of Muriel Spark', in *Essays on the Contemporary British Novel*, ed. by Hedwig Block and Albert Wertheim, Munich: M. Hueber, pp. 175–92.

Walker, Dorothea (1988), *Muriel Spark*, Boston: Twayne.

Waugh, Patricia (2010), 'Muriel Spark and the Metaphysics of Modernity: Art, Secularization, and Psychosis', in *Muriel Spark: Twenty-First-Century Perspectives*, ed. by David Herman, Baltimore: Johns Hopkins University Press, pp. 63–93.

Whittaker, Ruth (1979), 'Angels Dining at the Ritz: The Faith and Fiction of Muriel Spark', in *The Contemporary English Novel*, ed. by Malcolm Bradbury and David Palmer, London: Edward Arnold, 1979, pp. 157–79.

Whittaker, Ruth (1982), *The Faith and Fiction of Muriel Spark*, London: Macmillan.

Wickman, Matthew (2010), 'Spark, Modernism and Postmodernism', in *The Edinburgh Companion to Muriel Spark*, ed. by Michael Gardiner and Willy Maley, Edinburgh: Edinburgh University Press, 2010, pp. 63–73.

Reviews of Works by Muriel Spark

Anon. (1968), 'Shallowness Everywhere [Review of *The Public Image*]', *Times Literary Supplement*, 13 June, p. 612.

Byatt, A. S. (1970), 'A Murder in Hell [Review of *The Driver's Seat*]', *The Times*, 24 September, p. 14.

Cixous, Hélène (2001b), 'Muriel Spark's Latest Novel: *The Public Image* [1968; trans. by Christine Irizzary], in *Theorising Muriel Spark: Gender, Race, Deconstruction*, ed. by Martin McQuillan, Basingstoke and New York: Palgrave, pp. 207–9.

Holmes, Richard (1968), 'Into a Limbo of Poise [Review of *The Public Image*]', *The Times Saturday Review*, 15 June, p. 21.

Hope, Francis (1968), 'Mrs Spark in Rome [Review of *The Public Image*]', *The Observer*, 16 June, p. 24.

Hope-Wallace, Philip (1962), '*Doctors of Philosophy* [Review]', *The Guardian*, 3 October, p. 5.

Hough, Graham (1981), 'Heartlessness is Not Enough [Review of *Loitering with Intent*]', *London Review of Books*, 21 May, pp. 14–15.

Kakutani, Michiko (1997), 'Her Serene Tyranny, a Mistress of Mayhem [Review of *Reality and Dreams*]', *New York Times*, 16 May, p. 29.

Kermode, Frank (1970), 'Sheerer Spark [Review of *The Driver's Seat*]', *The Listener*, 24 September, p. 425.

Maloff, Saul (1968), 'Lady-Tiger [Review of *The Public Image*]', *Newsweek*, 21 October, pp. 108–10.

Nye, Robert (1970), 'Another Suicide [Review of *The Driver's Seat*]', *The Observer*, 24 September, p. 14.

Nye, Robert (1971), 'Gloria Deplores You Strikes Again [Review of *Not to Disturb*]', *The Guardian*, 11 November, p. 9.

Ostermann, Robert (1968), '*The Public Image* Makes its Point by Understatement', *National Observer*, 9 September, p. 7.

Smith, Ali (2004), 'Wave Your Hankie [Review of *The Finishing School*]', *The Guardian*, 22 March, <https://www.theguardian.com/books/2004/mar/20/fiction.murielspark> (last accessed 19 February 2016).

Stoppard, Tom (1962), 'Fine Hand at Work [Review of *Doctors of Philosophy*]', *Scene*, 29 November, p. 19.

Tomalin, Claire (1971), 'The Servants' Revenge [Review of *Not to Disturb*]', *The Observer*, 14 November, p. 33.

Turner, Jenny (1992), 'She Who Can Do No Wrong [Review of *Curriculum Vitae*]', *London Review of Books*, Vol. 14, No. 15 (6 August), pp. 8–10.

Tynan, Kenneth (1962), 'Straining for the Vital Spark [Review of *Doctors of Philosophy*]', *The Observer*, 7 October, p. 26.

Updike, John (1975), 'Topnotch Witcheries [Review of *The Abbess of Crewe*]', *The New Yorker*, 6 January, pp. 76–8.

Waugh, Evelyn (1957), 'Something Fresh [Review of *The Comforters*]', *Spectator*, 22 February, p. 32.

Wilson, Angus (1965), 'Journey to Jerusalem [Review of *The Mandelbaum Gate*]', *The Observer*, 17 October, p. 28.

Secondary Sources

Abel, Lionel (1963), *Metatheatre: A New View of Dramatic Form*, New York: Hill, 1963.

Abercrombie, Lascelles (1932), *Principles of Literary Criticism*, London: Victor Gollancz.

Arendt, Hannah (2006), *Eichmann in Jerusalem: A Report on the Banality of Evil* [1963], London: Penguin.

Arendt, Hannah (2005), 'Mankind and Terror' [1953], in *Essays in Understanding, 1930–1954: Formation, Exile and Totalitarianism*, ed. by Jerome Kohn, New York: Schocken Books, pp. 297–306.

Arendt, Hannah (1951), *The Origins of Totalitarianism*, Cleveland and New York: Meridian.

Bakhtin, Mikhail (1981), *The Dialogic Imagination*, trans. by Caryl Emerson and Michael Holquist, Austin: University of Texas Press.

Barreca, Regina (1994), *Untamed and Unabashed: Essays on Women and Humour in British Literature*, Detroit, MI: Wayne State University Press.

Barth, John (1984), 'The Literature of Exhaustion' [1967], in *The Friday Book: Essays and Other Non-Fiction*, Baltimore and London: Johns Hopkins University Press, pp. 62–76.

Barthes, Roland (1972), 'Objective Literature' [1952], in *Critical Essays*, trans. by Richard Howard, Evanston: Northwestern University Press, pp. 13–24.

Barthes, Roland (1968), *Writing Degree Zero* [1953], trans. by Annette Lavers and Colin Smith, New York: Hill and Wang.

Bauman, Zygmunt (1991), *Modernity and the Holocaust*, Cambridge: Polity Press, 1991.

Bennett, Alice (2012), *Afterlife and Narrative in Contemporary Fiction*, Houndmills and New York: Palgrave Macmillan.

Bennett, Alice (2009), 'Unquiet Spirits: Death Writing in Contemporary Fiction', *Textual Practice*, Vol. 23, No. 3, pp. 463–79.

Berger, John (1972), *Ways of Seeing*, London: Penguin.

Bergson, Henri (1911), *Laughter: An Essay on the Meaning of the Comic* [1900], trans. by Cloudesley Brereton and Fred Rothwell, New York: Macmillan.

Bernays, Jacob (2015), 'Outlines of Aristotle's Lost Work on the Effects of Tragedy, Section IV', trans. by James I. Porter, in *Tragedy and the Idea of Modernity*, ed. by Joshua Billings and Miriam Leonard, Oxford: Oxford University Press, pp. 315–28.

Booth, Wayne C. (1961), *The Rhetoric of Fiction*, London and Chicago: Chicago University Press.

Borges, Jorge Luis (2000), 'Pierre Menard, Author of the *Quixote*' [1939], trans. by Andrew Hurley, in *Fictions*, London: Penguin, pp. 33–44.

Briefel, Aviva (2009), 'What Some Ghosts Don't Know: Spectral Incognisance in the Horror Film', *Narrative*, Vol. 17, No. 1, pp. 95–108.

Brooke-Rose, Christine (2002a), 'The Author is Dead: Long Live the Author', in *Invisible Author: Last Essays*, Ohio: Ohio State University Press, pp. 130–55.

Brooke-Rose, Christine (1981), 'The Real as Unreal: Robbe-Grillet', in *A Rhetoric of the Unreal: Studies in Narrative and Structure, Especially of the Fantastic*, Cambridge: Cambridge University Press, pp. 291–310.

Brooke-Rose, Christine (2002b), 'A Writer's Constraints', in *Invisible Author: Last Essays* (Ohio: Ohio State University Press, 2002), pp. 36–52.

Butor, Michel (1968), *Inventory: Essays*, trans. by Richard Howard, New York: Simon & Schuster.

Cesarani, David (2007), *Becoming Eichmann: Rethinking the Life, Crimes, and Trial of a 'Desk Murderer'*, Cambridge, MA: Da Capo Press.

Cesarani, David (2004), *Eichmann: His Life and Crimes*, London: Vintage.

Cohn, Dorrit (1978), *Transparent Minds: Narrative Modes for Presenting Consciousness in Fiction*, Princeton and Guildford: Guildford University Press.

Craig, Cairns (1999), *The Modern Scottish Novel: Narrative and the National Imagination*, Edinburgh: Edinburgh University Press, 1999.

Crosland, Margaret (1981), *Beyond the Lighthouse: English Women Novelists in the Twentieth Century*, London: Constable.

De Lauretis, Teresa (1984), *Alice Doesn't: Feminism, Semiotics, Cinema*, Bloomington: Indiana University Press.

Debord, Guy (1983), *The Society of the Spectacle* [1967], trans. by Donald Nicholson-Smith, Detroit: Red & Black.

Doane, Mary Anne (1991), *Femmes Fatales: Feminism, Film Theory, Psychoanalysis*, New York and London: Routledge.

Doane, Mary Anne (1982), 'Film and the Masquerade: Theorising the Female Spectator', *Screen*, Vol. 23, No. 3–4, pp. 74–87.

Duchene, Anne (1959), 'The Method in the Novel', *The Manchester Guardian*, 20 March, p. 11.

Eaglestone, Robert (2017), *The Broken Voice: Reading Post-Holocaust Literature*, Oxford: Oxford University Press.

Eknoyan, Garabed (2005), 'The Kidneys in the Bible: What Happened?', *Journal of the American Society of Nephrology*, Vol. 16, No. 12, pp. 3464–71.

Eliot, T. S. (1969), *The Waste Land* [1922], in *The Complete Poems and Plays*, London: Faber & Faber, pp. 59–80.

Elsaesser, Thomas (2010), 'Performative Self-Contradictions: Michael Haneke's Mind Games', in *A Companion to Michael Haneke*, ed. by Roy Grundman, Chichester: Wiley-Blackwell, pp. 53–74.

Ewert, Jeanne C. (1999), '"A Thousand Other Mysteries": Metaphysical Detection, Ontological Quests', in *Detecting Texts: The Metaphysical Detective Story from Poe to Postmodernism*, ed. by Patricia Merivale and Susan Elizabeth Sweeney, Pennsylvania: University of Pennsylvania Press, pp. 179–98.

Farrimond, Katherine (2017), *The Contemporary Femme Fatale: Gender, Genre and American Cinema*, New York and London: Routledge.

Felman, Shoshana (2001), 'A Ghost in the House of Justice: Death and the Language of the Law', *Yale Journal of Law and the Humanities*, Vol. 13 (July), pp. 241–82.

Felman, Shoshana (2000), 'Theatres of Justice: Arendt in Jerusalem, the Eichmann Trial, and the Redefinition of Meaning in the Wake of the Holocaust', *Theoretical Inquiries into Law*, Vol. 1, No. 2 (July), pp. 465–507.

Ferrebe, Alice (2004), 'The Gaze of the Magus: Sexual/Scopic Politics in the Novels of John Fowles', *Journal of Narrative Theory*, Vol. 34, No. 2 (Summer), pp. 207–26.

Forster, E. M. (1927), *Aspects of the Novel*, New York: Harcourt, Brace.

Friedman, Ellen G., and Fuchs, Miriam, eds (1989), *Breaking the Sequence: Women's Experimental Fiction*, Princeton: Princeton University Press.

Freud, Sigmund (1955), 'The Uncanny' [1919], in *The Standard Edition of the*

Complete Psychological Works of Sigmund Freud, Vol. 17, ed. by James Strachey, London: Hogarth Press, pp. 218–52.

Freytag, Gustav (1895), *Technique of the Drama: An Exposition of Dramatic Composition and Art* [1863], trans. by Elias J. MacEwan, New York: Griggs.

Gasiorek, Andrzej (1995), *Post-War British Fiction: Realism and After*, London: Edward Arnold.

Genette, Gérard (1980), *Narrative Discourse: An Essay on Method*, trans. by Jane E. Lewin, Ithaca, NY: Cornell University Press.

Golden, Leon (1976), 'Towards a Definition of Tragedy', *The Classical Journal*, Vol. 72, No. 1 (October–November), pp. 21–33.

Greene, Gayle (1991), *Changing the Story: Feminist Fiction and the Tradition*, Bloomington: Indiana University Press.

Greven, David (2006), 'In a Pig's Eye: Masculinity, Mastery, and the Returned Gaze of *The Blithedale Romance*', *Studies in American Fiction*, Vol. 32, No. 2 (Autumn), pp. 131–59.

Greven, David (2013), *Psycho-Sexual: Male Desire in Hitchcock, De Palma, Scorsese, and Friedkin*, Austin: University of Texas Press.

Guppy, Shusha (1986), 'The Art of Fiction 91: Interview with Alain Robbe-Grillet', *Paris Review*, 99 (Spring), <https://www.theparisreview.org/intervie ws/2819/alain-robbe-grillet-the-art-of-fiction-no-91-alain-robbe-grillet> (last accessed 11 April 2015).

Guy, Adam (2014), 'Johnson and the *Nouveau Roman*: *Trawl* and other Butorian Projects', in *B. S. Johnson and Post-War Literature: Possibilities of the Avant-Garde*, ed. by Martin Ryle and Julia Jordan, London: Palgrave, pp. 35–53.

Hassan, Ihab (1987), *The Postmodern Turn: Essays in Postmodern Theory and Culture*, Columbus: Ohio State University Press.

Heath, Stephen (1978), 'Difference', *Screen*, Vol. 19, No. 3, pp. 51–112.

Heath, Stephen (1972), *The Nouveau Roman: A Study in the Practice of Writing*, London: Elek.

Henriot, Émile (1957), 'Un Nouveau Roman', *Le Monde*, 22 May, p. 12.

Hodgson, Jennifer (2013), '"She finds a metaphor for her condition without defining it": Ann Quin and the British "Experimental" Novel of the Sixties', unpublished PhD thesis, Durham University.

Hogan, Thomas (1959), 'Flight from Reality', *The Guardian*, 14 October, p. 4.

Holquist, Michael (1971), 'Whodunit and Other Questions: Metaphysical Detective Stories in Post-War Fiction', *New Literary History*, Vol. 3, No. 1 (Autumn), pp. 135–56.

Jameson, Fredric (1998), 'Postmodernism and Consumer Society' [1990], in *The Cultural Turn: Selected Writings on the Postmodern, 1983–1998*, London: Verso, pp. 1–20.

Jameson, Fredric (1992), *Postmodernism, or, The Cultural Logic of Late Capitalism* [1989], London: Verso.

Joyce, James (2000), *A Portrait of the Artist as a Young Man* [1916], Oxford: Oxford University Press.

Katz, Adam (2005), 'Narrative Thinking and Experiential Knowledge: The Example of Ronald Sukenick', *Texas Studies in Literature and Language*, Vol. 47, No. 3 (Fall), pp. 189–212.

Keats, John (1995), 'Ode to a Nightingale' [1819], in *Selected Poems*, ed. by Nicholas Roe, London: Everyman, 1995, p. 214.

Kermode, Frank (1968), *Continuities*, London: Routledge.

Kruse, Noreen W. (1979), 'The Process of Aristotelian Catharsis: A Reidentification', *Theatre Journal*, Vol. 31, No. 2 (May), pp. 162–71.

Lacan, Jacques (1977), *Écrits: A Selection* , trans. by Alan Sheridan, London: Tavistock.

Lane, Jeremy F. (2002), 'The Stain, the Impotent Gaze, and the Theft of *Jouissance*: Towards a Žižekian Reading of Robbe-Grillet's *La Jalousie*', *French Studies*, Vol. 56, No. 2, pp. 193–206.

Leenhardt, Jacques (1973), *Lecture politique du roman 'La Jalousie' d'Alain Robbe-Grillet*, Paris: Les Éditions de Minuit.

Leki, Ilona (1983), *Alain Robbe-Grillet*, Boston: Twayne.

Liggins, Emma (2015), 'Beyond the Haunted House? Modernist Women's Ghost Stories and the Troubling of Modernity', in *British Women Short Story Writers: The New Woman to Now*, ed. by Emma Young and James Bailey, Edinburgh: Edinburgh University Press, pp. 32–49.

Little, Judy (1983), *Comedy and the Woman Writer: Woolf, Spark, and Feminism*, Lincoln: University of Nebraska Press.

Lodge, David (1992), *The Art of Fiction*, London: Penguin.

Lodge, David (1977), 'The Novelist at the Crossroads' [1969], in *The Novel Today: Contemporary Writers on Modern Fiction*, ed. by Malcolm Bradbury, Manchester: Manchester University Press, pp. 84–110.

Lyotard, Jean-François (1984), *The Postmodern Condition: A Report on Knowledge* [1979], trans. by Geoff Bennington and Brian Massumi, Manchester: Manchester University Press.

McCarthy, Tom (2008), 'The Geometry of the Pressant', *Artforum International*, Vol. 46, No. 10 (Summer), pp. 392–5.

McHale, Brian (1987), *Postmodernist Fiction*, New York and London: Methuen.

Mäkelä, Maria (2012), 'Navigating – Making Sense – Interpreting (The Reader behind *La Jalousie*)', in *Narrative, Interrupted: The Plotless, The Disturbing and the Trivial in Literature*, ed. by Markku Lehtimäki, Laura Karttunen and Maria Mäkelä, Berlin and Boston: Walter de Gruyter, pp. 139–52.

Malina, Debra (2002), *Breaking the Frame: Metalepsis and the Construction of the Subject*, Ohio: Ohio State University Press.

Malpas, Simon (2004), *The Postmodern*, London and New York: Routledge.

Margolin, Uri (1999), 'Of What Is Past, Is Passing, or to Come: Temporality, Aspectuality, Modality, and the Nature of Literary Narrative', in *Narratologies: New Perspectives on Narrative Analysis*, ed. by David Herman, Columbus: Ohio State University Press, pp. 142–66.

Meaney, Gerardine (1993), *(Un)Like Subjects: Women, Theory, Fiction*, London: Routledge.

Meretoja, Hanna (2014), *The Narrative Turn in Fiction and Theory: The Crisis and Return of Storytelling from Robbe-Grillet to Tournier*, London: Palgrave.

Merivale, Patricia, and Sweeney, Susan Elizabeth (1999), 'The Game's Afoot: On the Trail of the Metaphysical Detective Story', in *Detecting Texts: The Metaphysical Detective Story from Poe to Postmodernism*, ed. by Patricia Merivale and Susan Elizabeth Sweeney, Pennsylvania: University of Pennsylvania Press, pp. 1–26.

Meyers, Helene (2001), *Femicidal Fears: Narratives of the Female Gothic Experience*, New York: State University of New York Press.

Miller, James (1993), *The Passion of Michel Foucault*, London: HarperCollins.

Moody, Nickianne (1996), 'Visible Margins: Women Writers and the English Ghost Story', in *Image and Power: Women in Fiction in the Twentieth Century*, ed. by Sarah Sceats and Gail Cunningham, London: Longman, pp. 77–90.

Morrissette, Bruce (1975), *The Novels of Robbe-Grillet*, Ithaca, NY: Cornell University Press.

Mullarkey, John (2013), 'Bergson and the Comedy of Horrors', in *Understanding Bergson: Understanding Modernism*, ed. by S. E. Gontarski, Paul Ardoin and Laci Mattison, London and New York: Bloomsbury, pp. 243–55.

Mulvey, Laura (1999), 'Afterthoughts on "Visual Pleasure and Narrative Cinema," inspired by King Vidor's *Duel in the Sun* (1946)' [1989], in *Feminist Film Theory: A Reader*, ed. by Sue Thornham, New York: New York University Press, pp. 122–31.

Mulvey, Laura (1989), 'Visual Pleasure and Narrative Cinema' [1975], in *Visual and Other Pleasures*, Houndmills: Macmillan, pp. 14–26.

Munt, Sally (1994), *Murder by the Book?: Feminism and the Crime Novel*, London and New York: Routledge.

Newman, Beth (1990), '"The Situation of the Looker-On": Gender, Narration, and Gaze in *Wuthering Heights*', *PMLA*, Vol. 105, No. 5 (October), pp. 1029–41.

Nicol, Bran (2009), *The Cambridge Introduction to Postmodern Fiction*, Cambridge: Cambridge University Press.

Owens, Susan (2017), *The Ghost: A Cultural History*, London: Tate.

Piette, Adam (2009), *The Literary Cold War: 1945 to Vietnam*, Edinburgh: Edinburgh University Press.

Porter, Dennis (1981), *The Pursuit of Crime: Art and Ideology in Detective Fiction*, New Haven, CT, and London: Yale University Press.

Porter, James I. (2015), 'Jacob Bernays and the Catharsis of Modernity', in *Tragedy and the Idea of Modernity*, ed. by Joshua Billings and Miriam Leonard, Oxford: Oxford University Press, pp. 15–41.

Ready, Robert (1975), 'The Logic of Passion: Hazlitt's *Liber Amoris*', *Studies in Romanticism*, Vol. 14, No. 1 (Winter), pp. 41–57.

Reznikoff, Charles (1975), *Holocaust*, Los Angeles: Black Sparrow Press.

Richardson, Brian (2006), *Unnatural Voices: Extreme Narration in Modern and Contemporary Fiction*, Columbus: Ohio State University Press.

Robbe-Grillet, Alain (1996a), 'A Future for the Novel' [1956], in *For a New Novel: Essays on Fiction* [1963] trans. by Richard Howard, Evanston, IL: Northwestern University Press, pp. 15–24.

Robbe-Grillet, Alain (1988), *Ghosts in the Mirror* [1986], trans. by Jo Levy, London: John Calder.

Robbe-Grillet, Alain (2000), *In the Labyrinth* [1959], trans. by Christine Brooke-Rose, London: Calder, 2000.

Robbe-Grillet, Alain (1959), *Jealousy* [1957], trans. by Richard Howard, London: Calder.

Robbe-Grillet, Alain (1996b), 'Nature, Humanism, Tragedy' [1958], in *For a*

New Novel: Essays on Fiction [1963], trans. by Richard Howard, Evanston, IL: Northwestern University Press, pp. 49–75.

Robbe-Grillet, Alain (1996c), 'New Novel, New Man' [1961], in *For a New Novel: Essays on Fiction* [1963], trans. by Richard Howard, Evanston, IL: Northwestern University Press, pp. 133–42.

Robbe-Grillet, Alain (1996d), 'On Several Obsolete Notions' [1957], in *For a New Novel: Essays on Fiction* [1963], trans. by Richard Howard, Evanston, IL: Northwestern University Press, pp. 25–48.

Robbe-Grillet (1977), 'Order and Disorder in Film and Fiction', trans. by Bruce Morrissette, *Critical Inquiry*, Vol. 4, No. 1 (Autumn), pp. 1–20.

Robbe-Grillet, Alain (1995), *Snapshots* [1962], trans. by Bruce Morrissette, Evanston, IL: Northwestern University Press.

Robbe-Grillet, Alain (1996e), 'Time and Description in Fiction Today' [1963], in *For a New Novel: Essays on Fiction* [1963], trans. by Richard Howard, Evanston, IL: Northwestern University Press, pp. 143–56.

Robbe-Grillet, Alain (1986), *The Voyeur* [1955], trans. by Richard Howard, New York: Grove Press.

Roe, Nicholas (1997), *John Keats and the Culture of Dissent*, Oxford: Clarendon Press.

Ross, Kristin (1995), *Fast Cars, Clean Bodies: Decolonisation and the Reordering of French Culture*, Cambridge, MA: MIT Press.

Royle, Nicholas (2003), 'The "Telepathy Effect": Notes Toward a Reconsideration of Narrative Fiction', in *The Uncanny*, Manchester: Manchester University Press, pp. 256–76.

Sarraute, Nathalie (1963), 'The Age of Suspicion', in *The Age of Suspicion: Essays on the Novel*, trans. by Maria Jolas, New York: George Braziller, pp. 51–74.

Sarraute, Nathalie (1970), *Between Life and Death* [1968], trans. by Maria Jolas, London: Calder.

Sarraute, Nathalie (1965), *The Golden Fruits* [1963], trans. by Maria Jolas, London: Calder.

Sarraute, Nathalie (1959), *Portrait of a Man Unknown* [1948], trans. by Maria Jolas, London: Calder.

Scholes, Robert (1967), *The Fabulators*, Oxford: Oxford University Press.

Shatz, Adam (2014), 'At the Crime Scene', *London Review of Books*, Vol. 36, No. 15 (31 July), pp. 21–6.

Showalter, Elaine (1985), *The Female Malady: Women, Madness, and English Culture, 1830–1980*, New York: Pantheon.

Smith, Alan Lloyd (1996), 'Postmodernism/Gothicism', in *Modern Gothic: A Reader*, ed. by Victor Sage and Alan Lloyd Smith, Manchester: Manchester University Press, pp. 6–19.

Sontag, Susan (1977), *On Photography*, London: Penguin.

Sternberg, Meir (1978), *Expositional Modes and Temporal Ordering in Fiction*, Bloomington and Indianapolis: Indiana University Press.

Stewart, Garrett (1996), *Dear Reader: The Conscripted Audience in Nineteenth-Century British Fiction*, Chicago: University of Chicago Press.

Stewart, Victoria (2011), *The Second World War in Contemporary British Fiction: Secret Histories*, Edinburgh: Edinburgh University Press.

Tani, Stefano (1984), *The Doomed Detective: The Contribution of the Detective*

Novel to Postmodern American and Italian Fiction, Carbondale: Southern Illinois University Press.

Toohey, Peter (2014), *Jealousy*, New Haven, CT, and London: Yale University Press.

Toynbee, Philip (1959), 'Enter the Anti-Novel', *The Observer*, 22 November, p. 22.

Trollope, Anthony (1996), *Barchester Towers, Vol. 1* [1857], Oxford: Oxford University Press.

Uglow, Jennifer (1988), 'Introduction', in *The Virago Book of Victorian Ghost Stories*, ed. by Richard Dalby, London: Virago, pp. xi–xvii.

Von Lang, Jochen, and Sibyll, Claus, eds (1983), *Eichmann Interrogated: Transcripts from the Archives of the Israeli Police*, New York: Farrar, Straus & Giroux.

Wallace, Diana (2004), 'Uncanny Stories: The Ghost Story as Female Gothic', *Gothic Studies*, Vol. 6, No. 1 (May), pp. 57–68.

Walsh, Richard (1997), 'Who is the Narrator?', *Poetics Today*, Vol. 18, No. 4 (Winter), pp. 495–513.

Waugh, Patricia (1988), *Metafiction: The Theory and Practice of Self-Conscious Fiction* [1984], London and New York: Routledge.

Wilson, Andrew (2010), *Beautiful Shadow: A Life of Patricia Highsmith* [2003], London and New York and Berlin: Bloomsbury.

Wood, James (2008), *How Fiction Works*, London: Jonathan Cape.

Yates, Candida (2007), *Masculine Jealousy and Contemporary Cinema*, Houndmills and New York: Palgrave Macmillan.

Zalloua, Zahi (2014), *Reading Unruly: Interpretation and Its Ethical Demands*, Lincoln: University of Nebraska Press.

Films Cited

Bicycle Thieves, Dir. Vittorio De Sica, Produzioni De Sica, 1948.

Carnival of Souls, Dir. Herk Harvey, Harcourt Productions, 1962.

The Driver's Seat, Dir. Giuseppe Patroni Griffi, Cinecoord International, 1974.

The Girl Who Knew Too Much, Dir. Mario Bava, Galatea Film/Coronet, 1963.

Halloween, Dir. John Carpenter, Falcon International Productions, 1978.

Hidden, Dir. Michael Haneke, France 3 Cinéma/Canal+, 2005.

Jacob's Ladder, Dir. Adrian Lyne, Carolco Pictures, 1990.

La Dolce Vita, Dir. Federico Fellini, Riama Film; Pathé Consortium Cinéma, 1960.

Last Year at Marienbad, Dir. Alain Resnais, Conicor, 1961.

Lost Highway, Dir. David Lynch, Ciby 2000, 1997.

The Others, Dir. Alejandro Amenábar, Cruise/Wagner Productions, 2001.

Index

Abel, Lionel, 70
Abercrombie, Lascelles, 136–7, 187n
Amenábar, Alejandro, 56
Amis, Kingsley, 3, 68, 184n
Angry Young Men, 2, 69
Arendt, Hannah, 108, 118
    Eichmann in Jerusalem, 119, 122–3,
        125–8
    'Mankind and Terror', 126
    The Origins of Totalitariansim, 121
Aristotle, 136–7, 187n; *see also*
        Bernays, Jacob; catharsis;
        tragedy
Atwood, Margaret, 55
Auden, W. H., 110
Auschwitz, 121, 124

Bakhtin, Mikhail, 91, 101
Ballard, J. G., 94
Balzac, Honoré de, 104–5
Barnsley, Alan, 16
Barrie, J. M., 25, 175
Barth, John, 10, 46, 50–1, 63
Barthes, Roland
    'Objective Literature', 105–6, 131–2
    Writing Degree Zero, 155–6
Baudelaire, Charles, 9–10
Bauman, Zygmunt, 126
Bava, Mario, 84
Beckett, Samuel, 43, 46
Berger, John, 84–5
Bergson, Henri, 29, 107, 112–14, 117,
        124, 135, 141; *see also* comedy;
        laughter
Bernays, Jacob, 137, 187n; *see also*
        Aristotle; catharsis; tragedy
black propaganda, 6–7, 90, 176; *see
        also* Delmer, Sefton; political
        intelligence

Book of Jeremiah, 166–7
Book of Job, 41–3, 71
Booth, Wayne C., 157
Borges, Jorge Luis, 46
Bradbury, Malcolm, 5, 61, 64, 92, 100,
        182, 186n
Brecht, Bertolt, 73, 159
de Breffny, Brian, 99
Brooke-Rose, Christine, 4, 25, 63, 140,
        154, 182, 183, 184n
Brown, Peter Robert, 18–9, 21, 24
Butor, Michel, 11, 104
Byatt, A. S., 147

Calder Publications, 104
Calvinism, 13, 16–17, 100, 179
caricature, 5, 42–5, 48–51, 52, 64–7,
        86, 94, 102, 112
Carpenter, John, 157
catharsis, 18, 95, 135–9, 142, 187n; *see
        also* Aristotle; Bernays, Jacob;
        tragedy
Catholicism, 2, 5, 11–17, 20, 23–4, 43,
        64–7, 92, 101, 106–7, 119–20,
        143–6, 178, 182
celebrity culture, 77–87, 88–90, 97,
        101
Cheyette, Bryan, 1–2, 77, 118, 121–2,
        141, 143
Christie, Agatha, 70
Cixous, Hélène, 84–6
Cohn, Dorrit, 157
comedy, 5, 13–15, 23, 29, 50, 69–70,
        107, 108, 112–14, 117, 124,
        135, 141; *see also* Bergson,
        Henri; laughter
commodification, 66, 81, 85, 94–100,
        101–2
Cooper, William, 3, 68, 184n

Coward, Noël, 70
Crace, John, 13
Craig, Cairns, 25, 41, 110

Day, Aidan, 107, 133–4, 144–5,
death
    anticipation of, 13, 34, 95–9, 106–7,
        142–8, 169
    denial of, 172–6
    and narrative agency, 28, 53–5,
        56–7, 137–8, 160–8
    omens of, 58–60, 173–6, 186n
    preparation for, 13, 35, 136–9, 176,
        184–5n
    as rebellion, 53–5, 81–2, 163–70,
        173–6, 180–1
    see also ghosts
Debord, Guy, 83, 93
Delmer, Sefton, 6; see also black
        propaganda; political
        intelligence
detective fiction, 30, 39–40, 42, 47,
        136, 142, 148–53, 159, 169–70,
        187n, 188n
Doane, Mary Ann, 169–70
domestic staff, 69–70, 71–2, 73–6,
        88–92, 96–102, 179
doubles/doubling, 57–60
Drabble, Margaret, 14–15
Duras, Marguerite, 11, 63, 103–4

Eichmann, Adolf, 29, 107–8, 117–30,
        131, 141; see also Hitler, Adolf;
        Holocaust; Nazism
Eliot, George, 3
Eliot, T. S.
    The Confidential Clerk, 40–1
    The Waste Land, 115
experimental fiction, 1–5, 11, 22–3,
        25–6, 28, 63–7, 68, 153–4,
        184n

Fallarino, Anna, 88–90, 95, 100,
        194n
fascism, 129, 131, 141, 178
Fellini, Federico, 82
Felman, Shoshana, 125
feminism, 5, 23, 57, 64–5, 71–3, 84–5,
        152, 169–70
femme fatale, 169–70
Flaubert, Gustave, 105
Forster, E. M., 43
Fowles, John, 25, 63, 163
free will, 14–16, 41–3, 53, 57, 65–7,

96, 119, 166–7, 182; see also
    predestination
Freud, Sigmund, 45, 59–60, 162
Freytag, Gustav, 96

Genette, Gérard, 37, 47, 51, 68
ghosts, 7, 10, 21, 27–8, 30, 34–62, 67,
        172–7, 180–1, 184–5n; see also
        death
Gothic, 10, 39, 48, 95, 145
Greene, Graham, 16, 20, 188n
Gregson, Ian, 10, 15, 64–6, 70, 85–6,
        92, 94–8, 100–2

Haneke, Michael, 161
Harvey, Herk, 56
Hassan, Ihab, 65
Hausner, Gideon, 125
Hazlitt, William, 175
Heller, Joseph, 66–7
Henriot, Émile, 104
Herman, David, 2–3, 5, 24
Highsmith, Patricia, 174
Hitler, Adolf, 127, 178; see also
        Eichmann, Adolf; Holocaust;
        Nazism
Hockney, David, 99
Hollywood cinema, 162–3, 169
Holme, Christopher, 99
Holocaust, 29, 107–8, 121–31; see also
        Eichmann, Adolf; Hitler, Adolf;
        Nazism
Holquist, Michael, 150
Hosmer, Robert, 91, 106–7
Hynes, Joseph, 16, 21–2

Irigaray, Luce, 23–4
Ivry, Benjamin, 118–9, 124

Jaeger, Werner, 136
Jameson, Fredric, 21, 92–4, 100, 101,
        134; see also simulacra
Johnson, B. S., 2, 25, 63, 140
Joyce, James, 45, 64, 186n
Judaism, 2, 8, 23, 119–27, 129–30
Jung, Carl, 41–2, 71

Kakutani, Michiko, 11–12
Keats, John, 172, 177
Kemp, Peter, 22, 65, 95–6, 111,
        120
Kennedy, A. L., 183
Kermode, Frank, 6, 15–16, 37, 106
Kristeva, Julia, 23–4

Lacan, Jacques, 84, 162–5
Lanchester, John, 165
laughter, 92, 112–14, 124, 135, 160, 164; *see also* Bergson, Henri; comedy
Lawrence, D. H., 97
Less, Avner W., 126
Lessing, Doris, 183
Levin, Ira, 71
Levy, Deborah, 183
Lindon, Jérôme, 104
Lodge, David, 3–4, 16, 144, 149
Lynch, David, 157
Lyne, Adrian, 56, 188n
Lyotard, Jean-François, 8, 67, 186n

McCarthy, Tom, 116, 157
McEwan, Nita, 58, 186n
McHale, Brian, 22–3, 51, 63, 150
McQuillan, Martin, 23–5, 48, 130–1, 186n
male gaze, 30, 96, 160–70; *see also* masculine anxiety
Malina, Debra, 68, 73
Malpas, Simon, 94, 97
Margolin, Uri, 155–6
Marvell, Andrew, 97
masculine anxiety, 148, 160–70; *see also* male gaze
Masefield, John, 7–8, 10, 27
masquerade, 169–70
Meaney, Gerardine, 22–3, 63
Medusa, 160, 164–5, 168
metafiction, 8–11, 22–3, 25–6, 28, 30, 32–3, 35–6, 41–51, 61–2, 63, 67, 77, 99, 136, 142, 144, 149, 165, 171, 180–81
metalepsis, 7, 27–8, 35–9, 49–51, 57, 62, 63, 68–70, 73, 76, 97–8, 100, 161, 179
metatheatre, 7, 10, 26, 28, 67, 70–1, 73, 76–7, 96, 100
modernism, 1–2, 45, 48, 64, 65, 93, 150
Moffatt, Sandy, 1
Monroe, Marilyn, 66, 100
Morrissette, Bruce, 132, 152
Mulvey, Laura, 84, 162–4, 169
Munt, Sally, 152
Murdoch, Iris, 12, 20, 188n

Nabokov, Vladimir, 46, 188n
narrative perspective
    as camera-like/surveillant, 83–4, 156–8

and detachment, 21, 77–87, 88–100, 104–8, 109–17, 131–40, 155–9, 175–6
as divine, 13–17, 20, 64–7, 142–7
as limited, 77–87, 88–100, 155–9, 160–70
as malevolent, 20–1, 131–3 145–8, 151–59
as objectifying, 105–6, 131–5, 139–40, 142, 149, 162–8, 180
as omniscient, 9, 13–17, 19–21, 24–25, 54, 143–5, 173–6
as posthumous/spectral, 21, 34–6, 36–51, 51–7, 172–6
as subjective, 19–20, 131–3, 155–9, 160–70
as voyeuristic, 21, 30, 81, 105, 131–3, 145–8, 151–3, 156–9, 162–8
Nazism, 6–7, 118–19, 121–9, 176, 178; *see also* Eichmann, Adolf; Hitler, Adolf; Holocaust
New Yorker, 24, 32, 123, 153, 185n
Nicol, Bran, 20–1, 24, 45, 67–8, 145–6, 160
nouveau roman, 2, 4, 6, 10, 21, 22, 25–30, 77, 103–41, 158–9, 165, 181, 184n, 187n
Nuremberg Laws, 121, 125
Nye, Robert, 14, 29, 92, 100, 120

Oates, Joyce Carol, 66

pastiche, 93, 95
Patroni Griffi, Giuseppe, 161
performance/performativity, 63–102, 135–40, 163–70
Perkins Gilman, Charlotte, 55, 185n
photography, 52–3, 79–87, 89, 96, 98–100
Pinget, Robert, 104
Poe, Edgar Allan, 150–1
political intelligence, 6–8, 89–90, 173, 176; *see also* black propaganda; Delmer, Sefton
pop art, 93–4, 99–100
postmodernism, 1–2, 4, 8–9, 21, 22–6, 28, 48, 51, 63–7, 67–8, 92–100, 100–2, 107, 134–5, 150–4, 184n, 186n
predestination, 13–16, 100, 142–7; *see also* free will
present tense narration, 106–7, 116, 139, 144–8, 153–9

prolepsis, 13–16, 19, 61, 106–7, 139,
    143–8, 156–60, 169, 178, 188n
Proust, Marcel, 22–3, 45, 105
puppetry, 15, 64–7, 70, 73, 85
Pygmalion, 173

Rankin, Ian, 107, 165
realism, 1–5, 6–10, 22, 26–8, 30, 45–6,
    55–7, 67–8, 72–3, 96–7, 101,
    104, 106, 127, 186n
Resnais, Alain, 128
Reznikoff, Charles, 122
ridicule, 4–6, 8, 73–4, 175–6, 182
Robbe-Grillet, Alain, 2, 11, 22, 29–30,
    63, 103–8, 109, 111, 115–7,
    124, 128–9, 131–5, 139, 140–1,
    147, 150–3, 154, 157, 162–3,
    168, 181, 184n, 187n, 188n
    For a New Novel, 104, 140
    'A Future for the Novel', 104, 117,
        131
    Ghosts in the Mirror, 129
    In the Labyrinth, 132, 187n
    Jealousy, 104–5, 107, 116, 128,
        132–3, 151–3, 157–9, 161–3,
        167–8, 188n
    Last Year at Marienbad, 128, 187n
    'New Novel, New Man', 132
    'Order and Disorder in Film and
        Fiction', 128
    *Project for a Revolution in New
        York*, 94
    Snapshots, 108
    Topology of a Phantom City, 181
    The Voyeur, 105, 128, 132, 151
Robinson, T. H., 41–2

Sage, Lorna, 15, 143, 146
Sansom, Laurie, 161
Sarraute, Nathalie, 11, 45–6, 103–5
schizophrenia, 84–5, 93, 134–5
Scholes, Robert, 3
sexual violence, 49–50, 53, 88–9, 95–6,
    138–40, 142–5, 148, 168
Showalter, Elaine, 23, 84–5
de Sica, Vittorio, 83
Simon, Claude, 104
simulacra, 93–6, 101; *see also* Jameson,
    Fredric
Smith, Ali, 17–18, 183
Smith, John, 123
Smith, W. Gordon, 63, 90, 91, 99–100
Snow, C. P., 3, 68
Sontag, Susan, 52, 80–1

Spark, Muriel
    The Abbess of Crewe, 15, 26, 66–7,
        77, 189
    adaptations of Spark's work, 99–100,
        161, 178, 189n
    archival materials, 7, 22, 28, 30,
        31–3, 39, 42, 44, 67, 74–5, 78,
        88–9, 91, 99–100, 120, 123,
        135–7, 139, 148, 156, 158,
        165–7, 172–3, 185n, 188–9n
    'Author's Ghosts', 36–7, 41, 182
    The Bachelors, 17, 65, 108–9, 176
    The Ballad of Peckham Rye, 27, 29,
        76, 100, 103, 107, 108–17, 124,
        130–1, 137, 140–1, 179–81
    'Bang-Bang You're Dead', 28, 36,
        57–60, 62, 67, 73, 76, 100, 181,
        185n
    'Chrysalis', 183
    The Comforters, 15–16, 20–3, 25,
        27–8, 32–3, 34–51, 61, 77, 136,
        179–82, 185n, 188n
    'Created and Abandoned', 50,
        185n
    Curriculum Vitae, 1, 7, 9, 31, 37,
        40–1, 59, 185n
    'A Dangerous Situation on the Stairs',
        67, 74–7, 89, 91, 100
    'The Desegregation of Art', 4–6, 8,
        182
    Doctors of Philosophy, 27–8, 63,
        67–77, 86, 96–7, 100–2, 182
    The Driver's Seat, 11, 14, 16, 18, 20,
        22–4, 29–30, 32, 77, 84, 88–9,
        92, 103, 106–8, 117, 129–30,
        130–141, 142–70, 179–80,
        188n
    The Finishing School, 17, 26
    'The Ghost That Was a Terrible
        Snob', 34
    'The Girl I Left Behind Me', 28, 36,
        55–7, 59, 61, 67, 181, 185n
    The Girls of Slender Means, 13, 18,
        26, 65–6, 69, 108, 153, 176
    'Harper and Wilton', 26, 36, 48–52,
        55, 61, 185n
    The Hothouse by the East River, 16,
        22–3, 26, 30, 90, 130, 171–83,
        188n
    'The House of the Famous Poet', 34
    'The Interview', 34
    'The Leaf-Sweeper', 34
    Loitering with Intent, 12, 20, 35, 65,
        182, 184n

The Mandelbaum Gate, 26–7, 29, 67, 77, 90, 103, 107, 117–31, 135, 140–1, 171, 181–2
'A Member of the Family', 177
Memento Mori, 13, 19, 24–5, 31, 35, 90, 108, 176, 184–5n
'The Messengers', 130, 138
Not to Disturb, 16, 18, 21, 22, 24, 27–8, 31, 67, 77, 88–102, 106–7, 110, 130, 179–80, 182, 188–9n
'The Party Through the Wall', 34, 177
'The Pearly Shadow', 34
'The Portobello Road', 28, 30, 36, 51–5, 61, 181, 185n
The Prime of Miss Jean Brodie, 6, 13, 16–19, 24, 26, 32, 65–7, 69, 74–6, 108, 153, 177–80
The Public Image, 16, 21, 24, 26, 28, 32, 65–7, 77–90, 92, 95–6, 100–2, 130, 163, 180, 186n
Reality and Dreams, 11–12, 18, 26, 65, 182
Robinson, 25, 108, 177, 188n
'The Seraph and the Zambesi', 8–11, 18, 183
Symposium, 182

The Takeover, 26, 189n
Warrender Chase, 31, 35, 61, 184n
Watling Street, 32, 188n
Stanford, Derek, 46
Stannard, Martin, 9, 31, 41, 148, 184n, 186n
Sternberg, Meir, 154
Stewart, Garrett, 159
Stoppard, Tom, 72–3
suspense, 153–9

Tomalin, Claire, 92–3, 100
tragedy, 10, 18, 35, 88, 95, 97, 108, 135–9, 142, 181, 187n; *see also* Aristotle; Bernays, Jacob; catharsis
Trollope, Anthony, 154–5, 156–7, 159

Warhol, Andy, 93–4, 99–100
Waugh, Evelyn, 16, 17, 39
Waugh, Patricia, 1–2, 8–11, 13–14, 22, 24, 63, 101, 144–5
Wax, Emmanuel, 35
Webster, John, 97–8
Whittaker, Ruth, 14, 17, 170

Zola, Émile, 105

CPSIA information can be obtained
at www.ICGtesting.com
Printed in the USA
JSHW062214091222
34656JS00002B/37

9 781474 475976